LEIGH HUNT'S
"EXAMINER" EXAMINED

Leigh Hunt
1810.

LEIGH HUNT'S
"EXAMINER" EXAMINED

Comprising
SOME ACCOUNT of that CELEBRATED
NEWSPAPER'S CONTENTS, &c. 1808-25

AND

SELECTIONS, by or concerning LEIGH HUNT,
LAMB, KEATS, SHELLEY and BYRON,
Illustrating the Literary History of that Time,
for the most part previously unreprinted

By EDMUND BLUNDEN

"The Examiner, he sits private there within."
BEN JONSON (1625)

ARCHON BOOKS
1967

92511

FIRST PUBLISHED 1928
REPRINTED WITH PERMISSION 1967
WITH A NEW PREFACE BY THE AUTHOR

Library of Congress Catalog Card Number: 67–11472
Printed in the United States of America

PREFACE

WHEN I left England in 1924 to take up a post in the Imperial University at Tokyo, I broke off an attempt to bring together the materials for a biography of Leigh Hunt, which would be in large measure inaccessible in the country to which I was going. During 1926, however, my friend and colleague, Takeshi Saito—probably the best Japanese authority on any subject concerned with the poets of romance whom England has produced—with great enterprise obtained a good set of Leigh Hunt's " Examiner," and with his customary generosity gave me the tenancy of it. Besides this, Professor Saito spent many hours of a busy life in assisting me to explore these capacious volumes. To him, therefore, I am principally indebted for the means of preparing the following pages, and there is nobody to whom I could express an obligation with greater sincerity of friendship and scholarly regard. *Beatus ille.*

The present work, it will be noted, is an outgrowth from the more comprehensive account of Leigh Hunt's life, which I can now look forward to completing. Its appeal must be rather to the precise observer of English literary movements a hundred years and more ago, than to the ordinary reader who might be entertained with the broader picture of Hunt and his long and remarkable career. Moreover, my concern has been with the writers' share of the " Examiner," and very little with the political or social affairs of which it was the dauntless critic. Nevertheless, the limited subject is a good one, as the " Examiner " was before its time in literary ideals and principles ; I trust that a sketch of that part of its work may not obscure its general brilliance and candour. The selections, which include for the sake of convenience, appreciation and honour the early declarations of the genius of Shelley and Keats made by their friend, and the gleanings of Lamb's taste and wit (I do not hesitate to claim them as his, and the reader will find my evidence in its proper place), are worthy of anyone's attention. And perhaps the literary lives of Shelley and Keats may receive occasional illumination from allusions now noted, since not even Miss Amy Lowell appears to have had the time for a scrupulous investigation of the " Examiner."

In reprinting Hunt's reviews I have resorted to the economy of cutting short some of the extensive quotations, and of omitting transitional sentences, necessary to their first piecemeal publication but now tedious. Other parts of his articles which do not strictly depend on their main matter, or which usefully paraphrased works, now famed and familiar, have also been discarded.

E. B.

April, 1928.

PREFACE, 1967

The book now republished may not even after forty years have lost its original claim to usefulness to readers attracted by the circle of Shelley and Keats, Lamb and Hazlitt, and the brothers Hunt who in many ways did great service to their literary gifts. *The Examiner* was a journal of progress and vision, and deserved a "biography", even though this one was principally limited to its literary and intellectual activities and to the period in which John and Leigh Hunt conducted it; for indeed it went on in other hands for half a century and more after that. Complete files of this Sunday newspaper of the last century are indeed rare, and even single volumes. The narrative and the selections made accessible will still, I think, save many readers, whether they are on particular trails or merely looking into the past and thinking over the history of imagination and art, a good deal of time and trouble.

That much more could be gleaned from *The Examiner* by those who can spend time over its often frightening bad print, I am aware; and I have refrained from trying to enlarge this book with the numerous small passages I have noted for quick allusions to favorite authors. Perhaps some things in the book could have been dropped now because writers on the eminent persons involved have made use of them, or for other reasons. The late P. P. Howe, whose life of William Hazlitt was from the first acknowledged as a masterpiece of accuracy and lucidity, was very angry with me for ascribing a protest against the Rev. W. B. Collyer to Hazlitt. I must have had some note behind that ascription, but the alleged mistake may be left for somebody to explain even in striking his pen through it.

There were three brothers Hunt concerned in *The Examiner*. We know too little of John Hunt, the "Roman centurion", the politically minded who founded more than one newspaper for the benefit of the cause of Reform. He was a character who asked for no honours or even laudations. He could write well, so I think, but at an early date saw that Leigh Hunt had a fluency and a fancy which would make such a paper as *The Examiner* at once free and memorable. The third brother, Robert, unlucky always despite his finding a place in Royal Academy exhibitions, was a competent art critic in his way, but it was he who made history in his day again by writing fearsome rubbish about William Blake. Blake duly put all three brothers into his wild world of deplorable wretches. Leigh Hunt, it seems, had one or two absurd anecdotes of Blake to tell.

It may be allowed me to mention that the set of *The Examiner* which I was invited by my friend Dr. Takeshi Saito to use, when we were both young, remains where it stood, as he does, in his Tokyo house. It was one of the rare books which he guarded with hope and some primitive equipment against air raids, once on a time. I am happy that no calamity occurred, and should anyone who comes on this new edition of my book feel that something more should be done about the brilliant Sunday newspaper read by Shelley and Keats it is certainly only a question of asking Dr. Saito for a sight of his collection—in Ushigome, Tokyo. There are libraries in Japan of every kind, but his "has to be seen to be believed."

Edmund Blunden

CONTENTS

PAGE

PREFACE   v

INTRODUCTORY   ix

PART I : NOTES ON THE VOLUMES
   1808, 1809 : Liberalism *v.* The Law of Libel   3
   1810 : Undiminished Brilliance   13
   1811 : Fixed and Flourishing   17
   1812 : The " Adonis of Fifty "   21
   1813 : Stone Walls no Prison   31
   1814 : Hazlitt, Barnes and the Editor   41
   1815 : L. H. at Liberty   48
   1816 : Poetry Abounding : Shelley and Keats   57
   1817 : Alarms and Excursions   67
   1818 : Controversies   77
   1819 : Lamb's Assistance   88
   1820 : The " Examiner " Ill at Ease   98
   1821 : Leigh Hunt's Editorship Ends   108
   1822 : Shelley, and the *Liberal*   112
   1823, 1824, 1825 : Dissolving the Partnership   117

PART II : SELECTIONS
  LEIGH HUNT
   Young Poets   125
   Poems by John Keats   129
   Lamia   141
   Adieu to Keats   158
   The Revolt of Islam   159
   The *Quarterly Review* and The Revolt of Islam   173
   Rosalind and Helen   184
   The Cenci   190

CONTENTS

	PAGE
Adonais	196
Prometheus Unbound	205
The Works of Charles Lamb	210
Velluti to his Revilers	224
Leigh Hunt's Last " Examiner " Article	234

ROBERT HUNT

An Outline Print of Lord Byron	242

CHARLES LAMB

Poor Gentlemen	244
Who Was Junius ?	246
" Debtor and Creditor "	248
Thalia to Mrs. Jordan	252
Sub-Pulpit Oratory	254
The Repair of St. Paul's	259

INTRODUCTORY

FOR the origin of the "Examiner" (a momentous birthday) the natural and authentic spokesman is Leigh Hunt in his *Autobiography* (ed. 1860, ch. IX). Youthful as he was when it began to appear on January 3rd, 1808, he had already had a considerable amount of practice in journalism, particularly in the columns of *The News* and *The Statesman*, of which his brother John was editor. John Hunt was senior to Leigh by nine years, and although notices of his life are scanty, doubtless through his own preference of privacy and impersonality, he was by all accounts a man of profound sense of duty, intrepidity and good taste. Apparently he did not write much himself in his papers, supplying rather the direction and the working methods. With him, then, "in joint partnership," the dashing, careless, fiery-spirited, and fancifully spectacular young Leigh Hunt "set up the weekly paper of the 'Examiner' . . . . It was named after the 'Examiner' of Swift and his brother Tories." It was of course by no means a Tory organ, but Hunt adds in explanation of his title that he did not think of Swift's politics, but of the "wit and fine writing, which, in my youthful confidence, I proposed to myself to emulate." For a man of his years, Leigh Hunt not only had wit and fine writing in unusual abundance, but also a surprising amount of general reading and a wide range of human interest (certainly often lacking in depth). Such were the founders of the "Examiner," while the object of the paper was chiefly "to assist in producing Reform in Parliament, liberality of opinion in general (especially freedom from superstition), and a fusion of literary taste into all subjects whatsoever. It began with being of no party; but Reform soon gave it one." In a general manner one may compare it with the talented

Nation of H. W. Massingham (too soon departed !), who, however, scarcely comprehended this part of Leigh Hunt's career when he remarked that had Hunt been living now he would have been esteemed as a pleasant writer of "middle articles." That touches the later Leigh Hunt.

The state of Europe in which the new journal was brought out must always retain its thunderously dramatic character. The "Examiner" commenced at the time when Bonaparte was at the height of his power. He had the Continent at his feet ; and three of his brothers were on thrones. His stubborn enemy, England, in spite of many moments at which a detached observer might have called her beaten, continued to fear and foil him. Few voices in England dared to speak in Napoleon's favour, and that was not unnatural ; the Hunts, at least, spoke as they thought and pleased, and directed the public as much against maladministration at home as against the bogey-man over the Channel. Their attitude called down upon the "Examiner" the dangerous and hated cry of "republicanism." Their point of view was expressed with such fine fury and unprecedented dexterity that the Government which they assailed soon took action against them. From the outset these men declared their intention of sacrificing themselves in any possible way that might lead to reforming the Church and State and to destroying the power of gilded ruffianism and ignorance. The appointment of the Prince Regent, that able sensualist (an ingenious writer has lately been endeavouring to persuade English readers that there was something almost saintly about him), soon arrived, to bring all the satire of the Hunts to its height and to provide them with the promised martyrdom.

The following brief chronicle may be of service to the reader as he pursues the story at some length in subsequent sections :

1808, January. John and Leigh Hunt issue the "Examiner."

1812, December. They are found guilty of a libel on the Prince Regent.

1813, February. They are imprisoned.

1815, February. Released. Subsequent decline of the fortunes of the "Examiner." Its literary character much developed.

1821, November. Leigh Hunt sails for Italy. John Hunt again imprisoned for political libel—2 years.

1825, October. Leigh Hunt returns to London. His brother presumes him to have forfeited his rights to the "Examiner" editorship. Dispute and estrangement.

From the dryness of that table we turn to the Prospectus* of the "Examiner" for refreshment. It was dated October, 1807. Dismissing rival prospectuses—"There is a flourish of trumpets, and enter Tom Thumb. There is an earthquake, and a worm is thrown up"—Hunt proposed IMPARTIALITY in large capitals, dwelt on the independent intention of the journal in politics, the theatre and the fine arts, assailed jockeys and cock-fighters, and uttered the solemn fiat, NO ADVERTISEMENTS WILL BE ADMITTED. "The public shall neither be tempted to listen to somebody in the shape of a wit who turns out to be a lottery-keeper, nor seduced to hear a magnificent oration which finishes by retreating into a peruke or rolling off into a blacking-ball."

---

* Accessible in Mr. Ingpen's edition of Hunt's *Autobiography*, 1903, and in Mr. Brimley Johnson's *Prefaces by Leigh Hunt*, 1927.

Part I
NOTES ON THE VOLUMES

1808, 1809: LIBERALISM *v.* THE LAW OF LIBEL

THE audacity of the proposals was maintained in the performance, as Sunday after Sunday John and Leigh Hunt struck out at "all abuses of power in the cabinet and in all offices under the crown." In October, 1808, the "Examiner" was prosecuted for an article on "Military Depravity," but shortly afterwards the nature of the case changed with circumstances and the charge fell through. Apart from politics, perhaps the main series of writings in the 1808 volume was Leigh Hunt's attack on "the bigoted part of dissent," in "Essays on the Folly and Danger of Methodism," which he reprinted as a pamphlet—now scarcely obtainable—the year after. And doubtless his papers on the drama and the actors of the season were of his usual quickness and force, but, like so much of Hunt's earlier prose, they have not been collected.

Among the early contributors were H. R. and B. F. The first, Harry Robertson, was a delightful and faithful friend of Hunt's, and a member of Hunt's "set" at Hampstead who has been neglected by literary historians. Treasurer at Covent Garden theatre, he seemed to Mrs. Cowden Clarke to combine "good temper, good spirits, good taste in all things literary and artistic." His subject, when he wrote for the "Examiner," was the opera. Barron Field is a little better known through the essays and correspondence of Lamb. He was among Hunt's earliest friends, but later on their paths diverged. Field wrote many things, including memoirs of Lamb and Coleridge, and, as has lately been discovered, a full Life of Wordsworth, which that poet's disapproval caused to remain unpublished, as it does to this day. With the assistance of these two intimates, the Hunts brought their "Examiner" in a few months to a powerful position and

3

circulation, measured by that day's scale. Carlyle testifies to the enthusiasm awakened by the new organ of reform: "I well remember how its weekly coming was looked for in our village in Scotland. The place of its delivery was besieged by an eager crowd, and its columns furnished the town talk till the next number came." Writing to his future wife in November, 1808, Leigh Hunt could report, "The paper gets on gloriously indeed: our regular sale is now two thousand two hundred, and by Christmas, or a few weeks after, I have little doubt we shall be three; and what is best of all, we shall now keep it to ourselves."

With the 1809 volume the "Examiner" could claim to be on solid ground, and our closer scrutiny may be begun. It is a quarto volume, in bulk and area much more convenient than our modern newspapers, and then "perfectly novel to this country," but printed without any mercy for the reader's eyesight, with coarse types on coarser paper.* The title-page reads:

THE EXAMINER
A Sunday Paper
ON POLITICS, DOMESTIC ECONOMY AND THEATRICALS
FOR THE YEAR 1809.

Party is the madness of many for the gain of a few.—*Swift.*

LONDON:
PRINTED AND PUBLISHED BY JOHN HUNT, AT THE "EXAMINER"
OFFICE, 15, BEAUFORT BUILDINGS, STRAND.
1809.

* Despite the Prospectus: "The types are newly cast in the foundry of Messrs. Fry and Steele, and the presses constructed by Mr. Matthews on the Stanhope plan, which produces an increased power in their mechanism, and therefore a more equal effect in the clearness and decision of the print."

There is a Preface, written at the completion of the year's issues for binding up with them, and signed with the " Indicator " mark, ☞, generally used by Leigh Hunt. The price of the paper was 8½d., of which 3½d. was the cost of the Government stamp. The contents were arranged in this manner : The Political Examiner (a leading article), Foreign Intelligence, The London Gazette (list of bankrupts, etc.), The Examiner (paragraphs of comment on recent affairs), Theatrical Examiner, Fine Arts, Police, Births, Marriages and Deaths ; other items were interspersed with more or less appropriateness. The Fine Arts were in the hands of Robert Hunt, another brother whose general notions were similar to those of the protagonists, but who can scarcely be reckoned a great artist or critic. Specimens of his own toilsome pencil may be seen coldly embellishing the volumes of *Classic Tales* which Leigh Hunt edited in 1806, but his portrait of John Hunt once exhibited at the Academy seems to have vanished with his other canvasses. Robert Hunt contributed to the " Examiner " for many years, and finally relapsing into penury, died as a poor and aged brother of the Charterhouse.

The very first article by Leigh Hunt in the 1809 " Examiner " defines the unity of the proprietors : " As they are brothers by birth, so it is their happiness to be brothers in sentiment, and it will be their pride to be brothers in suffering, if they can do one atom of service to the Constitution and help to awaken the eyes, the hands, and the hearts of Englishmen to the only effectual means of resistance against the common enemy." The business which led to this utterance was the ultimately cancelled prosecution of 1808, and in the same issue of the paper an announcement was made that the proprietors declined the proposal of " an entire stranger " calling himself " Scarecrow " to organise a public fund for their legal expenses. Whatever might happen, the editor was resolved to speak out on any subject, and the genuine versatility of Leigh Hunt as a young man quickly impresses

5

the explorer of these faded pages. His comments, even on forgotten matters, have life yet. Thus he compliments the Americans on their embargo policy, and adds, " It is more calculated to raise the American character than any one of their acts since the best times of Washington. It was the constant rule and advice of that sound practical reasoner never to interfere with the squabbles of the European States. The Americans have adopted it ; in spite of the clamours of merchants and the jostlings of stock-jobbers, they have walked out of the crowd to pursue their own peaceful occupations ; and who shall hinder them ? If they have no reason to fight against us, they have at least a right *not* to fight at all. Heaven grant that they may now have a little meditative leisure to 'prune their wings,' and grow a little polished both in the Senate and out of the Senate. I long to see some American books worth reading." (He was, of course, the son of an American.) Or he gives Sheridan in his rôle of politician and courtier a tremendous basting : as, " You came to give this illustrious cause the weight of your 'name.' The weight of your name ! Carve me out, ye powers of mirth, a square foot of solid air, that I may overwhelm that fellow Bonaparte ! Of all the pitiable drolleries that we see in this world, that of a beggar affecting to patronise is one of the most pitiable. Sir, you may have a name, but it has no more political weight in it, than your pocket. . . . We laugh at the idolatries of a mob of heathens, who could worship an insect, an onion, or a stone ; but here is a man, a polished man in a polished country, a wit, a senator, nay, a public satirist, who has bartered his liberty like the veriest slave on the coast of Guinea for something that turns his head ; who has passed his whole life in worshipping a red liquor enclosed in a coarse kind of glass ; and for the pleasure of being slapped on the shoulders and called ' a mad wag' has sacrificed the last comfort and honour of his old age." Such was the energy, the emotion, the imagery of the long and numerous political essays

6

in the "Examiner"; of which, however, this is not the place to give a comprehensive account.

Hunt's pen travelled readily over many subjects, and we find him during this year attending to such varieties as Public Monuments, Newspaper Principle, and the Chancellorship of the University of Oxford. On the first of these, he protests with as much zeal as our modern æsthetes, but with no æsthetic frigidity. His desire is not merely to ornament the town, but to honour worthy Englishmen. His business is less with the delight of the eye than the example of heroes. "Cooke, who carried the glory of England and the light of civilisation thrice round the world, has no monument. Locke, who taught us the noblest of all arts—the art of sound thinking—has no monument." On Newspaper Principle, no one could be more entitled to speak than this man whose fortunes were to be broken by his fidelity to independence and truth. It is curious to see that even at that date, according to Leigh Hunt, daily papers had largely to rely on the advertisers for existence. "It is the eloquence, not of the politician, but of the perruquier, the money-lender and the quack-doctor, which keeps their patriotic energies in motion." The Chancellorship at Oxford gave him the opportunity to commend culture to the Government, and to advance the claims of Lord Grenville "the cultivator and promoter of learning" against those of Lord Eldon— the man whose judgment was presently to deprive Shelley of his children. Incidentally, Hunt stigmatised a late Oxford edition of Strabo as "indeed appalling." We live in better times for classical texts, but we lack somewhat of the Leigh Hunt capacity to enjoy our advantages.

Passing willingly to the theatrical articles of 1809, we find them plentiful but not of unusual force. Some vivid criticisms of the actors of *Macbeth* appeared on January 15th; the following week an introductory article for a "Series of Criticisms on the Living Dramatists" began, "This is not quite so melancholy a subject as

7

Methodism," ended, "Now flattery is a vice, of which I am determined not to be guilty," but never had any successors. On February 26th the burning of Drury Lane Theatre was spiritedly described. A more cheerful occasion was the reopening of Covent Garden Theatre in September, in all the splendour of bronze Grecian lamps, Ionic pillars, casts of Minerva, Venus, Bacchus, Flora, and so on; yet this was the occasion on which the public showed its displeasure against the increased cost of admittance. Hunt describes the affair with gusto. "On Mr. Kemble's appearance in the dress of *Macbeth*, the character he was about to play, he was received with a partial applause, which was instantly drowned in a torrent of execration, and after plaintively bowing, and looking as tenderly disconsolate as he could, for a minute or two, he was compelled to retire. . . . Every species of vocal power was exercised on the occasion, and some persons seemed to pride themselves in shewing their invention at making a noise : in one corner of the pit you had a heap of groans, in another a combination of hisses, in a third a choir of yells, in a fourth a doleful undulating moaning, which, mingling with the other sounds, reminded you of the infernal regions, when in an instant the whole house seemed about to be rent asunder with a yah ! of execration, whenever Mr. Kemble presented himself from the side-scenes. When Mrs. Siddons appeared, and seemed to petition for a little compassion, there was a general groan of disgust ; but the death of her brother in the last act was followed by triumphant shouts of exultation, as if the spectators congratulated themselves on this temporary demise. After the farce, some persons, said to be magistrates, appeared on the stage, but soon vanished before the general indignation ; and it was not till two o'clock that the audience retired, growling as they went, like Homer's lions, at those who had laid toils for them :

  ' 'Twas the same the next night, and the next, and the next.' "

The contest closed in December with the capitulation of

the theatre managers. On November 5th Leigh Hunt began his critique (a very candid and practical exhortation to a young actress) with these words: "Tragedy seems entirely to have forsaken the country of Shakespeare and Otway. The last production of any celebrity was the *Douglas* of Mr. Home, at the first representation of which a Scotchman is said to have started up and exclaimed, 'Whar's your Wully Shakespeare noo?' He was struck, poor fellow, with the novelty of a drama that interested the passions, and still more with the novelty of such a production in his own country. And yet almost all the late Dramatists have claimed acquaintance with the impassioned Muse, from Thomson who made her a flower-girl, and Johnson who made her a school-girl, down to Whitehead, and Pye, and Reynolds himself, who have made her a non-entity." Since then, however, Melpomene has undergone even shabbier treatment, and Leigh Hunt himself with his *Legend of Florence* is almost the only mid-Victorian deserving her pardon.

By far the most notable article on Fine Arts in that year's "Examiner" was printed on September 17th, under the heading "Mr. Blake's Exhibition"; this, indeed, is the only criticism by the luckless Robert Hunt that anyone ever heard of nowadays, and has been rewarded with the yeasty epigrams of Blake and the voluptuous anger of Swinburne. It did not appear without premonitions. On June 4th R. Hunt had expressed his bewilderment at the wildly mixed style of Fuseli, whom Blake approved, particularly complaining of the "favourite large nose" with which Fuseli endowed his studies of Juliet. The Blake article began with an apprehension that insanity in England was rapidly increasing in popular regard, and presently continued, "Such is the case with the productions and admirers of William Blake, an unfortunate lunatic, whose personal inoffensiveness secures him from confinement, and, consequently, of whom no public notice would have been taken, if he was not forced on the notice and animadversion

9

of the 'Examiner,' in having been held up to public admiration by many esteemed amateurs and professors as a genius in some respect original and legitimate. The praises which these gentlemen bestowed last year on this unfortunate man's illustrations of *Blair's Grave*, have, in feeding his vanity, stimulated him to publish his madness more largely, and thus again exposed him, if not to the derision, at least to the pity of the public. That work was a futile endeavour by bad drawings to represent immateriality by bodily personifications of the soul, while its partner the body was depicted in company with it, so that the soul was confounded with the body, as the personifying figure had none of the distinguishing characteristics of allegory, presenting only substantial flesh and bones. This conceit was dignified with the character of genius, and the tasteful hand of Schiavonetti, who engraved the work, assisted to give it currency by bestowing an exterior charm on deformity and nonsense. Thus encouraged, the poor man fancies himself a great master, and has painted a few wretched pictures, some of which are unintelligible allegory, others an attempt at sober character by caricature representation, and the whole 'blotted and blurred,' and very badly drawn. These he calls an Exhibition, of which he has published a Catalogue, or rather a farrago of nonsense, unintelligibleness, and egregious vanity, the wild effusions of a distempered brain. One of the pictures represents *Chaucer's Pilgrims*, and is in every respect a striking contrast to the admirable picture of the same subject by Mr. Stothard, from which an exquisite print is forthcoming from the hand of Schiavonetti." To these heavy objections the critic appended several extracts from Blake's Catalogue, certainly incoherent and naively presumptuous, to a non-mystical apprehension.

B. R. Haydon, no less naively presumptuous but alas! not otherwise comparable with Blake, was at this period the artistic hope of the "Examiner" group, and Robert Hunt recommended Fuseli to study the "property" of his " hues, forms and expressions of passion " as exemplified in " Dentatus " (at the Royal Academy, 1809). Another painter then overrated by the Hunts and their friends was David Wilkie, who is warned, however, not to " descend too low into objects of disgust," " bloat and voracious bestiality," " gross Dutch taste." If Robert Hunt completely missed Blake, he did better with Turner—but as yet the Turner of " Rain, Steam and Speed " had not appeared to bewilder the old school.

Many miscellaneous curiosities in the " Examiner " at this time invite us to dally by the way. There are the elegant notes on the monthly fashions, which transform the dust-hued pages into brilliant colour-prints. Poets might envy that costumier's prose : March, the stormy month, must have repented and kindled to find that " The prevailing colours for this month are rose, green, and purple of various materials, silk, satin, and plain velvets, ornamented with gold or silver pearls, or embroidery. Satin caps and hats, with short white feathers, are generally worn. Small morning or walking hats, trimmed with silk frivolity, are an entirely new and very elegant article. . . . The Patriotic helmet, and the College bonnet, each worn with short white lace veils, are amidst the most novel and attractive. . . . The purple and the green beaver hat, somewhat of the Spanish form, turned up with a loop and acorn tassel of gold, falling towards the left eyebrow, and ornamented with a small Persian plume of the same colour, is making its appearance, and as a carriage decoration possesses much becoming attraction." Meanwhile, report came down from Scotland that a Mermaid had been seen, also a becoming attraction. " The face seemed plump and round, the eyes and nose were small, the former were of a light grey colour "—there is a deal of word-painting to this Mermaid, whom however the astute " Examiner " refuses to guarantee, though Miss Mackay and Miss Mackenger of Scotland watched her in the sun throwing back her thick green hair. Almost as remote as the

c

mermaid seems " Miss Linwood's Gallery of Pictures in Needle-work of worsted." This graceful artist had copied with exquisite feeling, despite the difficulty of the task, such pictures as Ruysdael's Waterfall and Morland's Farmer's Stable, even Dolci's Salvator Mundi; Robert Hunt grew quite lyrical in her praise. But it is time to resume the serious side of our subject.

Serious enough, even to the daring Hunts, was the new prosecution for libel, instituted against them at the beginning of December, 1809. The article announcing the impending action discussed the charge quite openly, and defied the Ministry with redoubled aspersions. With the trial still threatening, Leigh Hunt closed the year's work by writing the preface to the collected volume, from which we quote: " Two years have now elapsed, during which the ' Examiner,' though commenced with difficulty and continued with danger, has been increasing both in the number and confidence of its readers. The Proprietors therefore may be allowed to think, that the time of trial is over. . . . Two actions have been brought against them to grace the close of each year ; I say, *to grace*, not out of mere defiance to power or any disrespect to law, but because the object of both these actions was to overpower the most manifest truths respecting the most disgraceful measures. The first, after costing as much as it could in preliminaries, was done away by the expulsion of the Duke of York from office ; and the second is now in suspense, whether it will or will not be done away by the expulsion of ministers. Whatever be the issue, the tone and temper of the ' Examiner ' will still be the same—very indifferent to threats, and resigned to consequences—with a respect for nothing but truth and the constitution, and a most unwearied contempt for mean princes and corrupt place-men. . . . May the English people, by this time next year, after having so long been a spending nation, a fighting nation, and a suffering nation, recover some portion of their ancient and most valuable renown as a *thinking nation*."

12

1810 : UNDIMINISHED BRILLIANCE

THROUGHOUT 1810* the "Examiner" was continued with little modification of aim, scope, form or style. In the first number of the year, Leigh Hunt discussed the divorce of the Empress Josephine, and the domestic character of Bonaparte, concluding with a wish that the Emperor's son, if he had one, might be a better man than his father (this with the expressed hope that the Attorney-General would not find it to be a libel). In the same issue Hunt published a poem entitled *Walcheren Expedition; or the Englishman's Lament for the Loss of his Countrymen.* (The disastrous occasion of this is perhaps best referred to in *The Dynasts.*) Hunt's poem, rightly excluded from the Oxford edition of his verses, is derivative from *Ye Mariners of England* (Campbell) and others, but its patriotism is his own :

> " Ye brave enduring Englishmen,
>   Who dash through fire and flood,
> And spend with equal thoughtlessness
>   Your money and your blood,
> I sing of that black season,
>   Which all true hearts deplore,
>   When ye lay
>   Night and day,
> Upon Walcheren's swampy shore."

On January 21st he devoted his " Political Examiner " to some considerations on the New Year's Ode of the immortally incompetent Poet Laureate, Mr. Pye (at whom he had previously made one or two grimaces of amusement).

* The ambitious energy of Leigh Hunt at this period may be seen from the fact that in 1810 and 1811 he also edited a well-filled quarterly magazine, *The Reflector.*

The text of the Ode was given in the same number. It was pompous or grovelling by turns, of course, and Hunt had an easy task to exhibit it as " a complete specimen, if not of the best Laureat writing, at least of the true Laureat flattery and fiction." But, proceeding thence, he asked whether these routine compositions were not " libels on the dignity both of him that writes and him for whom they are written ? . . . In every point of view, the Laureatship is a ridiculous office : if the monarch is a great prince, the hired poet degrades him ; if an indifferent one, burlesques him ; and if a bad one, renders both prince and poet execrable." Time may have smiled presently when Leigh Hunt himself, grown grey and almost conservative, desired much to be the successor of Wordsworth, free, it is true, from writing verse to the command of the calendar. Meanwhile he was exercising his sprightly youth, and, reciting Gibbon's recommendation in the *Decline and Fall of the Roman Empire* (chapter 70, note) that the Laureateship should be abolished, he summed the office up as a " rank absurdity."

The libel action standing over from 1809 was dropped in March, but even at that the " Examiner " had suffered, as Hunt complains, to the tune of some ninety guineas in legal expenses—a substantial loss in those times. In September, Hunt reprinted from the *Stamford News*, then a journal of prestige and power, a lengthy protest against the detestable punishment of flogging refractory soldiers. The article was headed " One Thousand Lashes ! ! " It came before the fiery eye of the Attorney-General, with the result that on November 11th the Hunts once more informed their readers that their indictment was preparing. As before, they bore the threat of affliction very lightly, and more paragraphs and letters on the theme of Military Flogging were put forth unreservedly in their pages.

For the rest, the 1810 volume need not detain us. An article in the droll plain style of Lamb at this date, on " Poor Gentlemen," may well be Lamb's in fact, and is reprinted below. Robert Hunt, doubtless urged by Haydon, propounded " Suggestions on the Best Mode of Encouraging History Painting in England " (July 22nd), based on proposals published by other hands. R. H. Cromek contributed a life of Schiavonetti the engraver (July 1st), and a briefer memoir by the same hand of Charles Grignion, familiar to lovers of eighteenth-century books, followed his death at the age of 94 that November. " Of the elegant Art of English Engraving," wrote Robert Hunt, " he first planted the seed." A warm-hearted and able statement of the merits of George Morland, by R. S. T., enriched the paper on September 2nd. Among the theatrical notices, two or three give glimpses of Leigh Hunt's valuation of famous plays. *As You Like It* (January 7th), despite its wit, wisdom and characters, perturbed him by its plot— " unnatural, and probability and nature are offended at once, when the two young ladies, one in man's clothes and the other with a crook, go a shepherdizing, and in a Flemish forest too." *King John* appealed to him partly because " perhaps there is no other play of Shakespeare, taken altogether, which exhibits so equable and so elegant a flow of versification " (June 3rd). The Restoration Comedy did not yet appear to him as Lamb would have wished, placed " by necromancy " beyond the rules and expectations of our diurnal morality, and Vanbrugh's *Confederacy* enraged him " with its *indifference* truly abominable " towards virtue. Steele's *Conscious Lovers* he called " the best sentimental play in the language," praising especially its " charming strain of unaffected knowledge," and " nice and feeling discrimination."

Hunt duly completed the year with a " Postscript "— *exempli gratia*, " The ' Examiner ' closes its third volume under circumstances precisely similar to those at the conclusion of the two preceding years—an increase of readers and a Prosecution by the *Attorney General*. These circumstances may not be equally lucrative to the Proprietors, but they are equally flattering ; and alike encourage them

15

to persevere in a line of conduct which enables them to deserve the one and to disdain the other. Twice has the *Attorney General* been foiled on these occasions ; and it is not improbable, that his amiable perseverance may be fated to sustain a similar shock for the third time."

1811 : "FIXED AND FLOURISHING"

LITTLE change in the policy, system or appearance of the "Examiner" is visible in the volume for 1811. The number of letters from readers indicates the steadfast appreciation which had already been achieved. Leigh Hunt continued his political, theatrical and social articles with undiminished ardour and agility, and it was in this year that he attracted the praise of Shelley and his acquaintance too. Governed by our literary intention, we shall not pursue the political thought of Hunt with anything like the zeal due to it, but it is amazing to watch his idealistic industry and kaleidoscopic subject-matter. Politics is an essence that quickly evaporates, but the theatre preserves something of its spirit much longer. Hunt's criticisms of actors are admittedly of the first excellence, although he himself found the life of a dramatic critic " a tedious one " ; witness these reflections in the first number for 1811 : " The general business of a critic, in seating himself in the theatre, is to strengthen himself against the three approaching hours ; to indulge in the remembrance of what has been, and in the pictures of what ought to be, in an English theatre ; and to snatch, as far as the slamming of doors and the fluttering of loungers will suffer him, the occasional relief of the music between the acts, which, compared with the pieces it divides, is like stripes of gold-lace upon a threadbare drugget. To go to the theatre with these anticipations, and be presented with a piece at once new and tolerable, is about as agreeable and surprising as it would be to a London pedestrian to see claret gushing from Piccadilly pump or a laurel-tree starting up in Saint Giles's." Hunt's critiques concern rather the players than the plays, and in 1811 he attended few performances in which the play itself was of great value.

17

On March 3rd he published his notice of Kemble's revival of *Twelfth Night*, a play which he termed "inferior to the *Falstaff* pieces in invention, to *Much Ado About Nothing* in wit and interest, and to the *Taming of the Shrew* in effect and completeness of design." The paper as a whole is greatly to the purpose, and he is not least useful to posterity when he denounces a forgotten actor who, among other imperfections, delivered the lines, "If music be the food of love, play on " in the manner " of a mouthing schoolmaster hastening to finish the passage that he might proceed to lecture upon it—that is to say, upon what he neither feels nor understands." When Thomas Moore's opera *M.P., or the Blue Stocking*, was brought out, Hunt made it an occasion for a lengthy and adverse criticism (September 15th). Opening with a gesture of hopelessness at the degraded condition of the drama, the writer spoke of the anticipations of the public awaiting this opera, and their mortification : "The promised Monday arrives ; the house is filled : expectant congratulation runs from bench to bench ; the most rigid and critical faces thaw in the general smile ; the overture begins—why is it not over ?— the curtain rises—the actors come forward—and lo, instead of an opera worthy of its poet, a farce in three acts of the old complexion ! A string of common-places, the more unsightly from the few pearls mingled with them ! An unambitious, undignified, and most unworthy compilation of pun, equivoque, and clap-trap ! " After a good deal of such candour, Hunt urged Moore not to print his opera, and ended with a tribute to, and definition of, the poet's quality : "There seems to me to be an original path open to him in the union of fancy with ethics, or rather perhaps, I should say, of poetical ornament with observation of men and manners." In this kind of decorated criticism of life Leigh Hunt's own poetical talent was to be usually exercised.

Among the general articles occurs a powerful and prophetic declaration by Leigh Hunt on the theme of

18

"Negro Civilization" (August 4th). Hunt was a great believer in the accomplishment of the "too good to be true." "The history of opinion tells us never to despair of effecting the ruin of prejudice." On this occasion he welcomed the arrival of an interesting negro, Captain Cuffee, who was coming aboard the ship which he owned and commanded to London, to discuss the future of his race with "the Directors of the African Institution." Assailing with shrewd argument and ironical analogy those who mechanically asserted "the natural brutality of negroes," Hunt rejoiced in the apparition of the sable Cuffee as "one of the forerunners of an equal race of beings" and a sign of English achievement better than all the glories of Bonaparte, concluding with a demand for a monument to the Abolition of the Slave Trade, to be set up "on the coast of Africa": "It should be as magnificent as size, and as beautiful as art, could make it; and that no emblem might be lost, it should be useful as well as glorious, and form a mighty sea-mark for the mariner." A considerable correspondence ensued upon the creed voiced by Hunt.

On February 22nd "The King *v.* Leigh and John Hunt" was heard, the charge being "a seditious libel, to which the defendants had pleaded—*Not Guilty*." The Attorney-General having weightily denounced their tone and views as being pro-Bonapartist (a mean but astute appeal to the jury), Henry Brougham rose to defend them, which he did very eloquently; and in spite of the summing-up of the case by Lord Ellenborough as "an inflammatory libel," the verdict was, *Not Guilty*. This enraged various servile journalists in London, and Hunt replied particularly to a mendacious attack in *The Courier*. Coleridge, who had been the principal political writer for that newspaper, requested the Editor of the "Examiner" to "state, that he is not the author of the article in the *Courier* . . . and the Editor accordingly states it with great pleasure. Mr. C. will hear further from him on this subject." No further clash between the authorities and the Hunts occurring in

1811, the annual summary contained these sentences : " In completing the present Volume of the 'Examiner,' the Proprietors have to record a remarkable event, which has attended the fourth year of its existence, and which they are rather at a loss how to appreciate, whether as a compliment to their public spirit, or the reverse : it is the cessation of the usual notice on the part of his Majesty's Attorney-General—the non-appearance of a legal Information for the space of a whole twelve-month. When the rabble shouted their applause during the harangue of the Grecian patriot, he turned round and asked whether he had said anything foolish ; the silence of the higher powers is perhaps a worse compliment now-a-days ; and when the Attorney-General withholds his condemnation, we may turn round and ask whether we have said anything slavish." The reader was assured that the opposition to, and scurrilous abuse of, the " Examiner " had assisted to make it " fixed and flourishing."

1812 : THE "ADONIS OF FIFTY"

THE title-page of the volume for 1812 bears a new
address : Maiden Lane, Covent Garden—where
Voltaire had lodged once, and where stood the
"Cider Cellars" tavern, long frequented by jovial young
sportsmen and other students of devilled kidneys and London
stout. The price of the "Examiner" was raised during
this year from 8½d. to 9½d. But the principal novelty of
1812 was the conviction of the proprietors for libel—an
incident not the least important in the history of opinion
in England, and of great consequence to the career of
Leigh Hunt in particular.

The Prince of Wales had become Regent, but the air
buzzed with rumour of his follies and pettinesses, his
amours and his favouritisms. The Hunts were determined
to use their entire resources in order to relieve the country
from rulers whose bad habits infected the general welfare.
Charles Lamb joined them, though anonymously, in a
brief but punishing bombardment of the Regent, which
broke out in March. First Leigh Hunt launched a
studiously insolent essay called "Princely Qualities," pre-
tending to copy the *Morning Post* and other newspapers
which had poured out sanctimonious epithets by dozens,
and to justify the epithets by specimens of the Prince's
virtue in action ; only, on arriving at the epithet, he left
a blank space. "Generosity," "Patriotism," "Magna-
nimity" were all followed by blanks progressing in size,
"Hiatus valde deflendus," "Hiatus maxime deflendus,"
"Hiatus gemebundissime deflendus." This ingenious irrita-
tion was extended into a ridiculous dream in which Hunt
affected to mistake himself for the Regent—"the reader
knows what strange, incoherent things people will dream,
things as incongruous, for instance, as supposing one's self

21

to be a beast and a man at one and the same time, or a jackass and Alfred the Great, or a Prince and a box of peppermint," etc. The article was reinforced by a poem in the same issue, professing to be by the Regent, and full of imputed asininity. The following week the "Examiner" dealt with "The Regent's First Levee," and changed the treatment to the most specious loyalty, illustrated by a quotation (otherwise unpublished) from Hunt's own verse : as thus, "What sparkling consciousness of being and of making happy, like the bridegroom coming out of his chamber and rejoicing to run his course ! The clouds of war and of sorrow roll away from before him ; peace and prosperity look forth from his happy face ; a prospect, all radiance and renovation, bursts open upon the eyes of the people and turns their despondency into rapture !

> " So comes the Moon, silv'ring the sullen back
> Of a slow-moving cloud, and clears the rack !
> So morning beams upon the skirts of night,
> So balmy comes upon the fresh'ning sight,
> And reassures the land, and tips its tears with light ! "

Other Regentiana in that number were a burlesque letter from "Humphrey Hobnail" to "The Hexaminer Noosepaper," and Lamb's sharp, satirically picturesque verses—a pun on the large scale—"The Triumph of the Whale." In the next number the attack reached its height.

"The Prince on St. Patrick's Day," the celebrated article which sent the Hunts to prison, came out on March 22nd, 1812, with assistance—two epigrams—from the pen of Lamb the same day. Hunt spread himself fearlessly on the new subject, or rather the new instance. His anger was roused to unusual heat by the *Morning Post*, which had published some surprising nonsense intended as incense for the Regent's pleasure, and which addressed him in French, Italian, and Spanish to this purpose : " You are the *glory of the People*—You are the *Protector of the Arts*—You are

22

the *Mæcenas of the Age*—Wherever you appear, you *conquer all hearts*, wipe away tears, excite *desire and love*, and win *beauty* towards you—You breathe *eloquence*— You inspire the Graces—You are an *Adonis in loveliness!*" —there is more of it, but one wants no more. The Prince's health, proposed at a public meeting on St. Patrick's day, had been drunk amid hisses, and Sheridan, afterwards alluding to the circumstance with the intention of defending the Regent, had been told to "Change the subject!" Not unnaturally, then, did Leigh Hunt comment in acid phrase on the *Morning Post's* rhapsody : "What person, unacquainted with the true state of the case, would imagine, in reading these astounding eulogies, that this *Glory of the People* was the subject of millions of shrugs and reproaches! That this *Protector of the Arts* had named a wretched Foreigner his Historical Painter in disparagement or in ignorance of the merits of his own countrymen! That this *Mæcenas of the Age* patronized not a single deserving writer! That this *Breather of Eloquence* could not say a few decent extempore words—if we are to judge at least from what he said to his regiment on its embarkation for Portugal! That this *Conqueror of Hearts* was the disappointer of hopes! That this *Exciter of Desire* (bravo, Messieurs of the *Post !*) this *Adonis in Loveliness*, was a corpulent gentleman of fifty! In short, that this *delightful, blissful, wise, pleasurable, honourable, virtuous, true*, and *immortal* PRINCE, was a violator of his word, a libertine over head and ears in debt and disgrace, a despiser of domestic ties, the companion of gamblers and demireps, a man who has just closed half a century without one single claim on the gratitude of his country or the respect of posterity!"

This fusillade did not exhaust Hunt's ammunition. His paper on March 29th was entitled "Proceedings of the Regency," closing in fierce simplicity, "The rest of the week he [the Regent] spent, of course, in the usual manner, with the usual society ; and to-morrow he goes to St. James's

23

Chapel *to receive the Sacrament !* " Artful allusion and
epigram followed. On April 26th, Hunt's leader was a
discussion of the inevitable " Charge of Libel for Explaining
the True Character of His Royal Highness the Prince
Regent," the Attorney-General having fastened upon that
passage just now transcribed. The charge was greeted
with the now familiar attitude, " do your worst," with
resolution and independence, and a prime reliance upon the
equity of English law. In July the trial was postponed
by reason of a difficulty regarding the selection of the jury.
In November Hunt was still denouncing the unprincely
Prince, to whom at the end of the month he even addressed
his " Political Examiner " in the form of a letter. " Sir,
you have most unaccountably mistaken your men." " The
question is not between a Prince and a mere libel ; it is
not between the sovereign dignity and a popular piece of
presumption ; it is, as I have already stated, between the
Licentious Example of a Court and the Voice of Public
Virtue ; it is a question, how far those vices, which do not
come under the cognizance of the laws, are to be subject
to the controul of the public spirit. . . ." On December
6th, the Judge who was to preside over the trial of the
Hunts—Lord Ellenborough—was publicly harangued in
the same fashion, though with more of wit. " My Lord,
it is upon two distinct grounds that we object to your fitness
for the discharge of the judicial office ; we object to it,
firstly, inasmuch as you hold a situation under his Majesty
incompatible with the nicer feelings of independence
required in a Judge,—and secondly, inasmuch as you are
in the habit of evincing that species of temper, which is
familiarly termed passionate, and which is incompatible
with the very nature of judgment."

The trial was held on December 9th, and reported at
great length in the " Examiner " of the 13th and 20th.
The actual charge was that John and Leigh Hunt " with
intention to traduce and vilify his Royal Highness the
Prince of Wales, Regent of the United Kingdom, and to

24

bring his Royal Highness into hatred, contempt, and disgrace, on the 22d of March, in the 52d year of the King,
published a libel against the Prince Regent," the passage
given above. Brougham defended. His unfamiliar account
of Leigh Hunt as he then stood—at the age of 28—well
merits to be repeated. "He is a young man who lives
not in the neighbourhood of or within the view of a Court—
who has no political connexions—who scarcely knows any
public man personally, except, if I may so speak, the
individual who is his Counsel—who does not know the
face of any one man connected with the public affairs of
this country. He is a rigidly studious man ; a man not
advanced in life, being, I believe, considerably under thirty,
but always surrounded by books rather than by men.
His delight is to pursue his studies, which he does, in-
cessantly, from Sunday to Sunday, in his retirement ;
while he also prepares his weekly journal, the topics in
which are various, as those of a public journal ought to
be, including the history of the events of the times in
which we live, and among them, observations on general
politics. He is devoted to no Political Party ; he knows
of none ; of which we have a striking instance, by way of
illustration, in the motto he has adopted for his paper,
which is a quotation from Dean Swift, ' Party is the madness of many for the gain of a few,' and this you must have
found, if you know any thing of the journal which he
conducts. Among the political topics which occupy his
attention, there are some general ones in which we are
all interested, and in which he has been extremely vigilant.
I mean, the system of Military Punishment in this country ;
the Criminal Justice of it, and its Administration ; the
Liberty of the Press, and fair Discussion ; the purity of
the Principles of our free Constitution ; the Abolition of
the Slave Trade ; the Amelioration of the present Condition of the Poor ; the general Happiness of the Community, promoted as it would be by due attention to the
interests of the lower classes of it ; the general policy

25

adopted by this country with respect to our Army Abroad —topics equally interesting to all parties ;—and also the leading affairs of our Sister Kingdom." These and similar agreeable and sympathetic observations did not succeed in obtaining an acquittal, but though thus vanquished Hunt argued still—in the "Examiner." Descanting on the verdict, the resilient young writer made a mock recantation on December 13th (a *reductio ad absurdum*, to say that the Regent "has kept his word with the Irish—he lives with his wife—he is little advanced in years, young, indeed, rather than otherwise ; and, in one word, he is thin.") On the 20th and 27th he dissected Lord Ellenborough's summing-up, "an epitome of bad excuses."

This often chronicled trial overshadowed the other events of that year's "Examiner," in which nevertheless several admirable pieces of writing are found. Hunt was less regular at the play than was the case previously, yet he wrote with his wonted buoyancy and directness on several dramatic occasions. He eulogised *Julius Cæsar* and condemned Johnson's disparagement of it (March 29th), claiming incidentally that Brutus is the hero of the piece and should have given his name for its title. *The Beggar's Opera*, the tunes of which were with him unalterable favourites, elicited (September 13th) a criticism of Gay— indeed, of the Augustans generally : "The habit of appealing to common life, though it assisted the temporary views of the school in which Gay was formed, was a most serious injury to it upon the whole. If it abounded, as it certainly did to exuberance, in wit, the exuberance was of a most rank description ; and there grew up a vulgarity about their habits of mind, originating perhaps with Swift, the contamination of which even the purity of Arbuthnot could not escape, and which not only polluted the language of Pope, but appears to have materially kept down and depraved his imagination." Hunt was not present at the farewell of Mrs. Siddons, but he marked the event with a sketch of her most successful parts, "Queen Katharine,"

" Constance," and " Lady Macbeth." (" The sleep-walking scene in the last has been much and deservedly admired ; the deathlike stare of her countenance, while the body was in motion, was sublime ; and the anxious whispering with which she made her exit, as if beckoning her husband to bed, took the audience along with her into the silent and dreaming horror of her retirement.") That is typical of the imaginative height of Hunt's retrospect. He also gauged remorselessly the value of the " young Roscius," Master Betty, on his reappearance : " his merits are what they were before—of an extrinsic and chiefly mechanical nature. . . . In short, Mr. Betty is a good stage-walker."

Illness (Hunt's recovery from which presently made the first item of news in this important Sunday paper !) kept him in his room for several weeks, and perhaps obliged him to seek recreation in the florid translations from Catullus and Horace interspersed through the 1812 volume. That spring, when taking his walks abroad, he seems to have discovered Hampstead, and on June 7th he began his " suburban essays," which were to invite his enemies to so much mischievous sport, with an article on " The Regent's Park and Barracks." But as yet his pastoral mode was serving a political aim ; he was hymning " the gentle eminence of Hampstead, with the sloping sunshine of its fields, its grovy fullness at top, and the church-steeple looking out over the trees," partly for the pleasure of execrating the building of barracks in that quarter, and (by that approach) of ridiculing the ugliness of British barracks. A powerful picture of the soldiers' quarters at Dover finds room : " The Dover cliffs, unless they are very much altered since I saw them last, do really contain a set of barracks, hollowed out in the chalk, and furnishing habitations to a set of human beings, whose business, I suppose, is to defend the coast there and catch agues. Never did I make more painful or marvelling conjecture, than at what could have been the object of the speculative person who made this experiment at burying alive. The

D

robbers' cave in *Gil Blas* is a fairy palace to it. In crossing the Castle walks, you meet with holes in the earth as if made for coal-cellars, and looking down, fancy you see something moving, when lo !

> From out the hollow ground
> Slowly breathes a sullen sound.

These are windows of the barracks within, and the sullen sounds are the hum of the soldiers' voices. The front part is lighter, having a landing place on the face of the cliff, and opening upon the sea ; but as you get inwards, you seem bidding adieu to light and life together : the soldiers lie in burrows, like rabbits, one line of beds over another, and what with the damp, the darkness, and the narrowness, the sensation is truly stifling. Walking through the passages, I heard a strange, hollow kind of mumbling, just over head, and looking up, saw a man leaning out of the upper burrow, and reading prayers to his comrades inside, by the help of what light he could catch from one of the apertures." This graphic impression makes one fancy what Hunt might have made of the catacombs of the Western Front in 1916.

It was not often that this writer (though ready) appeared as an art critic, but on June 14th and June 21st, 1812, he went out of his way to assail the British Institution for its supposed illiberality to B. R. Haydon. First he admitted the artist's faults as a painter ; said that the hand of Macbeth's page, in the piece in question, was "for a pickaxe rather than a train or a feathered bonnet," that the head of the page was not of the same age as his limbs, and that Macbeth's muscles were "too much obtruded." But, against those too well-founded objections, he reckoned several credits, a nobly expressive "upper part of " Macbeth, an intensely figured Lady Macbeth "with her lifted finger, which throws a gigantic shadow on the wall," and *in parts* a Titianesque colouring and masterly drawing. The unfortunate Haydon had been considered and had considered himself certain of a prize of 300 guineas for the whole performance, and then after delays and rumours he had been sacrificed, offered a paltry 30 guineas, the price of his frame. Hunt divined that certain pugnacious letters from Haydon published already in the "Examiner" had brought on this black magic.

Another enthusiasm of Hunt's at this date, also destined to wither, or lose its excess of lustre, was for Lord Byron, whose *Address on the Opening of Drury Lane Theatre* was printed on October 18th. The public had received the effusion coldly, and Hunt assumed it to be no very favourable specimen of Byron's powers, and hinted that it was the production mainly of "his ear and his memory." After some elaboration of this proposition, he concluded : " If we may judge from the spirit of his Lordship's writings, he will not be sorry to see these free observations, nor perhaps to avail himself of what they advise. We like the independence of his opinions—we like the sturdy good sense, which in spite of some things that occasionally obscure it, looks out from the general features of his poetry ; there are certain passages of his more heart-felt effusions, which have even touched our sympathies to the core ; and on every account, we heartily wish to see his writings become all that they should be." Besides that article, literary interest clings to an elegy by Barron Field (November 8th) in the Wordsworthian manner, dignified and significant, showing wherein the author might evoke the appreciation of his friend Lamb ; and to a notice of a painting by George Dawe (the non-artist commemorated with such inspired malice by Lamb), illustrative of Coleridge's *Genevieve*. Robert Hunt notes it, " The young man on his knee singing to a Lady who is pensively and elegantly leaning on a pedestal, is an impassioned exemplification of the pleasing lines . . . [but] the figures are of an unseemly thinness, and the eloquently pleading lover has an effeminacy of appearance by no means calculated to aid his otherwise impressive suit."

The "*EXAMINER*" *EXAMINED*

It was with the certain prospect of the rigours of the law that Leigh Hunt this time penned his accustomed surview of the year's work. "The usual task of the little Prefaces affixed to these Volumes has been to call to mind the honour done us by an ex-officio information, and the pleasure afforded us by its disappointment. The former we have again to record: and if the latter, for the first time, has not accompanied it, the feelings that we anticipated in case of such a reverse have not deceived us." He apologised for his recent lack of attention to the theatrical department, and promised, "Arrangements will be made, that shall secure the entertainment of his Theatrical Readers during his imprisonment."

1813: STONE WALLS NO PRISON

THE imprisonment was not entered upon until February 3rd, 1813. While he was awaiting the sentence, Hunt did not specially propitiate his adversaries; he began the year with a mischievous political fable beginning "There was formerly on the north-eastern coast of China a large and beautiful island called Hing, which by some convulsion of nature disappeared," and proceeding with great invention and irony to show how this disappearance had been caused by the pranks of the King's son, Prince Chin-Hum, and his idiotic entourage. "My friends, this infatuated Prince had innumerable advantages both of person and opportunity. His head had arrived at a beautiful baldness without the help of tweezers; he was corpulent to a degree that might have excited envy in the handsomest figure in Pekin; . . . he appears in public not only with a scandalous profusion of false hair on his head, but with a sort of hairy muff all round his chin. . . ." Such was the irreverent imagery with which Hunt pointed his moral. His next article, though in more serious style, was as offensive, no doubt, to the Government with its title, "On the Censorial Duties of the Press with regard to the Vices of the Court." (It affords a curious example of the decline of the classics in England; what Sunday politician, except perhaps Mr. Garvin, would nowadays introduce his column, as the scholarly Hunt here does, with some Latin verses of Claudian?) The article was of great length, of surprising outspokenness furiously illustrating its theme, and of an essential rightness in its invocation of King Alfred's character, and Hampden's, and Marvell's—"romance and enthusiasm . . . in short, instead of a set of paupers, friars and slaves, enabled us to be a rich, an intelligent, and a free people." A subsequent

31

paper challenged the claim of the *Courier* that the Regent was a patron of the fine arts, concluding with the brevity of disgust, " his Royal Highness's historical artist is a foreigner of the name of Stroechling, a man not to be compared with Englishmen in any one respect, and a painter of indecent pictures."

The next " Political Examiner " was penned in gaol. On February 3rd " the defendants appeared in Court, whereupon Lord Ellenborough read the libel, and his notes upon the trial. The defendants then put in an Affidavit." In that document they said that their motives had been impersonal and honourable ; that their pecuniary resources (exaggerated in public gossip) were not large, the profits of the " Examiner " up to that date having been almost anticipated in various ways ; that previous prosecutions had reduced their means very severely, one trial totally exhausting one year's net profits from their journal ; and that the Court might fairly consider these things, if it fined the applicants, in mitigation of their penalty. The Court does not appear to have been induced an inch towards moderation by this affidavit. Mr. Justice le Blanc (and not Mr. Justice Grose, who was absent, but whom Leigh Hunt mistakenly names forty years later in his *Autobiography* as having delivered the sentence) prefixed to the judgment of the Court a diatribe on the baseness of feeding " the diseased taste of the public," and the need to make deterrent examples : then came the sentence, " that you severally pay to the King a fine of £500 each ; that you be severally imprisoned for the space of two years ; you, John Hunt, in the prison of Coldbath Fields, and you, Leigh Hunt, in the New Jail for the County of Surrey in Horsemonger Lane ; that at the expiration of that time, you each of you give security in £500 and two sufficient sureties in £250 for your good behaviour during five years, and that you be severally imprisoned until such fine be paid, and such security given." In his observations on this tyrannical sentence, Hunt paid a noble tribute to his

32

brother John, "a man almost proverbial among his friends
for soundness of understanding and uncontaminated dignity
of mind"; opined that, as to the separate prisons, "the
law is understood to have intended the heavier punishment
for me, as undoubtedly ought to be the case, if we are
worthy of any punishment"; and after some allusion to
his illness and the "clanking of the chains of felons" in
his new quarters reiterated his resolve to act like an
Englishman and "suffer any extremity rather than disgrace myself by effeminate lamentation or worse compromise."

To follow Hunt's details of his imprisonment in the
"Examiner," although by no means so Arcadian and
graceful there as in his chapter in the *Autobiography*, is
our best plan here. On February 14th he resumed the
editorial meditations on the sentence, with a serious cheer-
fulness that many men who have sneered at Hunt would
have fallen short of under such circumstances and prospects.
"Brought to trial as we were by an arbitrary method of
accusation, tried as we have been by a jury improperly
made up and under such a presiding spirit as ought *not* to
preside in a court of justice, and suffering as we now are
a punishment totally unfit for our conduct and habits,
it is nevertheless impossible not to feel ourselves the inhabitants of the freest country in Europe, and not to
recognize . . . in the decorum, the cleanliness, and the
considerate adaptation of my prison to the purposes for
which it was *intended*, a public feeling worthy of being
honoured and kept alive. The very circumstance of my
being enabled to acquaint the public in this manner with
my situation and opinions, makes me feel myself an
Englishman; and shall I cease to object to what is wrong,
because I am so ? No, I shall only be the more industrious
to leave no wrong unremedied, precisely for that reason."
With this preamble, he announced that his brother was
in good health and spirits; "and his room, though small,
he described as light and airy, and looking, if with no very

agreeable foreground, towards Hampstead and Highgate."
For his own case, a Committee had responded duly to the
petition of his physician and himself, and his family had
been allowed to join him. " We meet with every personal
civility, and if the keeper of my prison shews a disinclination
to act without authority, we are among the last persons
in the world to quarrel with any man for acting up to his
sense of duty." But Hunt protested against the thrusting
of a man convicted of a political libel into the same gaol
" with the lowest and vilest criminals," and pungently
satirised the extensiveness of the term " misdemeanour "
which levelled reformists with " inciters to robbery and
murder." And then, in his indeed admirable style of
courageous wit, he told the story again as " an Eastern
story," wherein certain princely pranks " in the land of
the Genii " infected a river there. Two bolder fish rose
to the surface to complain against " this fatal amusement."
A cadi named El-En-Burrah at once " seized the daring
fish with an angling-rod of magic parchment." The fish
were " separately dismissed to a dog-kennel " used to
control bad dogs—" very clean, and light, and airy, and
fit for dogs," but not for fish. " Of one of the fish I have
not heard all the particulars, and can only say that he
was a very stout fish, and went off to his prison with a
contemptuous silence. The other was pretty much of as
strong a spirit, but he was of a delicate and sorry kind of a
body, and he lay gasping at the bottom of his kennel for
want of water." In short, this fish requested a tub of
water, and urged that the law should observe the difference
" between a mackarel and a mastiff."

The subject was continued on February 21st and 28th.
The readers of the " Examiner " were informed not only
of their editor's illness and experiences, but of several
private proposals for a subscription to pay the fines. In
any estimate of Leigh Hunt's nature and conduct, it
must always be observed that he endeavoured to stand or
fall in money matters by his own exertions, until presently

his burdens and disappointments reduced him from that standard of independence. Still in the forefront of action and responsibility in 1813, he wrote with decision on behalf of himself and his brother against accepting any plan of subvention, although " one has been hinted to me, of a description so generous and considerate, that as it would be impossible for a public writer to accept it, who is afraid, not indeed of the fine spirit of others, but of his own gratitude, so it would be equally impossible that he should ever forget it." Probably this was the offer of Shelley, who had written from Wales to his friends, " boiling with indignation at the horrible injustice and tyranny of the sentence pronounced on Hunt and his brother." Hunt proceeded to say that he would nevertheless thoroughly agree with another who in his situation accepted such assistance at need, but that his and John Hunt's need was not yet great, and meanwhile " it becomes us not to be paid for performing our duty." The article succeeding mentioned that a Committee had met at Horsemonger Lane and, in view of the certificates of their own medical man and Hunt's usual physician, had sanctioned Hunt's transference to the Prison Infirmary. " To the Infirmary I am accordingly going; and there at least I shall be out of the worst associations of the place—out of the noise of these dinning fetters, these ruffian voices, this horrible laughter rising at intervals from women as well as men felons." From this personal picture the writer advanced into a redoubtable oration with this text : " We protest then against our sentence and all that led to it, as strongly and solemnly as the subjects of a free state like England can protest." There were six divisions of this challenge : " Firstly, because we were brought to trial by *an arbitrary instead of an equal method of accusation* . . . or in other words by the mere will and pleasure of one single person." (Under this head Hunt incidentally harangued the Attorney-General for having thrice put the " Examiner " to the expense of £100 without a trial.)

Secondly, the Jury "was an *improper Jury*, five of the persons on it being in the employ of Government, and one other a Jew under a false name." Thirdly, the Judge was "*an improper Judge*," a man too closely engaged in politics to try a political case, but also "a man of a notoriously bad and passionate temper." Fourthly, the principle of conviction was that rulers are above criticism. Fifthly, "the *truth* that was advanced on this subject . . . was declared to come under the head of *libel*." Sixthly, "*we have been made victims to the shameful vagueness and inequality of the laws with regard to punishment*." When these several pieces had been discharged, Hunt fell silent on the whole matter of imprisonment, and only tenuous allusions during the rest of 1813 indicated that he was not editing the "Examiner" next door to the genial "Cider Cellars" of Maiden Lane.

While Hunt was in prison, his old and favourite school-fellow Thomas Barnes devoted himself very eagerly to the "Examiner," contributing almost all the theatrical notices, and a series of parliamentary criticisms or portraits beginning on August 15th, 1813. These various papers, with their wide literary comprehension both ancient and modern, their strength of purpose, and their abundance of incisive phrase and cadence, all point out the author despite his anonymity as a remarkable journalist, and were duly fulfilled in his most prosperous industry as Editor of *The Times* from 1816 to 1841. Chance has deprived him of a biographer, but when the history of *The Times* is written it may be hoped that this original and powerful journalist and sterling Englishman will be brought fully into the light of common knowledge. Barnes was a dramatic critic of deep reading and feeling, and it is worth while noticing here by way of example how he received S. T. Coleridge's *Remorse* (January 31st). Having discussed the timidity of genius, Coleridge's successful triumph over it, and the story of the play, he wrote, "The fable is managed and developed with a rapidity which never languishes, an intelligibility which a child might follow, and a surprise which would keep awake the most careless attention. The skill indeed with which the situations are disposed, so as to create effect, would have done honour to a veteran dramatist; for this we suppose Mr. Coleridge is indebted to his acquaintance with the German drama, which in the hands of Schiller at least, redeems all its faults by its excellence, and among its other striking beauties, abounds in the picturesque. We never saw more interest excited in a theatre than was expressed at the sorcery-scene in the third act. The altar flaming in the distance, the solemn invocation, the pealing music of the mystic song, altogether produced a combination so awful, as nearly to overpower reality, and make one half believe the enchantment which delighted our senses." Of the characters, Ordonio, " a *Hamlet* corrupted by bad passions," greatly dissatisfied the critic, and on April 4th he published a further condemnation of that "contemplative assassin, who justifies murder by arguments drawn from the scale of being, or the doctrine of general utility," in the form of a panegyric of that cordial ruffian Punch. But he added that this " no more affects the excellencies of Mr. Coleridge's drama, than a burlesque of Scarron or Cotton can detract from the dignity of Virgil. If, however, Mr. C. is not content with the explanation, why then, poor souls, we must be content to be mangled in terrorem in that formidable essay about to be published in which he threatens, we are told, to prostrate—nay, perhaps, ' unless mercy seasons justice,' to annihilate all his unfortunate critical assailants." That essay belongs to Coleridge's prodigious onato-bibliography.

During 1813 Charles Lamb, who appears to have felt a measure of responsibility for the " Examiner " prosecution, anonymously supplied a number of short but valuable articles under the head of " Table Talk," and probably also the pleasant, absurd fabrication that the late comedian Suett was the author of the Letters of Junius. (It is now reprinted and claimed as Lamb's at p. 246). Yet the

"Examiner" was still mainly Leigh Hunt, who was able to reveal with pride that autumn that he had only three times missed his political front page. Much might be said of his writings on Napoleon, for example; but our path lies aside from that region of history, however fascinating it might be to view with Hunt the "State of the Civilized World at the Close of the Year 1812," to rejoice with him over England's "possession of such persons as Clarkson, as Lancaster, as Maria Edgeworth, as Romilly, as Bentham," and "on quitting Europe and casting a glance towards the Western hemisphere" to have "a thousand bright visions of future improvements and rising glories burst upon us."

Several mocking allusions had been made in the "Examiner"—as where had they not ?—to the Poet Laureate, Mr. Pye of Berkshire, and his death in August, 1813, gave Hunt an opportunity to frisk and curvet among the pleasures of absurdity. He admitted a kindness for such legendary gentlemen as Grand Falconers, Knight Harbingers, Bed-chamber Lords, my Lord Goldstick and "his friend the Whitestaff," but for poets-laureate none. "The office of Poet-laureat has the singular fatality of being impossible to be well bestowed; if a good poet accepts it, the office disgraces him; if a bad one, he disgraces the office." Considering nevertheless that someone would be called to succeed Pye, Hunt said he could think of nobody accepting "out of the pale of the Circus or *Morning Post*." He ran his eye over the names of possible selections. "A slight sort of chill came over us when we heard that Mr. Southey was just now to make his appearance in town; but notwithstanding his ambiguous revilements of the Reformers, and his condescending to dedicate something to Mr. Croker, we brought to mind the fine turn of his genius and the native purity of his heart, and our chill was converted into a glow of good-will and security. We can easily imagine the contempt with which Mr. Campbell would treat an offer of the thing; Peers, we believe, are not in the habit of being asked, or Lord Byron's would be about as bitter ; Thomas Moore, a poet in whom the former love of pleasure has not destroyed the spirit of independence or the resolution to do justice to his talents, would ask the Messengers if they recollected his country ; Wordsworth, a name which it is impossible to mention without feeling reverence for his real genius and indignation at his puerile abuse of it, would remember, we trust, his noble sonnet to Milton ; let us hope as much for a man of similar genius, Coleridge, in spite of his sorry distribution of panegyrics to the actors all round."   And, adding similar characterisations of James Montgomery, Rogers, and Scott, Hunt wound up with a lofty historical apology for poets as the guardians of virtue and independence.

What was his disgust when in September the news came that Southey was Poet-Laureate !   " Our readers," his article begins, " have seen how this business has terminated." The laurel " is planted on the primitive head of Mr. Robert Southey ! "   An amusing threnody follows, which must have taken the fancy even of the victim :   " We are to suppose that he at once cares for good example and countenances bad ;   that with an unaltered contempt for dependence he is dependent ;   with an unaltered scorn of worldliness he is worldly ;   and with his hymns to the Household Virtues still in his mind, and a horror of all dice-boxes, dress-boxes, and dram-boxes, he is to bow down at Court amidst the Headforts and Yarmouths, and to say over the hand that he kisses, in the words of the old poet,

> Questa è la bella man, che il cor m' inchioda,
> Questa è la man, che tutto il mondo loda,
> Questa è la man, ch' è la mia cara luce
>   Ch' io vidi in l'alto esempio imaginato.

> This is the heart-felt hand, that warms my lyre,
> This is the hand, which all the world admire,
> This is the hand, of which I've dreamt at night,
> Holding its proud example to the light."

39

The "EXAMINER" EXAMINED

The annual "Postscript" insisted upon the unrusting independence of the incarcerated proprietors; promised the subscribers a new type for the newspaper, the pages at the close of 1813 being indeed almost inscrutable; and complimented with sound critical phrase the writer of the criticisms "both on Senators and Actors." It is thus possible to identify Thomas Barnes, who is known as the author of the parliamentary criticism, in his character as dramatic critic also.

1814: HAZLITT, BARNES, AND THE EDITOR

THE next volume was enriched and enlivened by the accession of William Hazlitt to the list of contributors. There had never crept in any want of enthusiasm or courage in the "Examiner," the editor's writings at this stage being extraordinarily lively and challenging, but with the arrival of Hazlitt a tempestuous gale soon seemed to have sprung up. He began with "On Posthumous Fame" (May 22nd), "On Hogarth's Marriage-A-La-Mode," very direct and expressive, but eclipsed those achievements in his long review of Wordsworth's *Excursion* (August 21st, 28th and October 2nd). What glorious writing! What splendours and what thunder-clouds! The criticism concluded in a burst of disillusion meant to overwhelm Wordsworth's poetic nostrum of the simple cottager. "All country-people hate each other," begins this part of the performance. It ends, "If the inhabitants of the mountainous districts, described by Mr. Wordsworth, are less gross and sensual than others, they are more selfish. Their egotism becomes more concentrated, as they are more insulated, and their purposes more inveterate, as they have less competition to struggle with. The weight of matter which surrounds them crushes the finer sympathies. Their minds become hard and cold, like the rocks which they cultivate. The immensity of their mountains makes the human form appear little and insignificant. Men are seen crawling between Heaven and earth, like insects, to their graves. Nor do they regard one another more than flies on a wall. Their physiognomy expresses the materialism of their character, which has only one principle—rigid self-will. They move on, with their eyes and foreheads fixed, looking neither to the right nor to the left, with a heavy slouch in their gait, and seeming as if nothing would divert them from their path. We do not admire this plodding pertinacity, always directed to the main chance. There is nothing which excites so little sympathy in our minds, as exclusive selfishness." Such was the new voice joining in the "Examiner" chorus, inspiring at once awe and delight, or anger and envy. Hazlitt also contributed during 1814 to the discussion of Kean's acting, particularly in the part of Iago; and at this time were published as "Commonplaces" such luminous and even mystical writings of his as "On the Love of Nature" (November 27th), wherein he vies in prose with Words-worth's *Intimations of Immortality*.

As for Kean's Iago, a letter from P. G. Patmore had been published on May 15th—"desultory remarks" on a genius estimated in terms of resemblance to Shakespeare. Hazlitt took up the theme on July 24th and August 7th, his verdict being that Kean's Iago was "too much in the sun"— "conducted the whole affair with the easy intrepidity of a young volunteer officer, who undertakes to seduce a bar-maid at an inn"—his manner was "no less paradoxical than Mrs. Greville's *Ode to Indifference*." Then came a master's interpretation of Iago, and a disgruntled lover's sneer at Shakespeare's supposing Desdemona or any other woman to have fallen in love with Othello's moral excellence. Leigh Hunt retaliated on August 14th to the latter part, duly quoting Sonnet 116. Barnes in his usual "Theatrical Examiner" for September 4th replied to Hazlitt's rendering of the character of Iago as a malignant being in whose constitution no carelessness or gaiety could be mingled; he invoked the parallel of Milton's Satan ruining Eve with "insinuating obeisances"—"No bridegroom ever presented a more smiling mien,"—and Hobbes "when he said that laughter arose from a sense of superiority." A week later Hazlitt returned, amplifying his original criticism, and maintaining that Barnes had mistaken him; to which in the next number Barnes rejoined with no little shrewdness, closing this most instructive and dexterously conducted argument thus: "Our correspondent charges us with wandering from the subject of the play. Has he not himself furnished us with the example, and in his able portrait of 'the over-active mind dangerous to itself and others, and insatiably craving after action of the most violent kind,' was he not delineating some ideal being rather than the *Iago* of the poet? Perhaps he had some existing character before him: at any rate the picture bears a stronger resemblance to Bonaparte than to Shakespeare's Ancient."

The parliamentary sketches by Barnes continued in all their eloquence and candour through the year, and would be a mine for the historian or novelist of the Regency. At the end of one of them the author (veiled by his initial) very finely thanked the editor for having allowed him unchecked freedom in expressing "opinions which were at variance with your own." Their friend Lamb contributed a lengthy article on a play by Kenney, appending to it a poem in praise of Mrs. Jordan's acting; article and poem are not included in Lamb's works hitherto, but will be found below. It seems probable, too, that the following satisfactory epigram (March 6th) fell from Lamb's pen:

THE TWO K——S.

KEMBLE's an actor, on a studied plan:
KEANE's not the actor—but the very man.
DRAMATICUS.

Reading the files of such a periodical as the "Examiner" is the obvious means of developing a fever of conjecture and identification, and yet let us mention one or two suggestions more for the 1814 volume. The long letter "On the Custom of Stifling Children to Prevent their Catching Cold" (January 9th) appears from matter and manner to be one of humanitarian John Lamb's "literary exercises." It has the same fertile strength of heart and mind as his known work, the same spaciousness of expression, and reference to "good intellects"—the Bible, Shakespeare,

E

Goldsmith—that Mr. Lucas finds in his later contributions to the "Examiner."

Imprisonment did not greatly hinder Leigh Hunt from *his* literary exercises. (We shall leave his political ones, as usual, to other hands; the numerous and picturesque allusions to Bonaparte alone would make a volume.) His strong objection to Southey's revised politics found its outlet in parody and satire, particularly on the publication of the Laureate's first New Year Ode—" such an Ode ! "

O Robert !   O my glorious, natural Bob !

The versifying habit grew upon Hunt himself, and from this time a series of political satires in doggerel metre variegates his newspaper. His sonnets on Hampstead, flowery little pieces blooming like poppies, also showed how his mind was now proceeding. Meanwhile he was not at Hampstead but in the Surrey Jail, and on February 6th he published a cheerful article to mark the expiration of half his imprisonment and his brother's. He therein mentions that he came to prison at a time when the doctor ordered him to take much exercise and varied recreation; instead of riding, and country rambles, and the play, he had recurred to his " old medicine—patience; and what with this, and all sorts of schoolboy exercises, jumping, skipping, and top whipping, to the noise of which my family are content to listen rather with their hearts than their ears, I have managed to wear out the first twelve months of my confinement, and am tolerably confident of doing as much with the second."

On February 27th and March 6th he transformed his " Political Examiner " into a review of Maria Edgeworth's novel *Patronage*. " It is a new and striking thing to see a novel uniting politics with domestic life, and breaking down that barrier of dryness and mystery which interested men would keep round the former sphere "—but that, dear ancient Hunt, was many years ago. On March 20th he produced the first part of "A Surprising New Ballad" which illustrated the person of Lord Ellenborough in such grotesquely comic strokes that Part II did not appear: probably another action at law was thus averted. On June 19th his anti-Regential breast was again relieved in metrical composition of a playful cast but not without sting, beginning, "There be, Princes Three." Leaving this field awhile, he displayed that mellower touch which has not failed to give his essays a considerable public until now, playing on the then general passion for balloons and rockets in a kind of enigmatic contemplation of the moon —the paper is headed "Beautiful Spectacle," assailing "French Fashions," and laughing at the dreary routine of trivial conversation observable when many people meet outdoors, "which may be called the Englishman's Dialogue. It is scarcely necessary to repeat a catechism so well known; but as we do not remember to have seen it transcribed, and malicious foreigners have a trick of misrepresenting our commonest habits, we shall record it here to prevent mistakes. The initials usual on imaginary occasions, A and B, we shall take the liberty, for the better vitality of the discourse, and that no injustice be done to it, to translate into Adams and Brooks.

A. (Advancing as if he could not help it.) How d'ye do, Brooks.

B. Very well, thank'ee; how do *you* do?

A. Very well, thank'ee; *Mrs.* Brooks well?

B. Very well, I'm much obliged t'ye. Mrs. Adams and the children well, I hope?

A. Quite well, thank'ee.

(Here Brooks having to speak next, gives his neckcloth a twist and looks about a little; Adams in pain for his friend doing so likewise, or if he has a lucky switch in his hand, twirling the end of it upon his shoe.)

B. Rather pleasant weather to day.

A. Yes, but it was cold in the morning.

B. Yes, but we must expect that at this time o' year.

(Another brief pause, neckcloth twisted and switch twirled.)

A. Seen Smith lately ?

B. No, I can't say I have. (This *can't say* is a very characteristic phrase in English discourse, implying that the speaker prefers truth even to the comfort of having an answer to give, and that he wishes to Heaven he *could* say it. The question above put is a painful one to Brooks, because it seems to throw upon him the responsibility of having ideas ; but he luckily recollects, that if he has not seen Smith, he has seen Thompson.) Brooks in continuation—But I have seen Thompson.

A. Indeed—and how is he !

B. Very well thank'ee.

A. I'm glad of it—Well—good morning.

B. *Good* morning.

Here it is always observed, that the speakers, having taken leave, walk faster than usual for some hundred yards ; and lucky is he who has a corner to turn, and can begin, as it were, afresh, in another street."

In the last number of the " Examiner " for 1814 a new prospectus was inserted. The nearness of emancipation evidently gave the Hunts a fresh zeal for their work. Their former principles were repeated with distinctness ; their main intention was set forth anew as " the preservation of that PUBLIC SPIRIT, popularly and properly so called, which priding itself on the independent exercise of a sturdy common sense, and judging inflexibly of every thing by one obvious standard of right and wrong, tends to keep the community in proper condition, as a whole, by teaching every one to feel and assert his own political value, as an individual." Hunt promised, upon his release, to resume his visits to, and verdicts on, the theatre, and in making this promise he claimed quite correctly that it was partly his own work in the earlier volumes and in a previous journal (*The News*) which had made dramatic criticism so popular a department of the newspapers. He regretted that latterly through his imprisonment and Barnes' illness, the "Examiner" had been very incomplete in that department, but he declared that in other ways recent issues had been improved, with instances of "superior powers of writing to what the readers of a Paper, not vulgar in that respect, had hitherto met with. We allude to the Criticisms on the Members of Parliament by the friend above-mentioned, and to occasional articles on Literary and Philosophical Subjects by another under the signature of W. H. Both of these will be continued." The type would be renewed, and the hour of delivery made more convenient for "the early riser." These points having been made with much urbanity, the article ended with a *confessio fidei* that nothing else in the paper need be changed; but this was a delusion—the Index cried aloud for utter reformation. How the readers of the "Examiner" endured it year after year is a mystery; perhaps it supplied the place of acrostics and chess problems, or even detective stories.

1815: LEIGH HUNT AT LIBERTY

UNDOUBTEDLY the "Examiner" for January 1st, 1815, had more outward grace (though not to superfluity) than its predecessors, while in essence it justified its new garb. Lamb's well-known pretty verses in the style of Ambrose Phillips, "To T. L. H. a Child," were given over his initials, and with an introductory warning by Leigh Hunt that the reader was not to look for such delights in every number. "Verses indeed may be had in plenty; but poetry is not so easily obtained, and compared with the usual run of newspaper articles, is like a precious liqueur, which is seldom and charily drank, to the general drink at table. The following piece perhaps we had some personal reasons for not admitting, but we found more for the contrary; and could not resist the pleasure of contemplating together the author and the object of his address—to one of whom the Editor is owing for some of the lightest hours of his captivity, and to the other for a main part of its continual solace." A page or two on, Hunt in pleasurable anticipation recommended his "Theatrical Examiner" with a view to giving concisely his general opinions on the stage and the players hitherto known to him, and so providing a preface to his intended notes on the new plays.

"Departure of the Proprietors of this Paper from Prison." No less welcome a legend appeared above Hunt's political article for February 5th. "The two years' imprisonment inflicted on the Proprietors of this Paper for differing with the *Morning Post* on the merits of the Prince Regent, expired on Thursday last; and on that day accordingly we quitted our respective jails." Such changes invariably disturb the constitution. "In truth, habit will dispute a point with any thing; there is no soil, however foreign to

48

one's native feelings, but in the course of time will find fibres about us to grapple with it ; and the sudden departure to another, even though it be an old and congenial one, is in some measure like being torn up by the roots." With the knowledge of Hunt's subsequent excess of misfortunes, obstructions and estrangements, we may discern in this article the troubled voice of presentiment. Hunt endeavoured to strike up a lively air, presenting the fact of the £1,000 fine paid by himself and his brother in the form of a bill :

" To French Ornaments for a National Festival	£300	0 0
To Mons. Stroehling (not mentioned what)	200	0 0
To Alteration of Coats, Hats, &c., for the last month	100	0 0,"

and so on ; but he soon relapsed into a stubborn but subdued statement that the " Examiner " had done something for English Liberty.

An innovation of the new " Examiner " was the series of articles under the pleasant and serviceable title " The Round Table." Hunt opened the series with a paper explaining that the writers would assume no fictitious characters, but talk undisguisedly, as the natural beings they were : " one of us was even caught the other day acting the great horse with a boy on his shoulders ; and another [doubtless Barnes] was not a vast while ago accounted the second best cricketer in his native town." They would be personal, but not solitary and dictatorial : " we are, literally speaking, a small party of friends, who meet once a week at a Round Table to discuss the merits of a leg of mutton and of the subjects upon which we are to write." These friends may be identified as Barnes,* Hazlitt and Hunt from the further data, that " one of us is deep in the learned languages, another in metaphysics,

---

* Barnes, however, was hindered by unexpected pressure of work from taking his share in the " Round Table " ; see No. 14 of the series.

and a third in poetry." The writer concluded by honouring
the memory of King Arthur and aspiring to revive something of the chivalric glory in the ensuing essays. A
second paper defined the classes of subjects to be treated,
Manners, Morals, and Taste.

Hazlitt next addressed the Table on the theme of the
value of life: "the strength of our attachment to it is
a very fallacious test of its happiness." Then came Hunt
on the varieties of egotism. A would-be Squire's applica-
tion for admission to the magic circle, and "A Mechanic's"
onslaught on Malthus, provided the substance of Nos. 5
and 6. No. 7 was on Classical Education, by Hazlitt—a
beautiful utterance: "Rome and Athens filled a place in
the history of mankind, which can never be occupied again.
They were two cities set on a hill, which could not be hid:
all eyes have seen them, and their light shines like a mighty
sea-mark, into the abyss of time." But before the end
of his space the essayist had turned to the great subject
of women, their unreasonableness. This led to a long
and sprightly apology for the sex by Hunt in the next
number, ending in an offering of impassioned gratitude
to his mother. No. 9 by Hazlitt concerned human caprice
and melancholy; in the next, he turned to the happy
pages of the *Tatler* and preferred that work to the *Spectator*,
while Hunt in a sly note pointed out "the sort of stories
and characters which our brother W. H., who is supposed
to be so severe, is fondest of recollecting." Hunt followed
that with an encomium of "people who have nothing
to say." Correspondents—" Woman " and " Jane Wadkin "
—occupied the 12th article. Hazlitt then concluded his
stately analysis of human caprice and melancholy: "the
web of our lives is of a mingled yarn." No. 14 found
Hunt answering correspondents. After a long interval,
perhaps due to the deranging effect of Waterloo upon
Hazlitt's powers of action, the next number was a tribute
to "Lycidas," and a noble one, by that critic; leading to
another beginning "Milton's works are a perpetual in-

vocation to the Muses, a hymn to Fame," and closing with the slightly biassed opinion that Milton's blank verse is the only readable blank verse. No. 17, by Hazlitt, discussed manners and gibed at Wordsworth's poem on the indolence of gipsies; manners, poetical and cultural, occupied the same writer in No. 18; and next time he pounced on the characteristics of certain sects. Then he changed his ground to " John Buncle," glorying in it as " the English Rabelais," and turning from it to rejoice as fully in the " Compleat Angler." Hunt took his place, to speak of modernising Chaucer, and while he discommended the proposal he gave some examples in which he makes the feat look like child's play. Hazlitt resumed, at No. 22, to ridicule the Methodists, on which Hunt (No. 24) echoed his sentiments, and changed the subject to that of the poetic constitution. The intermediate number was a letter containing eighteen questions on and hostile to Malthus, signed Estesi—Coleridge's usual pseudonym, though it is not apparent from other signs that the letter was his. Thoughts on death by Hunt (a dignified and inspiriting essay); Bottom, Puck and other phantasies of Shakespeare, by Hazlitt (with a vociferous postscript, most amusing, against Wm. Cobbett); the doctrine of eternal necessity, by Hazlitt; parallel passages from several poets, by the same—these matters carried the series on to 28 numbers, and completed the sessions of the Round Table for 1815.

Between them Hunt and Hazlitt also supplied the theatrical criticism of the year. Hunt was fresh, brilliant and full of meaning when he wrote the five papers headed " Sketches of the Performers " in January and February, his union of grace and power therein rivalling the playhouse genius of Lamb, whose enthusiasms for Mrs. Jordan (for instance), Miss Kelly and Munden he heartily supported. The laughter of Mrs. Jordan in his still vocal pages " breaks in and about her words, like sparkles of bubbling water." (And unfortunately Mrs. Humphries there, although " a pretty woman," still " masticates a blank verse just as she might a parsnip.") But let us recapture a little of old Munden, most welcome shade of all the actors that ever shed tears of farewell—and Hunt's account is none the worse for being critical : " Certainly the work he makes with his face is equally alarming as well as droll ; he has a sort of complicated grin, which may be thus described : he begins by throwing aside his mouth at the corner with as little remorse as a boy pulling it down with his fingers ; when he jerks up his eyebrows ; then he brings his mouth a little back again with a shew of his teeth ; then he pulls down the upper-lip over the top-row, as a knight might his vizor ; and finally consummates the joke with a general stir round and grind of the whole lower part of his face. This accompanied with some dry phrase, or sometimes with a single word, the spectators always find irresistible, and the roar springs forth accordingly. But he is a genuine comedian nevertheless, with a considerable degree of insight into character as well as surface, and with a great power of filling up the paltriest sketches. We have known him entertain the audience with a real as well as sophisticated human for five or six minutes together, scarcely speaking a word the whole time, as in the part of a sailor in the opera of the *English Fleet*, and in one, we think, in an afterpiece called the *Turnpike Gate*, where he comes in and hovers about a pot of ale which he sees standing on a table, looking about him with ludicrous caution as he makes his advances, half afraid and half simpering when he has got near it, and then after circumventing it with his eyes and feelings over and over again, with some more cautious lookings about, heaving a sudden look into it in the most ludicrous manner imaginable, and exclaiming, in an under voice of affected indifference and real chuckling, ' Some gentleman has left his ale.' " One might almost be reading a sketch of our surely immortal Charles Chaplin. The astonishing keenness of Hunt's impressions is realised when it is recollected that this

verisimilitude was written after almost two years' absence
from the theatre. The " Sketches," Munden's son records,
" obtained a great reputation."

He was present at " his first play (new series) " on February
20th, when he had his first experience of Kean's acting, in
Richard II ; but either from too high expectation (a sort
of constitutional mirage frequently disastrous to Hunt in
this world), or from being too far from the stage, or from
some other cause, he was not deeply pleased. " Kean is
much farther gone in stage trickery than we supposed him
to be, particularly in the old violent contrasts when
delivering an equivoque, dropping his voice too consciously
from a serious line to a sly one, and fairly putting it to the
house as a good joke." The actor's voice he likened without
demur to " a hackney-coachman's at one o'clock in the
morning." On March 19th Hazlitt took the same actor
as his theme, and hoped that " the Editor " would come
to see Kean better both physically and intellectually. On
April 2nd he tilted at Munden (and his encomiast), calling
the comedian " a bad clown " ; and on June 4th both
our critics harmonised sweetly over the final appearance
of Bannister. Performances of *Comus, The Beggar's Opera,
The Tempest, The School for Scandal* were among the subsequent subjects of Hazlitt's careless, battering reviewal ;
but his principal achievement of the season was his bitter
explanation of the dearth of good comedies (August 20th) :
" We are deficient in Comedy, because we are without
characters in real life—as we have no historical pictures,
because we have no faces proper for them." What, then,
could Hazlitt have said, if he arrived in our modern midst ?
He goes on to argue that " the sweeping pall and buskin
and nodding plume, were never more serviceable to Tragedy,
than the enormous hoops and stiff stays worn by the belles of
former days were to the intrigues of Comedy. They assisted
wonderfully in heightening the mysteries of the passion,
and adding to the intricacy of the plot. . . . But now-a-days
—A woman can be *but undressed.*" And nowadays ?

53

At least we have no Stothard nowadays (to turn to the artists), on the publication of whose illustrations to Byron's poems Leigh Hunt expressed his delight—opposite Hazlitt's disgust with comedy. When one takes up any little volume of verse of that period with embellishments by Stothard and others, and notes that it was published in the common course, cheaply and as it were casually, the splendid set pieces of our latterday laborious and self-extolling presses (though they embody much fine character) seem to fade ; " how hardly shall they that have riches——" Hunt alludes especially to Stothard's pictures for Chaucer and Spenser, and his power of identifying himself with every author whom he illustrates ; " It is the same with the Works of Lord Byron, just published. The characteristics of this author are passion, melancholy, a fondness for the mysterious, an intense feeling both of the painful and the voluptuous. All these, and these only, are to be found in the designs for his productions by Mr. Stothard."

A few references to Byron, or poems by him, were scattered through the year. Hunt paragraphed his marriage (January 1st) : " A poet's honeymoon is worth mentioning : it is bound to be *quinta pars nectaris* " ; and on December 17th he celebrated the arrival of a daughter with a few observations on the posterity of poets. Never quite happy in his Byroniana, Hunt observed, " A Poet's enjoyments are matter of interest with the public, who are so much indebted to them for enjoyment themselves ; and we sincerely congratulate the Noble Bard on this addition to his works." Here follows a catalogue of the poets who had no children, and the few who had, with an opinion that modern poets were more fortunate in this than their forerunners ; " All of them, we believe, of any eminence have got children ; Campbell, Coleridge, Moore, Scott, Southey, Wordsworth, and now Byron. Mr. Moore lost a little girl a short time since ; but he has two others ; and there is something in the idea of a *poet's daughter,* which carries a recommendation with it beyond even the

usual charm of the sex. These also are the finest of titles ;
and Lord Byron will aggrandize his posterity more by his
name in the republic of letters, than if he had gathered
about it all the ribbons and coronets in the bestowal of
Courts." Byron gave Hunt three of his best lyrics, which
duly appeared : " Oh ! snatched away in beauty's
bloom " on April 23rd, " Bright be the place of thy soul "
on June 11th, and on July 30th " Farewell to the Land,"
with a caveat by the editor that neither he nor the author
endorsed all the sentiments therein.

This last poem was a note in the tumult of expression
after Waterloo, and we cannot leave the year of Waterloo
behind without glancing at the victory and its immediate
consequences with the eyes of an " Examiner " reader.
In his editorial notes of June 18th Hunt was saying that
" it is not yet completely ascertained that Bonaparte has
set out for the army, but nobody doubts that he has," and
(while the orchard of Hougoumont was singing with shots
and clanging with explosions) the newspaper was proposing
to the Londoners that Wellington and Napoleon might
" come in contact." The following number was almost
entirely a battle gazette, prefaced by a reminder from
Hunt that military victories are only " the medium of
things infinitely more important—the settlement of govern-
ments, and the general good or ill of the people." On
July 2nd he wrote fully of the whole situation, his mind
being rather more concerned with the painful mystery of
the cost of war than with the triumph of our arms. Three
weeks later the strenuous anxiety of thinking men was
greatly relieved, and Hunt was able to write on " Bonaparte's
Surrender of Himself to an English Man of War "; this
he did with words readily transferable to the prevalent
mood when in 1918 the other Great War closed : " We
are like drinkers in the last stage of their habits, who have
so long been accustomed to drams, that excitement is
succeeded by mere dullness." He hoped that Bonaparte
might be comfortably imprisoned in Great Britain, and

that in any event, in deciding what to do with him, "England should consult her own loftiness of character, and vindicate the real superiority she has claimed credit for "— should follow indeed Hamlet's order to Polonius to bestow the players "after your own honour and dignity." Discussing the dispatch of the prisoner to St. Helena, on August 13th, Hunt admired Napoleon's bearing in face of this unwelcome order, saying that it gave his claims "a certain grace, which puts us into an aukward kind of contrast," condemning the action of the Ministers as embodying "a petty fear, and a still pettier revenge," and finally declaring that the origin of militarists lay in the current system of education. "The causes of such men as Bonaparte are not to be found in the viciousness of the individual, nor are their effects to be done away by singling him out for abuse, to the impunity of all others resembling him. The causes are to be found in the admiration of all ranks of society for wars and soldiers in general—in that admiration which these very complainers persist in keeping up for their own purposes—in early habits of education—and in books of all kinds, schoolbooks in particular, in *Homer*, in *Plutarch*, in *Cæsar*, in *Xenophon*, and a hundred others which grave Christian divines continue to teach all over Europe. Edifying no doubt were the sermons which these reverend persons preached in all the churches in behalf of the Waterloo Subscription, and grievous their denunciations against the lust of conquest and the unbridled violence of the passions. Perhaps their text also, to render the moral more perfect, was taken from the history of David, or the hewing of Agag in pieces by the priest Samuel. But what then ? The next morning these very persons are as didactic as ever in behalf of the Cæsars and Alexanders, are giving out themes upon the glories of the Greeks and Romans, and flogging their scholars or their children for not knowing that *virtue* in the Latin language is the same thing as *valour*."

1816: POETRY ABOUNDING:
SHELLEY AND KEATS

IN noticing a performance of *Comus*, during 1815, Hazlitt
had made free with the characters of some contemporaries, Wordsworth being one; and Leigh Hunt had
quickly dissociated himself from that part of Hazlitt's
recreation. Wordsworth had even called on Hunt during
his brief residence in the Edgeware Road, and doubtless
a scene of mutual gratitude had left behind some feelings
of alliance, which are indicated by Wordsworth's appearance
among the poets of the " Examiner " early in 1816. That
gleaming sonnet with the self-descriptive opening " How
clear, how keen, how marvellously bright " was printed
on January 28th, and a fortnight later " While not a leaf
seems faded " followed. But on the next Sunday Wordsworth was advanced to the front page on account, as will
immediately be suspected, of his being one who combined
the poetical genius with political unreliability : " Heaven
made a Party to Earthly Disputes—Mr. Wordsworth's
Sonnets on Waterloo." The sonnets had appeared in
The Champion. Taking up the " Inscription for a National
Monument, in Commemoration of the Battle of Waterloo,"
Hunt raised objection to the classification of the French
armies as " that impious crew," and while he admired the
next piece " Occasioned by the Same Battle " as " very
varied and sonorous," he denied Wordsworth's right to
claim for " The Bard " the sole power of " comprehending
this victory sublime," and questioned his common sense in
fancying the angels to have joined in the huzzas after
Waterloo. The third sonnet was also a pæan on the
occasion, though superficially descriptive of the " Siege of
Vienna Raised by John Sobieski "; Hunt attacked it as

historically inept, and finished his day's work with " We
hope to see many more of Mr. Wordsworth's sonnets, but
shall be glad to find them, like his best ones, less Miltonic
in one respect, and more so in another." It was not long
before that somewhat pompous address to Haydon—
" High is our calling, Friend ! Creative Art . . ."—found
a place in Hunt's columns, " by the Poet's permission " ;
but thereafter the alliance with Wordsworth seems to have
lapsed.

The other eminent Lake Poets were rudely handled
by the reformists throughout 1816. Southey was an old
target. On February 4th his immortal " Blenheim " was
printed entire as an antidote to his account of Waterloo
in the *Quarterly*, a flourish before the full-sounding denun-
ciation of his " Lay of the Laureate " that July. Hazlitt
was of course the volcanic author of that torrent of
damnation. A parody of the poem called " The Laureate
Laid Double " was printed in parallel stanzas with it on
August 4th. Meanwhile Coleridge had been dragged to
the stocks by Hazlitt in the famous review of " Christabel,
&c." (June 2nd), with the cynical explanation of the mystery
of the story by allusion to a manuscript, and a line therein
not given to the public by Coleridge :

> " Behold her bosom and half her side—
> *Hideous, deformed, and pale of hue.*"

And there was thrown in the estimate of " Kubla Khan "
as showing " that Mr. Coleridge can write better *nonsense*
verses than any man in England. It is not a poem, but
a musical composition."

Still pressing on, Hazlitt met the announcement of
Coleridge's " Lay-Sermon on the Distress of the Country "
(September 8th) with spectacular ferocity and malicious
dexterity. The author of the as yet unpublished work
was bombarded with opprobious titles and epithets, " the
very Barmecide of knowledge," " the Dog in the Manger

of literature," " an intellectual Mar-Plot," " the Man in the Moon," " the Wandering Jew," in astonishing profusion, as fast as mill-wheels strike. When at the end of December the book came out as *The Statesman's Manual ; or the Bible the best Guide to Political Skill and Foresight,* Hazlitt once more fired away, but with evident difficulty, and the quotations which he makes in ridicule actually shine out unsullied by his mud-slinging. In Hazlitt's maltreatment of Coleridge there is usually a strain of Olympian jest or secret admiration which makes those papers seem amiable if they are compared with his white-lipped fury against Wordsworth at the close of 1816. " The spirit of Jacobin poetry," he wrote, " is rank egotism. We know an instance. It is of a person who founded a school of poetry on sheer humanity, on idiot boys and mad mothers, and on Simon Lee, the old huntsman. The secret of the Jacobin poetry and the anti-Jacobin politics of this writer is the same. His lyrical poetry was a cant of humanity about the commonest people to level the great with the small ; and his political poetry is a cant of loyalty to level Bonaparte with kings and hereditary imbecility. As he would put up the commonest of men against kings and nobles, to satisfy his levelling notions, so for the same reason he would set up the meanest of kings against the greatest of men, reposing once more on the mediocrity of royalty. This person admires nothing that is admirable, feels no interest in any thing interesting, no grandeur in any thing grand, no beauty in any thing beautiful. He tolerates nothing but what he himself creates ; he sympathizes only with what can enter into no competition with him. . . . He hates all science and all art ; he hates chemistry, he hates conchology ; he hates Sir Isaac Newton ; he hates logic, he hates metaphysics, which he says are unintelligible, and yet he would be thought to understand them ; he hates prose, he hates all poetry but his own ; he hates Shakespear, or what he calls ' those interlocutions between Lucius and Caius,' because he would have all

F   59 the talk to himself, and considers the movements of passion in *Lear*, *Othello*, or *Macbeth* impertinent, compared with the Moods of his own Mind; he thinks every thing good is contained in the *Lyrical Ballads*, or, if it is not contained there, it is good for nothing; he hates music, dancing and painting; he hates Rubens, he hates Rembrandt, he hates Raphael, he hates Titian, he hates Vandyke; he hates the antique, he hates the Apollo Belvidere, he hates the Venus de Medicis. He hates all that others love and admires but himself." Undoubtedly Ercles' vein; but Wordsworth or a piece of him manages to survive it.

While Hazlitt was roaring at the older poets, Hunt's more anticipative nature, now rapidly receding from political aspirations into literary luxuries, recognised some younger men as destined for greatness. He records that when Keats' sonnet "To Solitude," signed J. K., was published—in the "Examiner" of May 5th—he did not know the writer personally. That was Keats' first known appearance in print, and a truly creditable beginning it was. On December 1st* Hunt addressed his public on the subject of "Young Poets"—Keats, Reynolds and Shelley—an introductory essay written in haste but with infallible judgment. Shelley's description, "a very striking and original thinker," remains predominantly true; Keats' "ardent grappling with Nature" still surprises us as it did the maker of the phrase; and Reynolds, "too artificial," still takes his secluded graceful way like "the water gently gliding ever" in his most familiar piece. "Young Poets" will be found in the second part of this book. In it Hunt pays a passing tribute to the third canto of "Childe Harold"—not his only reference to Byron in the "Examiner" for 1816, although the others relate rather to Byron's affairs than his verses. There was, for example a long article (April 21st) on the separation of that poet and

* The "Notices to Correspondents" of November 3rd ran, " The Sonnet on Chapman's Homer by J. K., and a selection from the *Naiad*, the earliest opportunity."

his wife; therein Hunt attacked the malicious gossip of
the newspapers in general, and proclaimed "that our
Noble Friend with all his faults, which he is the last man
upon earth to deny, possesses qualities which ought to
crumble the consciousness of these men into dust." For
this friendly homily, which was at any rate a welcome
exception to the current abuse, Byron was not ungrateful;
but it is a sickly, awkward and loquacious paper. A postscript the week after claimed that it had helped to put the
scandalmongers to flight, announced Byron's departure for
the Continent, and repeated " our perfect conviction that
the separation will not be lasting." Hunt subjoined the
well-known copy of conversational verses " To the Right
Honourable Lord Byron on his Departure for Italy and
Greece."

These were, with some flaws, melodious, well-adorned
and cheerful verses, reminding us vividly that in 1816
Hunt was himself a " young poet " of importance. His
" Story of Rimini " had certainly enlivened the critics,
thrilled gentle hearts and young fancies, and given the
poets themselves a new enlargement of theme and fresher
conception of the effects of the English rhyming couplet.
Delighted with praises and literary friendship, Hunt was
now beginning to feel a tedium in public affairs, from which
the charming chances of poetry invited him more and more
to stray. In his poetry, whether it is liked or not, one
recognises the radiation of a distinctive personality, and
one recalls in its airs the fact that Hunt was a brilliant
pianist and " matchless fireside companion." His enthusiasm frequently quickens sparkling passages of verse (to
adapt his own lines);

> We see him then, half eagerness, half ease,
> Ride o'er the dancing freshness of the seas;

but his observation runs low long before the demand upon
it ceases, and he continues to rhyme and flirt with pretty
phrase as though his improvisation were a very good sub-

stitute for natural expression and matured truth. So it is with his exhilarating address to Byron, opening with striking fancy freshly but simply announced, and slipping away at length into words, words, words and false ingenuity. And yet the poem takes one's mind back to the frankness and fine ease of Drayton in his Epistle to Henry Reynolds.

> Not that our English clime, how sharp soe'er,
> Yields in ripe genius to the warmest sphere;
> For what we want in sunshine out of doors
> And the long leisure of abundant shores,
> By freedom, nay by sufferance, is supplied.
> And each man's sacred sunshine, his fire-side.
> But all the four great Masters of our Song,
> Stars that shine out amidst a starry throng,
> Have turned to Italy for added light,
> As earth is kissed by the sweet moon at night.

In Hunt English poetry found a sort of homebred Italian, who, for all his excess and gaudiness, diffused a vinous radiance through our cloudier habit of mind and measure, and transplanted a coloured fancy from the warm South.

During 1816 he contributed verse more frequently to the "Examiner" than in any other year, attracting of course the attention of various malevolent critics, but achieving more than once a hold on the reading hours of posterity. The poems to his two children Thornton and John have still their readers, and had their parodists. Among the translations (and Hunt is the first of our lyrical translators) that excellently bright one from "The Celebrated Canzone of Petrarch, beginning 'Chiare, Fresche, e Dolce Acque'" appeared in the newspaper on December 8th, with the date of completion November 25th and a note that the version was made in gratitude for "a print after Stothard on the subject of the fourth stanza" presented to Hunt. In lower style, and almost forgotten, are the series of seven letters in verse (uneasy anapaests) scribbled off by Hunt in hit-or-miss fashion that year; he calls himself "Harry Brown" and the cousin of Tom Brown, *i.e.* Thomas Moore, then behaving very friendly to Hunt ; the manner of writing is itself an allusion to Moore's "Postbag" poetry, and four of Hunt's letters are addressed to him, the others to Hazlitt, Barron Field and Charles Lamb.   Biographers have neglected these casual effusions which contain a good deal of personal notice, with several strokes of valuable wit ; and in the first of the series Hunt sketched the pleasures of indolence at Hampstead in such cool and gleaming tints that one may feel what vernal graciousness surrounded his immortal friendships of that period :

> How can I touch, and not linger awhile,
> On the spot that has haunted my youth like a smile ?
> On its fine breathing prospects, its clump-wooded glades,
> Dark pines, and white houses, and long-allied shades,
> With fields going down, where the bard lies and sees
> The hills up above him with roofs in the trees ?
> Now too, while the season, half summer, half spring,
> Brown elms and green oaks, makes one loiter and sing ;
> And the bee's weighty murmur comes by us at noon,
> And the cuckoo repeats his short indolent tune,
> And little white clouds lie about in the sun,
> And the wind's in the west, and hay-making begun ?

In truth it must have been difficult and even painful for Hunt, so roaming and rhyming, to revert to his business as editor of a Sunday paper, yet he contrived to throw some of his former intensity into his topical and controversial writings   The supply of "Political Examiners" with their challengings and championings, their oratorical imagery and indeed their modern point of view, whether the subject of the week were the Income Tax or Military Encroachment, Mr. Canning or the Holy Alliance, did not fail.   A slightly moderated energy of personal satire now observable might be due to Hunt's maturing age, but doubtless is more to be ascribed to the shadow of further legal spoliation hanging over the "Examiner."   In general, his comments on contemporary history retained that largeness and grasp for

which Hunt has so seldom received the credit of late years.
If he preferred as he grew older to descant on the excellences
and the happy evolution of humanity, is that a reason for
treating him as so many idlers in literature treat him—like
a shallow hedonist, a pious fraud ? The "Examiner" in
its early years is his enforced and hurrying struggle for
ideals ; his later life is the quiet confidence taught him by
experience. But this is going too far ahead; resuming
his editorial work in 1816, one finds especially revisitable
his two papers on the death and funeral of Sheridan (July
14th and 21st), which are more sympathetic and personal
than the introductory essay perfunctorily supplied by
Hunt to Moxon's edition of the dramatist in 1840. Indeed,
Hunt had previously called Sheridan rude names ; but
now it was, " We not only miss Mr. Sheridan in point of
intellect—we miss him also in that liberal and graceful
description of it which made pleasant the light which it
shed. We miss the graceful, the classical, the social, the
smiling part of public life—the *literas vere humaniores*—
the sunny side of *the town*." On September 22nd the
" Examiner " printed a correct copy of Byron's monody on
Sheridan, with a curiously detailed criticism of its failure,
in which are embedded notable observations on Byron :
" His talent does not lie so much in appealing to others,
as in expressing himself. He does not make you so much
a party as a witness," and " He is a Salvator Rosa, and has
no business with scene-paintings, bad or good." As he
was seldom found in the theatre during 1816, Hunt's
dramatic criticism was unusually scanty ; he wrote strikingly
of *Timon of Athens* and Kean in it (November 3rd)—hinting
by the way that the play's " representations of pecuniary
difficulty, and friendship put to the test," strongly appealed
to his own situation—and on December 8th he took the
opportunity of Bickerstaff's *Lionel and Clarissa* to charac-
terise that author's· " pleasant mediocrity," " indolent dis-
cernment of simplicity " and nimble, cheerful conversion
of plagiarism into the " Pereant qui ante nos " attitude.

64

To the " Round Table " Hunt contributed three sketches of types, " characters " almost, two of which, " The Old Lady " and " The Maidservant," reappeared in his collected writings and have justly delighted a great many readers.

The " Round Table," however, was becoming rather dull; it was often empty, and when it was not, it was almost always occupied by Hazlitt in solitary and minatory state. Admitted, that Hazlitt himself was a host. He could not take up such themes as inherent beauty, the artist's pleasure in art, the necessity and charm of pedantry, gusto in painters and writers, without scattering beams and flashes of intellectual and passionate glory. Best of paradoxers! when Hazlitt writes " Henry VIII was a good-natured monarch. He cut off his wives' heads with as little ceremony as if they had been eels," or " The definition of a true patriot is *a good hater*," one realises more clearly than ever the truth of Catullus's *Odi et amo !* Assisted, then, with an occasional relief by Hunt, Hazlitt advanced the total of " Round Table " essays to 47 in 1816, and added the final piece on January 5th, 1817; the series was then reprinted with additions by himself and Hunt in two pocket volumes, and duly bedevilled by the *Quarterly* for April, 1817

Minor contributors of 1816 were few, so far as this record need go. B. R. Haydon, who had in former years written extensively but drably here, appeared on March 17th on the arena, suitably flanked and supported by the Elgin Marbles; his trouble was Mr. Payne Knight and his confederate connoisseurs, whom he lashed and with much terminology abhorred for their unbelief. " To these divine things " (not Knight & Co.), he ended, " I owe every principle of Art I may possess. I never enter among them without bowing to the Great Spirit that reigns within them. I thank God daily that I was in existence on their arrival, and will continue to do so to the end of my life. Such a blast will Fame blow of their grandeur, that its roaring will swell out as time advances; and nations now sunk in barbarism, and ages yet unborn, will in succession be roused by its thunder, and be refined by its harmony. Pilgrims from the remotest corner of the earth will visit their shrine, and be purified by their beauty." In his Autobiography the painter says that this philippic, which he proudly transcribes, had a " tremendous effect on society," and saved the Marbles for the country, but ruined him by alienating the patrons of painting. Besides Haydon, mention must be made of Barron Field and Horace Smith. Field's initials are appended to a delightful poem, in the measure of George Wither or "Hudibras," published on August 18th. It is called "On seeing Mrs. K—— B——, aged upwards of Eighty, nurse an Infant," and is excusably included from another and later source in recent editions of Lamb's work. Besides the initials, the dating " Northiam, 1814," shows that it is not Lamb's, but it is kindred of his wit-melancholy.

> " Thou dost not to this age belong :
> Thou art three generations wrong :
> Old Time has miss'd thee : there he tarries !
> Go on to thy contemporaries !
> Give the child up. To see thee kiss him
> Is a compleat anachronism.
> Nay, keep him," &c.

Smith's "Sonnet, Addressed by the Statue of Jupiter, Lately Arrived from Rome, to his Royal Highness the Prince Regent," is excellent in the vein of casual grandeur, poetry subordinate to jest, then distinguishing English verse—the Ozymandias vein.

> " Found by the Priest of rival Deities,
> In penance here I stand, 'mid forms obscene
> Of Demon, Dragon, Monster, Mandarin.
> O King Restorer ! Rightful Lord *of these !*
> Me, too, restore—not to my Throne, but Tomb ;
> Be buried sleep, not living shame, my doom."

1817: ALARMS AND EXCURSIONS

THE appearance (fusty) and the spirit (fiery) of the " Examiner " were not much modified in the tenth volume, much of the importance and attraction of which relates to Keats and Shelley. We shall attend to the details of their implication, which have not been wholly chronicled hitherto. On January 19th the mystery of an editorial announcement made on October 6th of the previous autumn, " The Elfin-Knight, the first opportunity," was cleared up by the appearance of Shelley's Coleridgean " Hymn to Intellectual Beauty " in all its phantasmal radiance, thus prosaically introduced : " The following Ode, originally announced under the signature of the *Elfin Knight*, we have since found to be from the pen of the author, whose name was mentioned among others a week or two back, in an article entitled ' Young Poets.' The reader will think with us, that it is alone sufficient to justify what was there observed ; but we shall say more on this subject in a review of the book we mentioned." Hunt was interrupted by the " Westbrooke *v.* Shelley " action of January 24th, of which two days later he gave a short report and an opinion, as yet indeterminate, but illustrated by a quotation from Voltaire's History of Louis XIV on the persecution of the Huguenots : " Many Arrêts of the Council were issued, blow upon blow, to extirpate the remains of the proscribed religion. That which threatened to be the most fatal, was the order to tear their children from the pretended *Reformés*, to put them in the hands of the nearest Catholic relations—an order against which *Nature cried with so loud a voice*, that it was not executed." On February 2nd Hunt added that his report of the case was erroneous, that Shelley's " defence was chiefly made, and in a most impressive and spirited

67

manner, by Mr. Montagu," and that the case would be tried again in private.

Sonnets by Keats began to appear soon afterwards, but not very good ones. "To Kosciusko" was printed on February 16th, "After dark vapors" (certainly looking more like mastery) the week following; but then an interval occurred: "J. K.'s Lines are delayed, owing to the great pressure of temporary matter." Presumably the poems held over were the two Sonnets "To Haydon" and "On Seeing the Elgin Marbles," published on March 9th. And on the 16th Hunt acclaimed the pretty triviality "Written on a Blank Space at the End of Chaucer's Tale of 'The Floure and the Lefe'" with the foreword, "The following exquisite Sonnet, as well as one or two others that have lately appeared under the same signature, is from the pen of the young poet (Keats), who was mentioned not long since in this paper, and who may already lay true claim to that title:

> The youngest he
> That sits in shadow of Apollo's tree."

This was indeed the most glowing sunshine of the friendship between Hunt and Keats; it was at this time that Keats came running towards Hunt in Millfield Lane, with his new book of *Poems* in his hand to present to the still undiscarded "Libertas"—the dedication copy. Hunt's review of the book, announced on May 25th, duly began appearing in the next number, but on June 8th the continuation was "postponed, owing to the great press of temporary matter," together with a paper by Haydon, which had to wait until July 13th. The Keats article was continued on the 6th and concluded on the 13th. This particularity may be forgiven us, since the late Miss Lowell in her large book on Keats accuses Hunt of "shirking" the difficult problem of praising the young poet without attracting the mohocks of the North and the *Quarterly*, and of "pussy-footing." In fact the delay was one of those to which "Examiner" readers were inured, and even the vision of Keats had to wait while Reform was particularly in need of the paper's resources. Hunt's article can hardly be overpraised ; he is not blind to faults, but he discerns excellences with prophetic quickness. He writes of the Keats who is now realised—and he does that in the absence of Keats' chief poetry. Soon afterwards, Haydon's* jealousy and Hunt's dissatisfaction with "Endymion" provoked Keats into a bitterness in which he scarcely did justice to his first and foremost critic. On September 21st Hunt seems to have meant to recall Keats' confidence and regard by printing with Keats' sonnet on "The Grasshopper and Cricket," taken from the 1817 *Poems*, his own competitive sonnet on the same occasion and topic.

During the earlier months of 1817, Hunt and Hazlitt frequently directed their light artillery against their old enemies Coleridge and Southey, sending over now a single shot and now a salvo. On January 12th, Hazlitt, having just concluded an onslaught on those poets and Wordsworth, immediately proceeded as a correspondent styled "Semper Ego Auditor" to recall S. T. C. in his fabulous youth ; thus revealing the glow of affection for the author of the Lay Sermons, which was previously suspected in Hazlitt's maledictions. The bitter practical joke of republishing Southey's "Wat Tyler" at this date of course elicited Hazlitt's ironies (without any latent charitableness), and Southey's attempt to have it suppressed only redoubled the sarcasms : " In courtly malice and servility Mr. Southey has outdone Herodias's daughter. He marches into

---

* "As to Haydon's calumny of John Keats, that 'he had been drunk for weeks together, and would cover his tongue with Cayenne that he might the better relish his Claret,' in all our convivialities I never saw Keats intoxicated, and, from all I know of his tastes and habits, I have not the slightest belief in the Cayenne pepper story. Haydon soon disgusted Keats—and no wonder."—C. Cowden Clarke, " Examiner," July 9th, 1853.

Chancery 'with his own head in a charger,' as an offering to Royal delicacy." Presently Hunt took a hand, presenting the " Death and Funeral of the Late Mr. Southey " with doubtful propriety but indubitable zest. The procession was thus marshalled :

A Corporal and File of Soldiers to clear the way.
Penny-trumpets, two and two.
Jacobins with their coats turned.
A Deputation from the Royal Spanish Academy.
Ditto from the Inquisition, holding thumb-screws.
A Frenchman of the old regime in full costume, powdered and sallow-faced, out at elbows, taking snuff, and bowing on all sides.
A Deputation from the Papists at Thoulouse, dragging in the mud the Effigies of VOLTAIRE and CALAS.
A bag-wig and a tattered laurel held up on a cushion.
Renegadoes from Al- {THE BODY} Renegadoes from Al-
giers as Pall-Bearers. giers as Pall-Bearers.
MURRAY the Bookseller as Chief Mourner,
Holding down his head and looking sideways.
Dr. PARACELSUS BROADHUM COLERIDGE,
Holding an enormous white handkerchief to his eyes,
and supported by two Bottle-holders.
Dr. STODDART, a Civilian,
In a very weak condition, his supporters having left him out of weariness, as well as from the inconvenience occasioned by his dirty mode of proceeding.
JOHN WILSON CROKER, Esq.
Supported by Involuntary Contributions.
WILLIAM GIFFORD, Esq.
Supported by Gentleman Pensioners, but very irritable in his grief, kicking the mud on all sides of him and on the Ladies.
GEORGE CANNING, Esq. M.P. in a close Carriage.
Empty Carriages of the Ministers and Court.
Hirelings on Horseback.

Equally improper and more punishing was Hazlitt's idea (in a review of Southey's "Letter to William Smith," May 4th), " Mr. Southey publicly exposes his mind to be anatomised while he is living. He lays open his character

70

to the scalping knife, guides the philosophic hand in its painful researches, and on the bald crown of our *petit tondu*, in vain concealed under withered bay-leaves and a few contemptible grey hairs, you see the organ of vanity triumphant—sleek, smooth, round, perfect, polished, horned and shining, as it were in a transparency." With Keats, we would have had the grey hairs omitted, but the rest is glorious nonsense. The review continued in later numbers of smilar destructive force, and Hunt threw in a squib, according to which Southey's corpse lying in state in "Murrain's back parlour" had made a posthumous oration in honour of Southey's consistency.

Hazlitt's writings for the "Examiner" seem to have paused soon after these satirical diversions, but Hunt of course, and perforce, kept up his conjurer-like performance as politician, literary, musical and dramatic critic, and essayist. He published only two poetical pieces this year. The principal part of his political expression was the series of thirteen " Letters to the English People on their demands for Constitutional Reform," which were interspersed as occasion asked by fine phraseological essays on the treatment of Napoleon, the revolution in Brazil and the conquest of Chili—we must take a few scenic effects from his conquest of Chili, and ask our Sunday stylists to beat them if they can : "The imagination follows the contending armies through forests and up green plains, down again into beautiful vallies, and again up the sides of towering mountains ; it fancies them appearing and disappearing, scattered among crags, crowding through narrow passes, winding along narrow and horrible precipices, and alarming as they go the animals of those quiet regions with the clanking progress of soldiery, or the new thunder of drums and trumpets ; till at last, the still more thunderous novelty of artillery commences ; the smoke seems to shake and roll up the hitherto stationary clouds ; a new lightning flashes ; and you see men and horses riding at each other as if in the air, surmounting by turns crag above crag, and shaking out the wounded and the overthrown like warlike spirits tumbling from the clouds." Cinematography! thy date is clearly 1817.

At least he was on safer ground at the opera, among "Italian, and music, and dancing, and beautiful mythologies," listening to *The Maid of the Mill* and meditating on Mozart in Italy. "Titian lived beneath a sapphire sky, where every other colour shewed a proportionate intensity; and the Sacchinis and Paesiellos heard the sound of their lutes, and the voices of their mistresses, through an atmosphere thrilling with clearness. . . . Mozart, who of all the German composers had the greatest animal spirits, went there when he was a boy: he drank at the winy fountain, and seems to have been intoxicated ever after with love and delight." From this southern rapture he could depart far north to enjoy Allan Ramsay's *Gentle Shepherd* (even though cut down to make an afterpiece); but the irruption of China into Drury Lane annoyed him unusually, to our advantage. "We protest vehemently against the Saloon. They have absolutely filled it with Chinese pagodas and lanthorns, a series of the former occupying the middle, and a profusion of the latter being hung up on all sides, *adorned* with monsters and mandarins, and shedding a ghastly twilight! . . . What mummeries and monstrosities! On one lanthorn, a man like a watchman—on another, a dragon or some unintelligible compound of limbs—on another some Chinese pot-hooks and hangers! Then the pagodas rise one over the other, like the cardhouses of the little boys; and as if there were not monsters enough on the lanthorns, a set of huge tyger busts, or some such substitute for Grecian sculpture, gape down upon you from the sides of the ceiling, and only want some puppet-shew men to ventriloquize for them and make them growl, to render this exquisite attraction complete. What is the meaning? Some libellous fellows say, that it is a complimentary imitation of the Prince Regent," etc. Presently, taking up the playbill, he finds among the attractions (after

72

much prelusive pomp) " a ' Chinese walk ' ; and what is the Chinese walk ? Nothing but the usual walk up the Saloon, with a trumpery Chinese tap-room or tea-room at the *end* of it, over which is daubed on a board ' *Thè à-la-Chinoise*,' and where (stupendous to think of !) you can buy cakes."

The nature of much interpretation and even eulogy of Hunt's powers has seemed to mean that his sensibilities are inclosed within the borders of the fanciful and urbane. A magnificent simile in the paper just referred to reminds one of Dr. Johnson's remark, that Thomson could not have seen the candles burning except with the poet's eye ; Hunt is talking of the gaslights of London shops : " In some of them, where the gas is managed with taste, and shot out from a slender pipe, it is no extravagance to say, that it puts one in mind of what one fancies in poetry— of the flamy breath at the point of a Seraph's wand ;

> And in his hand a reed
> Stood waving, tipt with fire."

Sublimity arising from domestic facts, like the Arabian phantom from the common jar, was peculiarly his theme. In writing of Mozart's *Don Giovanni* (August 16th), he gave several instances of true sublimity and supernatural art. He contrasts the noise of Mars with the nod of Jupiter, the nod of Jupiter with Fate " that lay hidden." He separates the assault and battery phrases in David's Psalms from " the pestilence that walketh in darkness " and congenial immensities. He (of course) repeats the immortal symbolic story of the " still small voice " ; and indicates how " fierce as ten furies " is comedy beside " Black *it* stood as night." And as the culmination he invokes Job's friend Eliphaz, with the ghost " before mine eyes—*there was silence.*" It is evident that Hunt, for all his aerial lightnesses and several serious imperfections, was not in imaginative stature far below our greatest names.

73

But we stay too long. It will be enough to notice his powerful eulogy of Hazlitt's " Characters of Shakespeare's Plays," with the motto " *Sero sed serio* " above, printed on October 26th, November 2nd and 23rd; pointing out especially how Hazlitt heliotropically " changes his own humour and manner according to the nature of the play he comes upon," and enjoying the full range of Hazlitt's enjoyment.

The argumentative sounds of Haydon (despite friendship's cleavage) were not seldom heard during this year. Long afterwards J. M. W. Turner, being told the sensational news of Haydon's suicide, did not even trouble to look up from his newspaper, merely remarking and repeating, " He killed his mother." Presumably this strange oracle summed up Haydon's many skirmishes with the Academy, such as (on August 24th, 1817) the remonstrance headed " The Ananias Cartoon Taken from the Students at the Gallery by the Academicians," and a sequel to it on November 15th, in which the complainant urged with Kent in the play that " Anger has a privilege," and flagellated " malignity," " meanness," " brutality " and other qualifications of the R.A.'s. " Why do they fear the rise of Historical Art ? " Alas for Haydon and his cohorts of Daniel-Lambert heroes, they had no fear of that !

As the year advanced, a few more evidences of Shelley's career found their place in the " Examiner." Proclaiming Reform with his wonted energy, Hunt on March 2nd took the chance of noticing " A Proposal for putting Reform to the Vote throughout the Kingdom," and making an extract from it ; he concluded, " This wants no comment ; or rather we ought to say, that we deny ourselves the luxury of making any, out of respect to the feelings of this noble nature, whom we have the honour and the happiness of knowing. While there are Englishmen like these, the old breed is not extinct ; and when they come forth, the new cannot long remain in possession of our green and glorious country." On August 31st there was a comment on

" Westbrooke *v.* Shelley," correcting the illusions of a contemporary newspaper that Shelley was a fool and the lady with whom he was living was not his wife. A selected passage from " Laon and Cythna " luminously signalled the publication of that poem. And on December 28th E. K., clearly the " Elfin Knight " previously seen in romantic solitudes, communicated his well elaborated conclusion that William Godwin had been " to the present age in moral philosophy what Wordsworth is in poetry," with a stirring picture of the qualities of his novel *Mandeville*, a criticism electrical with Shelley's nervous rapidity of imagination. Here should appropriately be quoted a note of Hunt's to an article on the philanthropist Owen, styled " the first mild and unequivocal *voice*, that proclaimed the incompatibility of *charity* with *faith*." That claim is thus annotated : " A few years back, a young man of extraordinary talents, now living, proclaimed the same opinion at a publc meeting in Ireland ; but he did it indignantly, and in such a manner as to rouse the *angry* self-love of others, and so lost the effect which older years would have given him." Such was the youth of Shelley.

But the conspicuous interest of this part of " Examiner " history is the outbreak of deadly war between its group (especially their leader) and *Blackwood's Magazine*. A great amount of ink was shed, and has since been shed on the subject ; yet the action of the " Examiner " is not correctly noted in most authorities The trouble began with the October number of *Blackwood's*, and on November 2nd the newspaper answered thus :

" To Z. The Writer of the Article signed Z, in *Blackwood's Edinburgh Magazine* for October, 1817, is invited to send his address to the Printer of the ' Examiner,' in order that justice may be executed on the proper person." A fortnight passed. Then a much more prominent notice was printed " TO Z," followed by extracts from the offensive article, ending " *The very Concubine of so impure a wretch as Leigh Hunt would be to be pitied, but alas ! for the Wife of such a Husband! For him there is no charm in simple Seduction ; and he gloats over it only when accompanied with Adultery and Incest*"; a specimen of literary criticism to which the footnote was, "The anonymous Author of the above atrocious attempt to destroy the personal character of the Editor of this Paper, is again called upon to avow himself; which he cannot fail to do, unless to an utter disregard of all *Truth* and Decency, he adds the height of Meanness and COWARDICE. Should this however be the case, those who have published the foul Scandal—if they persist in skreening the Author from a just punishment—must prepare to abide the consequences of their delinquency." The next week, November 23rd, Messrs. Baldwin, Cradock and Joy (the London agents for *Blackwood's*) communicated their disavowal of any part in the management, or knowledge of Z's identity; of which Z also seemed ignorant. The Hunts waited, but in vain; and on December 14th the sign-manual of Leigh Hunt appeared beneath some forceful sentences headed "Z." "This poor wretched lying and cowardly creature has now had more than ample time to come forward, and has not done so. He has, to be sure, published a second edition of his atrocious nonsense, in which some of the worst of his insinuations are withdrawn; but he, or his employers, must not think to escape, while the same venomous malignity survives in the remaining parts of the reptile. Reptile indeed he is, and most unhappy creature must be, to feel excited to pour forth misrepresentations, which could not be falser, if he had cried out, in his anguish, at the blackness of the green leaves or the hatefulness of affection." Hunt further expressed his gratitude "to two gentlemen, strangers to him" for hastening to his defence, one in *The Edinburgh Magazine*, the other in a pamphlet entitled *A Review of Blackwood's Edinburgh Magazine for October*, 1817.

"Z" and his associates of course proceeded gaily with their Cockney School studies, but Hunt does not seem to have fallen into a sadness or fast because of them, However, he again made public allusion to his masked assailant, and on April 12th, 1818, printed a notice, "Attack on the Editor in a Magazine." He began with a statement which may seem singular, yet is borne out by his similar testimony in the Harold Skimpole episode of many years afterwards : "I must here observe, that I have never been in the habit of attending to these things, and that all the notices of it, except the last, came from my brother ; who being at the Examiner-Office when the libel reached him, and moved with a zeal for me which a friend may reasonably feel beyond the party attacked, thought it worth while to call for the author, and possible that the call would be attended to. The call was repeated in vain. I made one myself in terms strong enough to rouse up any decent animal from his hiding-place, and endeavoured to persuade myself that I ought to feel something more than mere scorn—but all to no purpose." Here follow various humanitarian reflections on the question of retribution, to which Hunt avowed himself opposed. "Still," he continues, "I fancied that the author could scarcely help coming forward. I had never disguised myself from individuals, or from the public. I had particularly left word at the Office, that any one who thought himself aggrieved by me, and who demanded my name and residence, should be told them ; and out of a simplicity, which it will take still more disappointment, I hope, generally speaking, to do away, I was trusting enough to imagine that an individual, evidently ignorant of all noble theories, and who had taken pains, in language that recoiled

77

upon himself, to misrepresent my actions, my motives, my very reading, nay, my personal manners, and very walk, would nevertheless have spirit enough remaining to avow himself and come forward He did not. He contented himself, instead, with addressing to me a letter, in which, after a certain growling and mean fashion, he recanted— that is to say, in which he had the face to pretend that he had *not* attacked me in my private character and person— in which, with habits of falsehood equally disgusting, he pretended to confound all the absurd particulars of his libel with some general questions equally ridiculous— and which he concluded by saying that he did not mind being called a coward, and should not come forward." Finally Hunt wrote that Z might now avow his identity with impunity : " my pity for him, with very great sincerity, is still stronger than my contempt."

Some years afterwards, when he was on the point of departing for Italy, Leigh Hunt wrote a Political Examiner on the subject of the calumnies not only of *Blackwood's Magazine* but of two other journals less literate and more scoundrelly (at that time an astonishing feat of nature)— the *John Bull* and *The Beacon*. In that serious remonstrance, proper to be considered at this point, Hunt gives something more of the inner history of the original " Z " incident. "When *Blackwood's Magazine* was first set up, he was one of those whom it attacked in its most gratuitous and atrocious manner. Not only were his manners and habits misrepresented to the least and idlest circumstance, but a sorrow in the history of a friend, which men of the smallest gallantry and goodness of heart would have known how to respect by their silence, precisely because it was liable to the misconstructions of the malevolent, and which had they known all the circumstances, they would have treated with more than respect because they knew it, was made to bear upon him as if of a different nature from what it was, and of his creation. The Editor had the permission of that friend to explain all circumstances, had

78

occasion rendered it necessary ; but the reader, especially if he ever happened to come into possession of a secret which it became all his manliness to keep, and which the most cruel and even ruinous malignity would hardly provoke him to allude to, lest it should be confounded with what it was not, will easily conceive that he may have accepted a permission very generous to give, without thinking it so proper to be made use of. The Editor, therefore, scandalously as he was assailed, would have left the scandal to worry itself to death, as he had been accustomed to do the minor ones of *Blackwood's* predecessor the *Satirist*, had not his brother, the Proprietor of this Paper, felt himself unable one evening when a new number of the *Magazine* was brought to him, to refuse his indignation and brotherly love the satisfaction of calling upon the calumniator to come forward. . . .

" The fellow was then threatened with the law, and a person comes to London from Mr. Blackwood, offering to compromise the matter with money, if we would drop proceedings. Finding however that our object was to get at the individual, whom they were prepared to go to any law expense rather than to give up, and that we did not wish to hamper with him booksellers and others, who as we then thought might be comparatively unconscious and innocent persons, this wretched individual, though eating his own words, returns to his trade of scandal, and expressly refuses to come forward at the name of ' coward ! ' We confess we were not prepared for an excess of meanness of this sort. . . . We must not omit to mention, that when the calumniator was first called upon in the ' Examiner,' an anonymous letter was written to the Editor from Edinburgh, informing him that his libeller was a certain person whom it named. He immediately wrote to this person, to ask him if he was so ; when he received an answer complaining in an unequivocal manner of the information, as a trick done to injure the writer. We afterwards believed it was more ; and that however happy

79

to include an injury to another by the way, the letter was meant to sound the Editor as to his real inclination to meet the ' coward ' in case he had come forward. . . .

" We must confess, that when the death of the late Mr. Keats was hastened by the unprovoked and brute persecutions of this envious and miserable publication (for that envy has a great deal to do with its scandal, we have long had no doubt, seeing the men of virtue and genius whom it has attacked), we had a great desire to aid in the work of its exposure ; but Mr. Scott of the *London Magazine* (for whose unfortunate death it has to answer) had already done so much towards it, and our own illness and cares rendered it so painful to us to do what little with our pen we did, that we waited from time to time till the good work fell into the hands of the *Scotsman,* and has been finished. We will own further, that as far as our own wrongs go, we are apt to be perplexed by certain notions of revenge, respecting which, for persons whom these hypocrites delight to hold up as such enormous infidels, we happen to hold some very singular Christian opinions. We wish we knew any of these brawlers for Church and State that did. But it is their fate to exhibit every indecency against which they declaim."

But let us revert to the year 1818, and there gather what is observable of other aspects of the campaign. It has been declared, for instance, that Hunt failed in his duty to Keats when the young poet was made the victim of *Blackwood's* and the *Quarterly,* and a critic has even defied us to discover any attempt by Hunt in 1818 to publish his faith in his friend. Mistaken or malevolent notions concerning Leigh Hunt die hard in England, as may quickly be seen by reference to the footnotes and indexes of the definitive Byron edited by Lord Ernle and the late E. H. Coleridge ; we may therefore be the more particular in the correction of this ungenerous ignorance. By way of introduction, it will be admitted that in 1818 a prolonged and sonorous protestation in favour of Keats in the "Examiner" would probably have called down still more insolence upon him, so that by not defending him directly Hunt was taking the most unselfish course, and doubtless the course which Keats wished him to take. Yet Hunt could not be silent.* The *Quarterly* containing the ugly article on "Endymion" and Keats' mind and work in general came out towards the end of September ; and on September 27th Hunt's "Political Examiner" was an apology for the absence of the customary reforming manifesto, in which he found means to have at the editor of the *Quarterly*, with this footnote : "We congratulate, most *sincerely*, our young friend JOHN KEATS on the involuntary homage that, we understand, has been paid to his undoubted genius, in an article full of grovelling abuse." This brief but incisive expression was supplemented on October 11th by the reprinting of an article from "the *Alfred* Exeter paper," occupying nearly four columns, and preceded by Hunt's still brief but ungrudging tribute to Keats : "A manly and judicious letter, signed J. S., appeared in the *Morning Chronicle* the other day, respecting the article in the *Quarterly Review* on the *Endymion* of the young poet Mr. Keats. It is one of several public animadversions, which that half-witted, half-hearted Review has called indignantly forth on the occasion. 'This is the hastily-written tribute,' says the writer, 'of a stranger, who ventures to predict that Mr. K. is capable of producing a poem that shall challenge the admiration of every reader of true taste and feeling ; nay, if he will give up his acquaintance with Mr. Leigh Hunt, and apostatise in his

* On June 7th the following announcement was made : "A Literary Notice next week on the excellent Works of Charles Lamb which have just appeared. The succeeding notice will be on *Frankenstein ;* the next on *Endymion*, by John Keats ; and the one after on the various productions of the author of *Melincourt*." But to our regret not one of these papers at that time materialised ; "The Literary Notices were not resumed, because the book-season, as it is called, had passed, and it was found that they would have been of little comparative use. They will appear towards winter." (August 30th.)

friendships, his principles, and his politics (if he have any), he may even command the approbation of the *Quarterly Review*.'—We really believe so; but Mr. Keats is of a spirit which can afford to dispense with such approbation, and stand by his friend." Whether Hunt knew that Reynolds was the author of the *Alfred* paper is obscure; it was nobly written, in a style similar to Hazlitt's, and doubtless at that juncture had a better effect on public opinion than Hunt's own eulogies of "Endymion" and Keats could have had.

And indeed, not relaxing the glorious expectancy with which he regarded Keats, judging him by classic standards, and anticipating the poet's own far-seeing dissatisfaction with "Endymion," Hunt was not able to eulogise the work. He did the best he could under such circumstances, opening his columns not only to Reynolds' eloquent praise, but also (November 1st) to a notice from *The Chester Guardian*—a finely discerned and well-worded criticism, evidently by a good hand. To one part of Reynolds' essay, Hunt wrote a friendly reply; Reynolds argued that Moore, Wordsworth and others would not survive as poets, because of their egotism, their insistency on "the moods and miseries of one person"; and Hunt answered that this individual or autobiographical peculiarity, though "not necessary to the lasting nature of poetry," would help to preserve theirs—"It is to Mr. Keats's poetry what particular companionship is to solitude, both excellent things, when genuine; and we are mistaken if he himself does not partake more of both than his intelligent critic supposes."

Shelley's "Ozymandias," announced by Hunt as a fine sonnet on January 4th, was printed over the signature "Glirastes" on the 11th, and three weeks later Horace Smith not unworthily took up the subject, anticipating (as so many more and earlier writers did) Macaulay's New Zealander. "Marianne's Dream also is not forgotten among our poetical stores"—so Hunt wrote, but the poem did not find its way into the "Examiner." A sonnet " To the Author of ' The Revolt of Islam ' " was included on February 8th, in which there is nothing remarkable ; but Hunt's review of the great vision was certainly so. Having first selected from " this extraordinary Poem " a passage at the beginning of Canto XII, italicised in Hunt's fashion of critical delight, the friend of Shelley then published in three numbers of the paper a description, exemplification, philosophic and poetic estimate of the work. After this noble salutation of genius, the " Examiner " was comparatively silent on literary topics, as has been mentioned, for many months, and Shelley departing to Italy was for a time out of the picture.

Controversy indeed spoiled the quality of the journal that year, and Hazlitt's absence was sadly to be felt. Reports of his lectures on poetry were frequently given, with quotations and determined commendations—" It was not a little striking, that though the *subjects* on which he treated necessarily decreased in interest every lecture— (he began with Shakespear and ended with Southey !)— his audience continued increasing to the last " ; probably John Hunt was the author of these excellent little notices. We could have known a great deal more of the literary life of that day had John Hunt written his memoirs. Another figure of the background to whom the curiosity of posterity often reverts without much result was concerned with the " Examiner " of 1818 ; that was John Lamb, an old correspondent. On November 8th and 22nd and December 6th his very stalwart and yet capricious letters on " The Corn Bill " were printed. Mr. Lucas has attended to this subject, and made it known that Charles Lamb pasted into his commonplace book the second of those letters, " Gleaning Made Robbery." By a coincidence, or pleasant thought of Hunt's, which must have been unusually agreeable to Charles Lamb, this letter was printed side by side with a theatrical notice (Mrs. Gould in *Giovanni*) by Charles himself, using a † as his mark. Apart from a note on December 20th on Miss Kelly (to which the editor later replied, " Our Correspondent, it appears, was mistaken when he said he observed Miss Kelly among the spectators at Mr. Kenney's Comedy on the first night ") that was Lamb's only contribution of the year.

The theatrical criticism was almost always written during 1818 by Hunt, who maintained his own distinctive exhilaration both in likes and dislikes. It was his faculty to be entertained ; it is not a common faculty ; he seemed to be perennially going to his first play, and accordingly his comments have a genial intentness and glittering gratitude in them which most regular critics all too quickly exchange perforce for a mechanical plus and minus system. Not that Hunt was unable to condemn. Take, for example, his Theatrical Examiner of January 11th, which begins, " Next to the avaricious and fatal mistake of building such large theatres . . ." and proceeds to damn the selection of plays put on at Christmas. " First, for instance, comes the half-witted tragedy of *George Barnwell,* in which prostitutes are held up to detestation, and young men are warned how they kill their good old uncles for the sake of that all-precious and all-worthy commodity, money." The Drury Lane Ghost distresses him ; at one minute " walks on the water and ' rides the storm ' on horseback, and at the next plays tricks with the *Clown,* and walks off surreptitiously with a beef-steak." At Covent Garden the pantomime from *Gulliver's Travels* gives him occasion to protest, like Hamlet's humble friend, against the revival of child-performers in plays—" it is destroying all the unconsciousness and best bloom of their time of life " ; but then he warms and rarefies in the cheerful fantasy, so that one wishes much to have been a fellow-spectator—" The scene in which the lovers first make their appearance in Brobdingnag, is the corn-fields mentioned in *Gulliver ;* and the enormous golden corn cuts a beautiful magnificent figure, and makes us see for an instant as we may suppose insects to see ; who, if they do so, must live in a glorious world indeed, of colours, and shapes, and overtopping splendours. It is almost impossible indeed for a spectator of this pantomime not to feel the *best* part of the lesson which is read us in *Gulliver*. . . ." Another instance of his very lively impressions and his absolute confidence in man's diviner powers is in his account of " Cosi fan tutte " (August 2nd), where he first tells the story in a few swift and unsparing sentences, then agrees to think it a very fine one ; we quote the conclusion : " [Garcia] is over-vivacious, if not in his gestures, in his attitudes ; and while standing still, as an Irishman would say, keeps writhing and bending himself about like an elephant's trunk. He makes also such doleful mouths when he is pathetic, that he appears to taste the bitterness of his sorrow literally in his mouth. He seems to want a lump of sugar after it.

" What an inexhaustible succession of beautiful airs and harmonies is there in Mozart ! One combination after another does not start out with a more sparkling facility in the far-famed Kaleidoscope. The first thing you hear in the present opera is the ardent trio, beginning *La mia Dorabella*, in which the lovers praise their mistresses, and insist that the old gentleman shall give proofs of their possible infidelity ; then comes, like a gentler note to the same purpose, the other of *E la fede delle femmine*, the sounds of which absolutely talk and gesticulate ; then the happy and polite one of *Una bella serenata*, with that gentlemanly willingness of assent on the line *Ci sarete, si signor*, like a bow itself ; then the triumphant noises of *Bella vita militar ;* then the little sobbing farewell, and entreaty to write every day, *Di scrivermi ogni giorno ;* the invocation for gentle winds on the voyage, *Soave sia*, with those delicious risings of the voice, like a siren's from the water ; the exquisite laughing trio, *E voi ridete*, with its slippery rhymes, its uncontroullable and increasing breathlessness, and the grave descending notes of the pitying old gentleman in the base ; the quiet triumph, and lingering enjoyment of *Un aura amorosa ;* the nodding and gentle giddiness of *Prendro quel brunettino ;* the breathing

85

passion of Secondate ; the smiling insinuation of *Il core vi dono.* What do we not owe to an art and a master like this, who as it were spoke music as others speak words ; and who left his magic imprinted for ever in books, for the hand and the voice to call forth, whenever we want solace in trouble, or perfection in enjoyment ! " We are lingering too long on this ground, or there should be quoted the same gallant spirit's reflections on Marlowe's *Jew of Malta,* with the concluding critical hymn to Shakespeare ; or those on Kean's *Othello,* "the master-piece of the living stage " ; in short, the Theatrical Examiners of Hunt in 1818 and other years contain a great number and variety of unreclaimed table-talk, often defective in some minor point, but altogether asking to be assembled in one illuminative and care-charming anthology.

On July 26th J. P. Collier began a series of " Criticisms upon the Bar," beginning with a complaint of the decline of legal eloquence ; his first paper is adorned with quotations from Wither and Shirley, the next from Spenser, Webster and Sir Thomas Browne, others from Chapman, Daniel, Brathwayte, T. Churchyard ; yet the arguments are realistic and the criticisms piercing. A certain majestic gravity, without frowning, characterises Collier's judg-ment and expression, and his prose is but little defaced or dismantled by his subsequent aberrations. With no claim to be supplying a series of essays, poor Benjamin Haydon was " in evidence," proposing with his wonted tattoo that every new church should be supplied with altar pictures, now addressing his civic ideals to the building committees, now to the Government ; discoursing to the advantage of all who heard him on the Cartoons of Raphael ; but presently his multiplied differences with Hunt caused him to cease these large-scale literary recreations in the " Ex-aminer." Probably the insertion of a long letter in his praise (November) did something to restore the native hue of his friendship ; the writer, James Elmes, took advantage of the arrival of some casts, presented to Haydon by the Imperial Academy of St. Petersburgh, to summarise the painter's rise to fame. Meanwhile, Robert Hunt, patient soul, continued to extol historic painting and its votaries, not, however, ignoring those " English rusticities " of men like Nasmyth and Stark and Vincent which nowadays cast a spell on those who see without the suspicion of a thrill the swollen muscles and horrid lightnings, the wildernesses and the precipices, the heavy-jowled warriors and the justly infuriated horses of many antiquated attempts on the sublime, where indeed these have not disappeared in rolls of canvas into cellared oblivion.

THE "Examiner" hailed the next year with a first article entitled "State of the World." "This is the commencement, if we are not much mistaken, of one of the most important years that have been seen for a long while," the case standing in neat tabulation thus, "In short, the world has now

1st. The experience of despots.
2d. The experience of *French* revolutions.
3d. A sense of its wants.
4th. A knowledge of its means.
5th. The examples of North and South America.
6th. An universal press, with a hundredth part of which Luther undid the despotism of Authority.
And 7th. The astonishing growth of that experimental philosophy, which has such an effect both on the production of means and the diffusion of knowledge; and which its illustrious father, Lord Bacon, prophesied, would alter the world.

(We shall return to this subject in our 4th Number of the present year.)"

Hunt did not, and we shall not, preferring the literary side of the history, unless certain great events appeared to metamorphose or redirect literature along with everything else.

Two not very great events disturbed the course of the "Examiner" in 1819. The first was an action against the paper by "the Hon. Charles Spencer Churchill, commonly called Lord Churchill," for libellously stating in 1818 that the plaintiff had "occasioned the death of Miss Sherwin, by furious and negligent driving"; and although the jury agreed with this opinion, they gave Lord Churchill £50 damages on two side-issues, and additionally the costs fell upon the " Examiner." A second action was brought against the Proprietor (it is to be noticed that at this stage John Hunt alone appears as the Proprietor) by a Pall Mall bookseller named Stockdale, whose grievance was that a report of proceedings at a Paddington Vestry (when he had been told he could not be trusted with the public's money) was libellous, and could only be atoned by £2,000 damages. In point of fact John Hunt, who had been present at the Vestry proceedings, as Charles Ollier testified, had performed a service to the public, and the impecunious Stockdale (one of the numerous queer fish who diversify the Life and Letters of the trustful Shelley) withdrew with small dignity from the contest.

To the literary eye the 1819 " Examiner " was a fruitful and satisfying year's work, and not least because Lamb came forward as a frequent contributor. Hunt had several times referred to his powers the previous year, calling him " the profoundest critic living," so that his renewed assistance must have been especially gratifying and inspiring. Now on February 7th Hunt reprinted Lamb's letter on Miss Kelly from the *Bristol Journal* (edited by their friend Gutch), prefixing some few words—" We should have guessed the masterly and cordial hand that wrote [it], had we met with it in the East Indies. There is but one praise belonging to Miss Kelly which it has omitted, and which it could not supply ; and that is, that she has had finer criticism written upon her, than any performer that ever trod the stage." The next week, Lamb " came pat as the catastrophe in the old comedy " with the beautiful triflings and toyings of " Valentine's Day." In March Hunt redeemed his promise of a year before to write on Lamb's two volumes of " Works " and did it triumphantly, as may be seen in the second part of this book ; in a manner, Hunt was as early on the scene when Lamb's genius arrived as when Shelley, Keats, Tennyson, and many others of less renown first appeared in literature. To continue—Lamb's unanswerable theory on the question "Who first invented *work?*" that sonnet with the extraordinary alliterative passage on Satan's endless labours, was given on June 20th; his paper on Brome's "Jovial Crew" and Miss Kelly's part in it, on July 4th; another on the "Hypocrite," with further deeply significant tribute to Miss Kelly, on August 1st; and the next week still more praise of Miss Kelly— "But what have we to gain by praising Miss Kelly?"— in a notice of "Belles Without Beaux." On the last occasion Hunt wrote an amusing and affectionate foreword, mentioning that he had written "a long, elaborate and critical account . . . dear, nine, closely-written octavo pages!" when "a better critic" sent in the remarks following. On August 22nd Lamb brought off a mild joke at the expense of one "Dion," who had been publishing a set of criticisms of London preachers under the general title of "Pulpit Oratory," by introducing "Sub-Pulpit Oratory (No. 1)," a study of "Mr. Moses Mims, Parish-Clerk of St. Brides, Fleet-Street" signed "Dion Junior." Possibly this parody (which is now for the first time ascribed to Lamb, and therefore is included below) upset the original Dion, for his sketches of pulpit orators were discontinued, and very regrettably Dion Junior also broke off. As C. Lamb, he printed the witty sonnet written at Cambridge, on August 29th; as * * * *, his review (chiefly extracts) of "Falstaff's Letters," September 5th; then on October 3rd without signature the punitive sonnet "Saint Crispin to Mr. Giffard," which modern tastes, after our display of rectitude and moderation in personalities since 1914, have affected to disapprove. And further, a review of Charles Lloyd's "Nugae Canorae" was "reluctantly postponed" to October 24th (again, there was a large proportion of quotation); "On the Acting of Munden," the nonpareil, appeared on November 7th; and the noble sonnet on Miss Kelly's performance in "The Blind Boy" transcribed from the *Morning Chronicle* appropriately con-

cluded Lamb's very freshening, vivifying effort for the
" Examiner " that year.

Hazlitt too occasionally rejoined and enriched the
symposium; here, on February 7th, was his immortalising
elegy on " John Cavanagh, the famous hand fives-player "—
" He who takes to playing fives is twice young," and he who
reads Hazlitt is equally rejuvenated. His dejection, his
injustice and bitterness are better than the idealisms of
most men; his is a book like that noted one in the Pilgrim's
Progress, which seemed rather bitter eating, but proved
sweeter when it was down. His " Character of the Country
People " (July 18th) is indeed a gloomy verdict of magnificent half-truth. " Even their tailors (of whom you might
expect better things) hate decency, and will spoil you a
suit of clothes, rather than follow your directions. One
of them, the little hunch-backed tailor of P—tt—n, with
the handsome daughter, whose husband ran away from
her and went to sea, was ordered to make a pair of brown
or snuff-coloured breeches for my friend C. L.; instead
of which the pragmatical old gentleman (having a will of
his own) brought him home a pair of ' lively Lincoln green,'
in which I remember he rode in triumph in Johnny
Tremain's cross-country caravan through Newberry, and
entered Oxford, ' fearing no colours,' the abstract idea of
the jest of the thing prevailing in his mind (as it always does)
over the sense of personal dignity." Besides these papers,
Hazlitt's influence frequently invigorated the " Examiner "
by way of Hunt's reviews of his books, or the hearty
appreciations of and selections from his lectures. The
controversial dexterity of Hunt as a reviewer is well seen
in the opening of his applause of Hazlitt's Letter to William
Gifford—" We said a little while since, that if the creature
yclept Gifford did not take care, he would be picked up
by the fingers of some person indignant at his perpetual
creeping malice, and held out to the loathing eyes of the
community, sprawling and shrieking. Here he is. Mr.
Hazlitt has got him fast by the ribs, forcing him, with

various ingenuity of grip, to display unwillingly all the deformities of his moral structure. They may now see 'the nature of the beast.'" If Hunt had had the opportunity to respond to some of his recent critics, they would have had to call for reinforcements quite early in the day. But doubtless Hazlitt was needed to inspire his satire to the full.

Of Keats during 1819 almost* the only trace in the " Examiner " seems to be his shrewd and cautious approval of Reynolds' counterfeit " Peter Bell " (April 25th)—the article in which he writes of " the sad embroidery of the *Excursion* " contrasted with " the coarse samples " (so the word is printed) " of Betty Foy and Alice Fell." The real " Peter Bell " by Wordsworth was punished by Leigh Hunt the following week, yet with due regard to its occasional excellences, such as the description of Peter's " savage wildness " ; but Hunt objected utterly to Peter's being reformed to " a proper united sense of hare-bells and hell-fire." When Reynolds' musical sketch, *One, Two, Three, Four, Five, by Advertisement* was successfully brought out at the English Opera House in July, Hunt was there to enjoy it without knowing who the author was, despite which he recognised " a writer too good for his task." Reynolds' aim had been " to exhibit a particular talent in particular situations," namely a young actor named Reeve in imitations of contemporary favourites—an entertainment with which Hunt was on the whole delighted, and in describing which he says one of his many admirable things about Munden's curiously creative art.

No article or poem by Shelley came to the " Examiner " readers this year except through the reviews of Hunt, who

---

* The following fine figure may merit rescue from an essay by Hunt on Barry Cornwall's *Dramatic Series*, where he is speaking of the new eagerness of " the younger part of society for genuine poetry : " A remarkable instance of this was witnessed by the public the other day in the young poet Keats, who burst suddenly upon them like a shape out of the old world of imagination, and threw the mere party critics into all their flattering convulsions of rage."

followed his warning to the author of " Peter Bell " with his congratulations to the author of " Rosalind and Helen " —his millennial mind easily conceived that "You might be made to worship a devil by the process of Mr. Wordsworth's philosophy; by that of Mr. Shelley, you might re-seat a dethroned goodness." Hunt's recognition and interpretation of Shelley's cloud-compelling genius were his highest critical achievement, and their triumphant newness of sensibility never withered through his long life. It was with a peculiar sense of Shelley's pre-eminence in his own life that he took the trouble later in 1819 (September 26th and the two next issues of the journal) to hold up the *Quarterly Review* on account of its malignancy to *The Revolt of Islam*. In this impassioned defence of Shelley at that time there glows a friendship unassailable by those who have hinted that Hunt "could not have known Shelley well in so short a period," and insinuate that in any event their unity could not have lasted. Having completed this important message to after-time, Hunt soon took up *Don Juan*, First and Second Cantos, which he discussed with vigour and admiration (paying Byron the compliment of saying "His genius is not naturally satirical"); yet perhaps he protested too much on the text of the morality of the poem; he saw his enemies sneering, and he forgot the verse itself in his wrath.

This record refers so frequently to Leigh Hunt that the reader may at times wonder whether he wrote all the "Examiner," and indeed he wrote an extraordinary amount of it; he was its editor, political essayist, literary essayist, theatrical critic, miscellanist—Novello's daughter Mary might be excused for thinking he also wrote the Bankrupts, Accidents and Offences, Agricultural Reports and Price of Stocks. It is extraordinary that so volatile a man, with his Spenser ever in his mind, and his fancies running free, or "still climbing trees in the Hesperides," could stand in the shafts so long and pull with such cheerful endurance; but in such puzzling circumstances the

93

character of Leigh Hunt by his son, prefixed to the Autobiography in 1860, may be consulted with benefit.   Long
after he had given up the "Examiner" he showed in his
Tatler a daily (and nightly) power of vivacious industry
which is even more astonishing, and even more opposed to
the caricatured traditions of his temperament, than his
first editorship.   No attempt has been made in the present
work to register or to rescue all his meritorious and now
unknown writings in the "Examiner," and naturally much
that is there readable would not be so out of its environ-
ment.   At any rate Mr. Milford has recovered from these
scarce pages all the poetry and practically all the light,
carabineering satires of "Libertas."   During 1819 Hunt
published in his paper a translation—*the* translation—of
the *Jovial Priest's Confession*, by Walter de Mapes; otherwise his Hudibrastics, Skeltonics, ballads and bellman's
verses of that season (the Peterloo period) had sunk into
obscurity till the reanimating touch of an invincible editor
gave their wit and skill a new chance in life.

Some novel papers in prose were left by Hunt, and
have been left by his occasional selectors, in the 1819
volume.   On March 21st a report on *The Automaton
Chess-Player*, then exhibiting in London, was printed, but
it is probably not by Leigh Hunt, and the subject is
somewhat hollow;   a little later the gay editorial pen,
certified by the ☞, hailed the neanderthal bicycle,
"The Pedestrian Carriage."   This machine was a seat
and two wheels, on the bicycle plan, propelled by the feet
acting on the ground, at a rate ("almost beyond belief")
of "eight, nine and even ten miles within the hour";
weight about 50 pounds, and price £8 to £10; supplied
by Mr. Johnson, 75, Long Acre.   Hunt, prophetical, called
this production "one of the many fresh instances of the
progress of experimental philosophy," and dipped into the
future without, however, noticing the inevitable approaching
noise of motor-cycles, lorries, tanks and Mr. Morris's effect
on Oxford.   "If numbers of persons were to adopt the

use of this new invention, it would make a considerable change at once in the health of the community ; and six or seven such inventions, acting upon their other daily habits, might alter their whole appearance as a people. Only think of numbers flying backwards and forwards in summer time upon these light and elegant machines, and almost realizing the old stories of Pacolet and his Wooden Horse. Many seemed inclined to do so the moment they saw it : but then the question was, as usual, who shall begin ? Will it not be want of modesty ? . . . However, this difficulty is done away ; for it seems that there have already been individuals sensible and modest enough to make no fuss about the matter, but mount and set off at once,—with a sense, not of themselves and what others shall think of them, but of the utility and pleasure of so cheap, lasting and desirable an invention. A friend of ours saw a gentleman dart upon one of them across the Strand,—we think, into Somerset-House. Others have been seen in Hyde Park, and others gliding by Vauxhall. We hope, in the course of the summer, to see them scudding about in all directions, to the great discomfiture of in- digestion, bad spirits, paleness, leanness and corpulence." The hope is apparently an innocent one.

Having recreated his fancy in a humorous study of parliamentary peculiarities called " Breaking Up of the Great School," Hunt under his pen-name Harry Brown brought out three numbers of what he styled

PRÆTERNATURAL HISTORY

HISTORIA PRÆTERNATURALIS
SIVE
HENRICULI FUSCI LIBELLUS AUREUS
Animalia Humanæ Species Degeneriora Tractans
Accedit Hominis Ipsius Descriptio, Viri Feminæque.

The zeal, sprightliness and invention of his satire were seldom more abundant. His topics were, first, " The

Bicaud, or Two-Tailed Gabbler " (lawyers) ; then, " The
Oesophagus, or Glutton " ; and after that, " The Fire-
Threatener, Star-Gazing Howler, Field-Preacher, or Bête
de Chauvin," from which we make an extract. " This
animal has in general a coarse rusty black skin, a poll with
coarse flat short hair, dirty paws, a nasal cry, and a sullen
and selfish expression of face, occasionally opening into
a horrible hypocritical grin. You doubt whether it is
going to smile or bite. It will bay the sky, as a dog does
the moon ; and if any one makes signs to know where its
stock is (for it is extremely fond of hiding money), it has
the remarkable habit of pointing upwards towards the
same place, as if its treasure lay there. Dogs have dreams,
and many animals a sort of foresight. There is reason
to believe that the Fire-Threatener does actually retain
a notion of the immortality of the soul, common to the
original human stock ; a perception, that would be
wonderful in so despicable a brute, did not vanity and
selfishness sometimes jump to the same conclusions as a
nobler aspiration. The confused notions of another world
in the mind of the Fire-Threatener have evidently as
little humanity as possible. During thunder and lightning,
or other awful aspects of the sky, it will grovel in the dust,
or hang up its entreating paws like a begging dog ; but
when the weather is serene, and the sun and the flowers
sparkle, and all creation looks fair, it seems to turn with
contempt from the lovely face of things, as who should
say, ' What a miserable world ! ' It exhibits the same
aspect when a human being is buried, and the weeping
relations are looking up to heaven with tears of hope ;
but at the burial of one of the Fire-Threateners (for they
cover their dead like some other beasts) they point upwards,
and groan, and howl, which is their way of expressing
both misery and satisfaction. They also exhibit the cruelty
and vindictiveness of their natures, by pointing to a fire
whenever they see one, and then making signs and grins
to those who avoid them, expressive of satisfaction at the

fancy of seeing them in it; a piece of courtesy which they generally conclude by turning up the whites of their eyes, and making other gestures, indicative of transport, apparently at the thought of being out of it themselves. From all this it is pretty clear, that if they have really a notion of such a thing as heaven, they fancy it must be exclusively peopled with Fire-Threateners; and as Fontenelle said that even man made God in his own likeness, it is to be supposed that the Fire-Threateners make him in theirs. What a hell of a paradise!"

As an antidote to that, the reader may like to have a glimpse "of that beautiful spot near Wimbledon, called, Combe Wood, which was so thickly set with primroses, that it seemed as if they had been put whole into the ground for a surprise. You could scarcely step in some places without treading upon them. Their beautiful pale yellow was interspersed with the bluebell and wild hyacinth; the trees were thick out in leaves; the birches, with their silvery bodies and light dishevelled boughs, stood here and there, bending their graceful figures, like ladies of the wood."

BESIDES the inordinately heavy labours of the "Examiner," Hunt had now attempted to master his financial adversities by other periodical ventures. One of these, perhaps, was not very onerous to compile— his *Literary Pocket Book*,* now one of the scarcest *desiderata* ; he had published the first volume in good time for 1819, through his friends Charles and James Ollier, who paid him £200 for the copyright. Throughout 1819 his "Calendar of Nature" had been transferred serially from the *Pocket Book* to the "Examiner." The 1820 edition was advertised (at 5*s.*) as containing : "Lists, enlarged and amended, of the living Writers, Artists, and Musicians of England, France, Italy, Germany and America ; of eminent persons from the most remote eras ; House of Commons ; Universities ; Musical Performers and Teachers, with their addresses ; Medical Lecturers ; Teachers of Languages ; Performers at the Theatres, &c. ; together with a newly-written Calendar of the Seasons ; the Bon Mots of Beau Brummell, now first collected ; a Diary, with blank pages for observations ; Original Poetry ; Walks round London ; Anecdotes and Extracts, &c." Another pleasing though exhausting enterprise, in which also Keats and Shelley had a hand, was the editing of the weekly *Indicator*, that justly celebrated little journal. "The 'Examiner' is Hunt's tavern-room for politics, for political pleasantry, for criticism upon the theatres and living writers. The *Indicator* is his private room, his study, his retreat from public care and criticism, with the reader who chuses to accompany him." In short, the heyday of the "Examiner"

---

* " In this catalogue of *books which are no books—biblia a-biblia*—I reckon Court Calendars, Directories, Pocket Books (the Literary excepted) " . . . Elia, *Detached Thoughts on Books* ; text of 1822.

had faded, returns were less and the editor's needs were more, and he was in the common quixotic case, planning the repair of his household fortunes by an indefinite term of overwork. It is not then a matter for surprise that 1820 was the last year of Hunt's satisfactory and regular editorship of the "Examiner," and that in the close of 1821, after months of indisposition, he temporarily withdrew from the office in search of Italy, Shelley, Liberty and indeed the Golden Age once again.

Another sign of the times or of the tightened belts of the "Examiner" staff was the inclusion of an advertisement page—to the retrospective eye, by no means the least engaging and indicative of each "Examiner's" sixteen pages (price 10*d.*), but then considered as heresy and schism, the accursed thing, by some conservative readers with memories. "Mr. Editor. At last, after twelve years then, we are to have a whole page of Advertisements, notwithstanding your protestations to the contrary. . . . As there are only 15 daily papers that present us with advertisements six days in the week, why, the proprietors of the 'Examiner' are willing to make up the deficiency. Have the goodness just to notice in your next number whether it is likely the Advertisements will be continued. I am, yours very truly, T. H." (On computation one sees that this is not an early bibliographical item of Mr. Hardy's.) Poor, prehistoric, unevolutionary T. H.; does his ghost ever catch sight of the modern newspaper? Could he not dimly realise the true business of the Press?

Hunt began the year 1820 with an article in a strain known to some modern newspapers and by hearsay to Dr. Robert Bridges. It is headed, "Non-Appearance of the Laureat to Celebrate the National Happiness," and it opens, "Where is the Laureat all this while? Where is the Ex-Jacobin . . . ?" The article is excellent if we admit that its justice or injustice makes no difference now. "He avoids the lyre, as if it were a frozen railing; or the bars of a prison where there is no getting out; or of a

99

fire that burns one's fingers; or as an old tin-kettle kicked
about in the snow; or the ribs of a dead ass; or a chair-
back discarded at Court. He receives his salary, and
' makes no sign.' " Presently Hunt had ample scope for
his political paradoxes and amusements, for this was the
year of the trial of Queen Caroline, and the " Examiner "
reformists had still no particular objection to lambasting
their office effigy of the Prince Regent on any occasion—
here was a marvellous occasion.

This was also (what secures the attention of more people
nowadays than even the unhappy Queen before the House
of Lords) the last year of John Keats in England and the
year in which *Lamia, Isabella, etc.* were published. Presumably Leigh Hunt had seen the poem of *Isabella* during
1818 or 1819, for on January 2nd, 1820, he severely handled
his friend Barry Cornwall's version of the same tale of
Boccaccio—*A Sicilian Story*—with the air of having a
confirmed opinion on the only possible meaning and poetic
treatment of it. In view of Keats's wonderful presentation
of this famous tragedy, what Hunt said to Cornwall and
the reading public before the *Lamia* volume appeared may
be repeated with a curious impression of its concealing a
premonitory review of Keats. " We have indeed a quarrel
to pick with Mr. Cornwall with respect to his Sicilian
subject. It is the only instance in which we have known
him give up his faith in a sentiment; and it is unluckily
a great one. In Boccaccio the heroine's lover is killed by
her brothers, who observe her afterwards constantly
cherishing a pot of basil. She waters it not only with
water but her tears, and the basil flourishes with extraordinary luxuriance. They get possession of it, dig it up,
and find the head of the slain lover. This, it is true, is
ghastly enough : but then the very ghastliness sets off the
unconquerable beauty of the love. The treasuring of so
appalling a thing only shews the intensity of the sentiment.
The head of her slaughtered lover was dear and precious
to the fond girl's heart for numberless reasons ; and had

it not been so, it would have become so by its fate. To
that very horror she would have delighted, and did delight,
to give more than the worshipped sacredness of a relic.
Now Mr. Cornwall has exchanged this head for a heart.
He has even discarded the poor pot of basil, and turned
t 1at unpresuming herb into a tree. The heroine therefore
does not even carry about the relic with her zealous and
fond cherishing. She sits under the tree in good set style,
and does nothing ungenteel, or what might be thought
eccentric by 'the circles.' We are sorry for this, because
Mr. Cornwall has a genius that ought to vindicate nature
always, as it is inclined to do; and not consult things of
the moment, fit only *for* things of the moment. A real
poet makes us melancholy, when he denies Nature, to
accommodate to sophistication. He is emphatically her
servant and helper; and if he forsakes her, with love too
in his heart, who shall bring back to her service the vain
and yet hopeless world ? 'I have ventured,' he says in a
note, 'to substitute the heart for the head of the lover.
It appeared to be a ghastly thing to preserve, though
perhaps the former may be the more commonplace thing
of the two.' We scarcely knew whether this note mends
the matter or otherwise; for here Mr. Cornwall had
thought about it, and yet chose the worser part; and
besides the heart is not 'the more commonplace thing of
the two:' it is the only commonplace thing. The head
remains in Boccaccio an original, a solitary, a noble, and
an affectionate thing."

When the *Lamia* volume arrived, Hunt's review of it
was printed in his *Indicator,* but he made some allusions
to it also in the " Examiner." First on July 23rd he said,
" A fine volume of poetry, ' good and true,' has just appeared
from the pen of Mr. Keats, one of the youngest poets in
years and oldest in powers of any now living," to which he
added the promise to give in the following number " a
happy piece of criticism from another journal "; it was
given, and proves to have been Lamb's golden-tongued

welcome to the triumphing youthful glory of Keats. Whether Hunt knew Lamb's hand does not appear, but he remarks editorially, "The poet and the critic are worthy of each other—a rare coincidence, when the first is good." Probably he did not identify the writer, and the *New Times* whence the article was transcribed was usually no friend of the "Examiner." Lamb's review was the finest utterance that he ever made in praise of a younger contemporary, and there are several records* (Crabb Robinson's, John Mitford's and one or two more) to show that he retained particularly his delight in the riches of "Saint Agnes' Eve," and frequently challenged the chimes at midnight with his commendations of it years afterwards. Probably no more adequate characterisation (radiant with the inspired pleasure of the original) has ever announced a new volume of poetry to the world. And one can hardly think of a more desirable manuscript in the range of English criticism than the doubtless destroyed autograph of this magnificent eulogy, for the restoration of which from newspaper oblivion we owe even more than usual gratitude to Mr. E. V. Lucas. Before passing from this *Lamia* volume, let us mention that a publication reviewed by Robert Hunt in February, 1820, may have had some share in the begetting of the *Ode on a Grecian Urn* (May, 1819), or if it was not early enough to have done so, some other production by the same hand may have done. Under the heading "Englefield Vases" R. H. wrote most agreeably and delightedly, beginning, "Among the Engravers who essentially increase our Literary pleasures by submitting to the eye what the Author verbally describes, Mr. Moses holds a distinguished place as the ablest of our Engravers of Outlines. His Altars, Vases, Pateræ, and other like

---

* The especial affection of Lamb for Keats's best poetry might be the subject for a pleasing essay. He desired that others should share it. For instance, "I have heard him repeat some of Keats's beautiful lines in the Ode to the Nightingale, about the 'pastoral eglantine,' with great delight." (Barry Cornwall's *Charles Lamb*, 1866, p. 222.)

Publications, shew a fine eye for proportion and grace, and a hand that never fails to second his correctness of vision and his muscular knowledge. He is now engaged on the conclusive number, the 6th, of the Englefield Vases. These beautiful Vases are painted with figures in funeral ceremonies, festivals, &c., fancy ornaments of honey-suckles, &c., all which, in the Prints, meet the eye with a decided and varied relief from the surrounding and darkly-engraved ground of the Vases. . . ." Is there not some semblance of identity between these graces and those of Keats's Urn ? An investigation might repay the trouble, if to gaze on Mr. Moses' softly-shaded prints should turn out to be trouble !

Of Shelley the readers of the "Examiner" had but scanty glimpses during 1820. When *The Cenci* was published, Hunt mentioned it in a hurried column (meant to be a mere provisional review) together with Hazlitt's *Lectures on the Literature of the Age of Elizabeth* and a novel entitled *Isabel* by Charles Lloyd. The paragraph on Shelley runs thus : "Of Mr. Shelley's Tragedy, called the *Cenci*, which to say the least of it, is undoubtedly the greatest dramatic production of the day, we shall speak at large in a week or two. It is founded on a most terrific family story, which actually took place in Italy : but sentiments of the most amiable, and refreshing, and exalting nature nevertheless breathe in a certain under-tone of suggestion through the whole of it, as they always do in the works of this author. The Correspondents who have written the joint epistle to us, under the signature of *Short and Sweet*, will perceive that we agree with them as to the propriety of criticising this play, however strongly a particular and affectionate circumstance has connected it with our self-love. Nicety is a great thing with us ; but a friend is a still greater, especially if he be also a friend to the whole human race." A little while later, however, Hunt relinquished his intention on account of illness, contenting himself with noting that "The *Cenci*, we understand, had nearly gone through the first edition some weeks ago." There was even a danger, then, that Shelley would become a popular writer! A sonnetteer named Arthur Brooke, of Canterbury, expressed this more quaintly (on November 5th) by talking of the fire of Hope which flashed from Shelley's "electric wire," rhyming with the now almost obsolete "wild and mighty lyre."

An event of the year involving several figures of the "Examiner" group was the exhibition of Haydon's expansive "Picture of Christ's Triumphant Entry into Jerusalem, which has been nearly Six Years on the Easel"; it was shown together with other examples of the artist "at Bullock's Great Room (Upstairs to the Right), Egyptian Hall, Piccadilly"; admittance, 1s—catalogue, 6d. We should like to own a copy of the catalogue, if only for the passage which even the excitedly admiring Robert Hunt ventures to call rather rhapsodical: "How does he feel the miserable incompetency of his own imagination, who struggles to see that face in which all that is visible of the Deity is reflected. Pure! Serene! Smiling awfully and sweet! Bland! Benignant! Lovely! Sublime in its beauty! Compassionate in its grandeur! Quivering with sensibility! Terrible in its composure! Omnipotent in its sedateness!" To this premonitory instance of the style of Mr. H. G. Wells, Hunt instantly adds his own sage observation on Haydon's Christ—"The colour of the hair approaching nearly to red will not be generally liked." The picture quickly began to take up almost as much space in the "Examiner" as it did in the Egyptian Hall, J. Landseer writing long letters to defend it against critics who objected to the inclusion of a sneering Voltaire and a sheepish Newton among the antique Hebrews. Hazlitt, Wordsworth, Keats and Haydon himself are readily identifiable in the throng, as may be proved by reference to the reproduction in Miss Lowell's *John Keats*, and some of the women of the Keats circle are there waiting to be recognised.

Altogether the literary value of the 1820 volume was almost comprised in the editor's best writings. Lamb indeed on January 16th printed his amusing comment on Barron Field's *First Fruits of Australian Poetry* ; a *Sonnet to a London Steeple* (May 28th) is also included among the uncertain items in his Works ; he would probably be the L. who signed the following quatrain, in allusion to the Queen's trial :

TO THE UPPER HOUSE.

How can your Lordships bore the Judges so ?
Why all this stooping to " the Courts BELOW ? "
Are then the Bishops dumb ? or can't they prove
The better precepts of the Court ABOVE ?

It looks like his in metre, point and politics.—Apart from these brief and rare visitations of friends, Hunt was usually left to keep up the " Examiner's " literary standard by himself. The profusion of prose and verse which he completed, on the side of the luckless Queen, is now scarcely to be read with profit, honourable though its chivalry and ardour must still appear. Of far greater interest now is his account of King George the Third, or would be if it were not mewed up in a forgotten file. Perhaps some historian now preparing to pay to George III that ultimate expression of his country's unfading friendship and admiration, a real biography (with economy, let us hope, in the tints of " fairy fiction ") will call up Leigh Hunt from the 1820 " Examiner " to enliven his pages ; notwithstanding that Hunt is quite sharply critical of the old King's limitations. Another Political Examiner on a quite different subject—" Petition against the Sale of Sunday Newspapers "—might be valuably read nowadays, but the nature of Sunday newspapers having slipped appreciably cavewards, Hunt's Shelleian arguments against the Vice Society's cant do not suit our times as they suited his. He went to the theatre, and wrote about it with much of his former gaiety and grace, throughout the year ;

in a brilliant paper on *Twelfth Night* at Covent Garden, full of entertainingly illustrative fancy, he descants with such happiness on a topic of perennial novelty that we must quote him : " We must be allowed to say that Miss Tree's leg is the very prettiest leg we ever saw on the stage. It is not at all like the leg which is vulgarly praised even in a man, and which is doubly misplaced under a lady—a bit of a balustrade turned upside down ; a large calf, and an ancle only small in proportion. It is a right feminine leg, delicate in foot, trim in ancle, and with a calf at once soft and well-cut, distinguished and unobtrusive. We are not so intolerant—we should rather say ungrateful and inhuman on the subject of legs, as many of our sex ; who without the light of a good ancle can see nothing else good in a figure. We have a tender respect for them all, provided they are gentle. But it is impossible not to be struck, as an Irishman would say, with a leg like this. It is fit for a statue ; still fitter for where it is. It helped to complete the applicability of the lines which Mr. Bishop* has selected from *Venus and Adonis :*

> Bid me discourse, I will enchant thine ear
>   Or, like a Fairy, trip upon the green ;
> Or, like a Nymph, with bright and flowing hair,
>   Dance on the sands, and yet no footing seen."

On November 19th Hunt, who was nothing if not personal, and whose " we " was almost the only veil between him and the mind's eye of his reader, was obliged to make a sad announcement. He would be unable to write for a month ; his ill-health had forced him " from the bustle and excitements of his numerous literary avocations " ; and then he flung his farewell expressions of contempt at the Ministry in return for their attitude to Queen Caroline, and withdrew to Hampstead, his Spenser

---

* The performance of *Twelfth Night* was enriched with musical interpolations—glees and songs—under the direction of Mr. Bishop.

and his medicine. This gave John Hunt the chance and indeed the necessity to supply the more aristocratic portions of the paper, which he did, political manifesto and theatrical impression alike, with ability awhile, presently calling in other hands. What strikes one in his writings is his familiarity with Shakespeare, and his sympathy and unity with such views as Lamb's upon the acting of *Lear*. Nor was he dejected in tone although, late in November, the Attorney-General came down once again on the "Examiner" with a prosecution on account of some loud remarks about the Queen's trial. Indeed, a warrant for John Hunt's arrest had been issued by some tartarly lawyers, but that was stopped. John Hunt, confronted with this new trouble, lifted his voice "even louder," and still his Shakespeare bore the burden of his song. "We are quite willing and prepared to meet Sir Robert and his masters in this quarrel; and if we are allowed anything like fair play—if neither pettifogging nor packing be resorted to—we have a perfect conviction (such is the goodness of our cause) that we shall give this Royal gamecock a signal beating, even on his own dunghill.

 Berowne. Hide thy head, Achilles; here comes Hector!
 King. Hector was but a Trojan in respect of this.
 Boyet. But *is* this Hector?
 Longaville. His calf is too big for Hector.
 Dumaine. More *Calf*, certain."

Of this spirit was John Hunt, to whose deep manliness Hazlitt bore witness in the congenial, sturdy dedication of "Political Characters," and who, although the *Dictionary of National Biography* leaves him out of account, is one of the first men in metropolitan circles of a hundred years since whom one would like to have known.

1821 : LEIGH HUNT'S EDITORSHIP ENDS

"THE Editor, in returning to his work (Feb. 25, 1821), has the melancholy task of noticing the Verdict against the Proprietor of this paper, his brother." But John Hunt had not gone down without a very fine defence,* spoken by himself, and concluding in a manner justifying the fair name of an Englishman : " My fate, in a certain degree, is in your hands. However earnestly I may desire, as well for the sake of others as my own, *that* freedom from personal restraint so dear to us all, whatever your determination may be, I shall be content ; satisfied as I am, that the Cause of Reform will be benefitted either by my acquittal or condemnation. Yes, I say even by my condemnation ; for the spectacle of a man's being sent to a dungeon for uttering, on public grounds, ' the truth, the whole truth, and nothing but the truth,' must inevitably serve to accelerate its final triumph. It is by no means necessary, Gentlemen, that an humble individual like myself, should remain in the possession of his liberty, and the enjoyment of his quiet home and family comforts ; but it *is* necessary, that there should at all times be found, in England, men who will make a firm stand for the public liberty, regardless of private considerations, and in despite of personal dangers." This patriot of the old school, being found guilty and having appealed in vain, was sentenced to a year's imprisonment in Cold-bath Fields, and to find security at the end of that term, to keep the peace, in £1,000. The " Examiner " was further disabled by the

* " Just published, price One Shilling. REPORT of the TRIAL of the KING *v.* JOHN HUNT for a Libel on the House of Commons. . . . The Defence Verbatim ; with a Preface, being an Answer to the Attorney-General's Reply, by Henry L. Hunt, the Son of the Defendant. Printed for William Hone, Ludgate-Hill." March, 1821.

108

persistent illness of Leigh Hunt, as may be seen by the following extract from the number for March 25th :

"On Friday the 23d of February, at Rome, after a lingering illness, died John Keats the poet, aged 25.

"In consequence of the renewed illness of the Editor, his little weekly paper entitled the *Indicator* is dropped for the present."

At the end of April Leigh Hunt made a brief reappearance in reference to the controversy between Byron and Bowles over the qualities of Pope's poetry, and announced that he would soon return to his usual work. But it was July 8th when his readers next heard from him, in an article on the death of Napoleon jointly composed by his brother and himself, and rounded with a sonorous and passionate specimen of Hazlitt's enthusiasm for the Corsican. Soon afterwards a series of " Sketches of the Living Poets," in which Leigh Hunt was far from being at his freshest and strongest, was begun. Only Bowles, Byron, Campbell and Coleridge were ever included, and with the articles some grimly unsatisfactory woodcuts were inserted. Inevitably there are remarks of brilliance and insight in these Sketches, as when Bowles' placid current is described—" His forte is his piano "—or Campbell's classicised verse, " He gives the finest glances about him, and afar off, like a bird ; spreads his pinions as if to sweep to his object ; and is pulled back by his string into a chirp and a flutter." These articles, a few clever topical verses, and an occasional " Political Examiner," made up Hunt's work in his journal for that year. Incidentally he paid his compliment to " A Lie ; alias Elia " in the *London Magazine ;* he played with the proposal of a Royal Academy of Literature (" Mr. Shelley, who can reason as well as feel, and who certainly will never turn his back upon his old independence, will never be among them ") ; and he expressed his contempt for his old enemy *Blackwood* still furiously raging and assisted by other prints of even duskier character. On November 15th Hunt and his family sailed for Italy—

a change which was probably not sufficiently debated, in respect of " Examiner " arrangements, with John Hunt, and brought about a series of difficulties in Leigh Hunt's life, including the regrettable breakdown of his friendly relations with Byron, and what of unhappiness sprang from that mismanaged affair.

When we have said that John Hunt was in the grip of the Law, or the politics behind the Law, during the year 1821, and that Leigh Hunt was out of action through sickness almost all the time, there remains little besides to notice in the story of the newspaper at that date. It began to be thin and commonplace in literary quality, and " lived on scraps." Few notable contributors came to the rescue ; " no friendly Lamb, nor Hazlitt stirred." On July 15th the " Examiner " had the honour of printing Shelley's well-known letter on the piratical republication of *Queen Mab*—not a recantation, but bordering close upon that. " I have not seen this production for several years." An example for some of the moderns to try and imitate ! Another correspondent of the year was the indestructible Haydon, who with great vehemence defended himself against a writer in the *London Magazine*, the author of the statement : " I was told the other day of a living Artist who, when a child was run over by a cart before its loved home, and the bankrupt mother stood rigid in stone staring with maniac agony on her crushed darling, calmly and deliberately gazed on her ' to study the expression ' as he called it." Haydon agreed that he had been enabled to give the real mother in his *Judgment of Solomon* an expression of " agonized faintness " by an experience somewhat similar, but refused the endowment of a cold ferocity. We must remember that he lived before the discovery of Art for Art's Sake. Haydon also sent the " Examiner " some comments on Sir Joshua Reynolds, curious and intense : " His men are all gentlemen, his children such quizzing cherubs that one longs to roll about with them on the carpet, and his women creatures of such spotless purity, that a man in their presence would be constantly trembling lest a *thought* should ever pass through his mind inconsistent with their delicacy." Again let us remember the semi-barbarous, unpsychological age in which Haydon was writing.

THE absence of the two Hunts powerfully dulled the light of their journal during the early part of 1822, nor did their substitutes rise to the occasion. The inclusion of numerous excerpts from other periodicals, a dismal penurious habit which during that decade dominated most of the Press, showed that the original vitality of the " Examiner " had been largely spent. Some fighting articles by John Hunt, and a series of ten " Fables for Grown Children " by " the late Editor "—with one exception unreprinted—still attested the former character of the work. In May Leigh Hunt, still somewhat out of form, writing without his usual grace and rapidity, opened a series of " Letters to the Readers of The Examiner," parts of which are worthy of remembrance. The first Letter was explanatory of Hunt's situation, health ("already better for breathing air a little more southern "), literary intentions (the *Liberal* was already the victim of "the idlest misrepresentations "), and fidelity to the " Examiner." The second Letter interpreted Byron's *Cain,* and marked out several of its poetic beauties ; the third analysed the *Quarterly Review,* and concluded with an invitation to Hazlitt to give the public his own views on that leviathan, and a promise to say a few words on behalf of Shelley who had also been traduced in its terrific pages.

This promise was carried out in the two succeeding Letters, intended to refute the *Quarterly's* strictures on *Prometheus Unbound,* and very valuable to the ordinary mind halting between two opinions. The *Quarterly* was trying, said Hunt, to avoid discussion of Shelley's doctrines by drawing attention aside to his " profanity." " The Reviewer is collecting passages to prove his author's enmity to the Christian faith—an enmity, by the bye, which Mr.

Shelley always takes care to confine to the violent consequences of faith as contrasted with practice, there being
in the latter sense no truer Christian than himself.   The
poet exclaims

> O, that the free would stamp the impious name
> Of * * * * into the dust ! or write it there
> So that this blot upon the page of fame
> Were as a serpent's path, which the light air
> Erases, and the flat sands close behind !

These *four* stars, which in fact imply a civil title, and not a
religious word, as the allusion to ' the page of fame ' might
evince, are silently turned by the Reviewer into *six* stars, as
if implying the name of Christ :

> O, that the free would stamp the impious name
> Of * * * * * * into the dust ! "

Exposing this and similar malicious minutiæ, Hunt went
on to point out the poetical pre-eminence of Shelley apart
from "metaphysics and polemics," and to this end he chose
in special *To a Skylark*, reprinting it entire, "for it is as
fitting for the season, as it is true to the musical and
etherial beauty of its subject," and afterwards exulting
in it.   " I know of nothing more beautiful than this—
more choice of tones, more natural in words, more abundant
in exquisite, cordial, and most poetical associations.   One
gets the stanzas by heart unawares, and repeats them like
' snatches of old tunes.' "   A fortnight later, the sixth
and last of the Letters appeared, " On Mr. Shelley's New
Poem, entitled Adonais " ; it is reprinted in the second
part of the present work.

On July 14th Keats' *Lines Written in the Scotch Highlands*
were printed, as the result of their previous unlucky,
mutilated appearance in the *New Monthly*.   The poem was
thus recommended by the " Examiner " : " Exclusive of
its rare poetic merits, it is valuable as an index to the mind
of the lamented Author, while under the excitation of the

powerful scenery of the Highlands." Unusual and solitary
as it is, the piece is classed by Mr. de Sélincourt among
those which he thinks unworthy of Keats. Three weeks
after this relic's emergence, a most unlooked-for obituary
sadly surprised the loyal readers of the "Examiner." It
ran: "Those who know a great mind when they meet
with it, and who have been delighted with the noble things
in the works of Mr. SHELLEY, will be shocked to hear that
he has been cut off in the prime of his life and genius. He
perished at sea, in a storm, with his friend Captain WILLIAMS,
of the Fusileers, on the evening of the 8th ult., somewhere
off Via Reggia, on the coast of Italy, between Leghorn
and the Gulf of Spezia. He had been to Pisa, to do a kind
action, and he was returning to his country abode at Lerici
to do another. Such was the whole course of his life.
Let those who have known such hearts, and have lost them,
judge of the grief of his friends. Both he and Capt.
WILLIAMS have left wives and children. Capt. WILLIAMS
was also in the prime of life, and a most amiable man,
beloved like his friend. The greatest thing we can say in
honour of his memory (and we are sure he would think so)
is, that he was worthy to live with his friend, and to die
with him. Vale, dilectissime hominum! Vale, dilectissime ; et nos ama, ut dixisti, in sepulchro."

Towards the end of 1822 the fortunes of the *Liberal*
engaged the fraternal attention of the "Examiner" and
the wrath of the enemies of all liberalism whatsoever.
Mindful of his Shakespeare, John Hunt commented, "The
little dogs and all, Tray, Blanch, and Sweetheart, see, they
bark at us "; he responded more definitely to John
Murray's circulating a letter alleged to be Byron's "in
which his Lordship speaks in the most disparaging manner
of some friends connected with him in the *Liberal*." And
he took up with masterly anger the question of Byron's
epigrams on Castlereagh in the *Liberal,* noting that the
Courier which raged with mock passion over these had
recently " exulted over the death of one of the most amiable

114

and enthusiastically beloved men that ever existed. Yet Percy Shelley had oppressed and injured none." His extracts from the *Courier* should not escape reprinting, as a specimen of the polluted opinion on Shelley at that time : " Shelley, the writer of some infidel poetry, has been drowned; *now* he knows whether there is a God or no," and, " Of the infidel Shelley we should speak in no compromising terms, were he still capable of future mischief. But he is dead, and the world has no more to do with him. His pernicious writings are the legacy he has left us— and with them we shall deal as freely as we would with the obscenities of Rochester or the impiety of Voltaire." Meanwhile the Vice Society was prosecuting W. Clarke, the Strand bookseller, for republishing *Queen Mab,* and the man was convicted amid judicial expressions of horror at the immorality of the poem. Clarke was said to have sold over five hundred copies of his pirated edition.

The outcry against the *Liberal* roused Hazlitt, who, seeing that John Hunt was conducting the direct defence, gave his assistance indirectly in a long letter (printed in three instalments) called " Canting Slander : to the Rev. William Bengo Collyer "—a performance marked by all his usual formidable intensity. Collyer's magazine the *Investigator* had included an article with the alluring title " Licentious Publications in High Life "—" an abusive attack upon the publishers of the Works of Sir Charles Hanbury Williams, upon Lord Byron, and upon the late Mr. Shelley." Hazlitt mainly concerned himself with Byron and *Don Juan,* which he instantly proclaimed " a work of extraordinary power and beauty, abounding in passages (to say nothing of the wit and satire) of great sweetness and delicacy, and—until you and such as you polluted them by your gross, debasing comments—innocent and moral." With Shelley, Hazlitt was not so surely in sympathy, and his comments are not so extensive; he, however, drew forth from the *Investigator* a detestable passage on Shelley's life, called it " a string of *atrocious*

falsehoods," and summed up thus : " I must take my leave
of you for the present ; and I cannot perhaps convey in a
stronger manner a notion of the feelings with which I
view the abominable slander uttered by such a person as
yourself against a noble enthusiast in good, whose least
quality would outweigh the sum total of your merits,
than by expressing my conviction, that had you and the
object of your calumnies lived at the time of the foundation
of Christianity, Percy Shelley would have been among the
most devoted and disinterested followers of the benevolent
Jesus, postponing every selfish consideration to the service
of his master and his doctrines of love and gentleness ;
while *you* would have been a ' Scribe or Pharisee,' probably
a ' Chief Priest,' certainly a ' Hypocrite.' "

1823, 1824, 1825: DISSOLVING THE PARTNERSHIP

THE development of the section of the "Examiner" devoted to book notices into a separate journal entitled the *Literary Examiner*, meant that little but politics appeared in the "Examiner" for 1823. Throughout the year John Hunt was awaiting his trial for the publication of Byron's *Vision of Judgment*, alleged to be libellous. One of Leigh Hunt's two unreclaimed contributions was a mock indictment of various authors for similar misconduct, a piece of nonsense with a point in his fluent, brilliant, youthful spirit. His other article was a clarendonising sketch, humorously anticipating Byron's future cantos of recklessness, called "Arrival of Don Juan at Shooter's Hill."

After the failure of the *Literary Examiner* the essayist again appeared in the columns of his old journal, sending from Italy the series known as "The Wishing Cap Papers," reminiscences of old friendly scenes and metropolitan haunts, occasionally varied with abstract matters and arguments. Between March and the end of 1824, twenty-one of these, greatly varying in merit and attraction, were printed. "No. I: Introduction" was a genuine example of his generous, egotistical-modest, beaming, quick-witted way. His motive was thus expressed: "I used to think that with all my love of particular places, I should not care where I went, provided I could take my friends with me. But I find it otherwise. The fine buildings in Genoa made me long to take a walk down a London alley. The vineyards and olives of Tuscany gave me a calenture for my old green fields. Walking about under the galleries and government-offices of Florence, I yearned infinitely to be at the Examiner Office in Covent-garden; *and so here I am.*" He showed the strength of his affections by including among the first of his imaginative pleasures "A Walk in Covent Garden" with peculiarly vivid notice of Lamb's evening parties, and "Piccadilly and the West End" culminated for him in the house and cheerful circle of Vincent Novello. We shall cull these flowers of cordiality.

"C. L[amb], why didst thou ever quit Russell-street? Why didst thou leave the warm crowd of humanity, which thou lovest so well, to go and shiver on the side of the New River, inticing thy unwary friends to walk in? Were friends and sittings up at night too unattractive? And was there no other way to get rid of them? Reader, we have not waked the night-owl with a catch, for C. L. is not musical. He will put up with nothing but snatches of old songs. Mozart is to him an alien, and Paesiello the Pope of Rome. But we have drawn three souls out of one card-player; and might have waked all the ghosts in our neighbourhood at Will's and Button's, seeing that there is no pride in the next world, and some wit left in this. What would I not give for another Thursday evening? It was humanity's triumph; for whist-players and no whist-players there for the first time met together. Talk not to me of great houses in which such things occur; for there the whist-players are gamblers, and the no whist-players are nobody at all. Here, the whist was for its own sake, and yet the non-players were tolerated. But the triumph went further. Here was R[ickman], to represent among us the plumpness of office, and the solidity of the government. My brother Reformer, W. H[azlitt], came to rest his disappointments and his paradoxes. Vain expectation! With him contended A[yrton], the most well-bred of musicians, who hates a paradox like an unresolved discord. Another A. [Alsager] was there, the best of neighbours, especially if you happen to be confined to your room. Item, a third A. [Allsop], the most trusting of linen-drapers, who lent a poet a hundred pounds. I do not know whether he has been paid. I hope not;

for he deserves to enjoy the interest for ever, and in his case it is a rich one. M. B[urney] was one of us, having his hands in his waistcoat pockets like his friend, and talking well upon episodes. And thou, M. L[amb]—why have I not the art, like the old writers of dedications, of at once loading thee with panegyric and saving the shoulders of thy modesty ? an art, by the by, which was so conspicuously concealed, that nobody would have suspected them of having it. There also came old Captain B[urney], who had been round the world with Cooke, and was the first man who planted a pun in Otaheite. Nevertheless, though I met him fifty times, I never had the courage to address him, he appeared to be so wrapped up in his tranquillity and his whist. He seemed to be taking a long repose from his storms. The jovial face of Colonel P[hillips], blooming with a second youth, made me bolder. He had been round the world also, when a boy, and had challenged his lieutenant for not standing closer by his captain. This illegality completed my confidence. With K[enney] we rejoiced over his successful plays, and tried to be indifferent over the others. He has humanity enough to remember with pleasure, that on the latter occasion we mustered up (some of us at least) as great an appetite at supper as if two plays had succeeded at once. It is more than we could have looked for, had a critic written them, instead of a poet. But somehow these poetical observers see farther into the niceties of us than your metaphysical."

"The west end of London, for an obvious reason, is of little interest in a classical point of view, compared with other parts of the town. One or two writers like Gibbon do nothing for so great a quarter. Even Covent Garden is not the most inspired ground. The most sacred places are now occupied by the money-changers of Cornhill and the Borough. Of these in my next. But oh ! for the evenings again that I have passed there, especially at a house at the other end of Oxford-street. The N[ovellos] lived there, the most catholic of catholics, for their spirit

embraced the whole world. There we should have waked
the night-owl with a catch, had an owl been within hearing.
The watchman did instead. The solitary passenger who
was astonished at our Laughing Trios, was not the less
so at the majestic rolling of the organ that would follow it ;
just emblem of the devotion for all good things which
we had in our hearts. There came J. G[attie], a set of airy
crotchets in the shape of a man ; and H. R[obertson],
(always ready with his tenor, his joke, and his breathing
nod of acquiescence) for whom I shall have another pang
on my conscience if I do not write to him (not because he
will die, but because he will think my friendship is dead,
which it can never be)—and C. C[larke], who groaned a
hundred times of an evening in the fullness of his satisfaction—(I hope to hear shortly that benevolent grind of
his epiglottis)—and the G[liddons], pleasant specimens of
humanity ; and Kate H., a beauty fit to take coffee with
the party in the Rape of the Lock :

> ' On her white breast a sparkling cross she wore
>   Which Jews might kiss, and infidels adore.'

And it was as catholic too as that of Belinda. Kate was
tall, had a fine black head of hair, with eyes to match, and
a face made for a portrait. When she came home from the
play, and sat down in her long scarlet mantle, showing
only her throat and fine curls, and sparkling smiles, you saw
how many eyes had been looking at her from the pit. A
husband carried her off to a distance, and we never saw her
again, which was unfair : I wonder how these husbands
reconcile it to their consciences. C. L[amb] came there
sometimes ' to wonder at our quaint spirits,' with a quainter
spirit of his own. He would put up with no anthems but
Kent's, and with no songs but *Water parted from the Sea.*
His sister humbly suggested, at a beautiful passage in
Mozart, that she thought there was some merit in that.
He would not hear of it. What was the consequence ?

120

Why, that he got loved by everybody in spite of his in-
tolerance ; which, with him, is apt to have more humanity
in it than the liberality of other men."

So heartily and sometimes profoundly Hunt's fancy
continued to revisit his beloved London, and to resist with
regret the lovely vistas of Florence and " sunburnt mirth "
about him, until his difficulties and his sense of defamation
and disaster concerned with the *Liberal,* and an illness
which may be estimated by the fact that it reduced his
beautiful handwriting to painful illegibility, got the better
of him. Two of the later essays departed so far from the
original notion of the Wishing-Cap as to be simply long
letters from a friend at Rome, probably Charles Armitage
Brown, descriptive of " Actors and Artists " and " Illumin-
ations and Ceremonies " there, with slight comments by
Hunt. However, the whole series was substantial, and
gilds the commonplaces of the year's " Examiner." The
principal occurrences particularly affecting the journal and
its promoters were the long delayed trial and then again
delayed sentence of John Hunt (this time not imprisoned,
only fined !) for publishing " The Vision of Judgment,"
and the death of Byron. The latter event naturally
obtained an extraordinary amount of attention through
the Press, not only of England but of Europe. What the
" Examiner " contributed to the occasion does not appear
to be of permanent importance. John Hunt spoke of
Byron with great admiration and honour, defending him
against the charge of misanthropy : " His face was indeed
enough, to any one with the least notion of physiognomy,
to refute the absurd falsehoods circulated respecting his
natural disposition : never was any face so made up of
sensitiveness, so full of those little swellings which denote
quick emotions." At first inclined to protest against the
burning of Byron's autobiography, the " Examiner " readily
announced itself in error when informed that the author
himself did not wish the Memoirs published. In its pages
(August 22nd) Byron's physician Bruno corrected some of

Fletcher's statements about his master's last moments; while as a supplement a creditable lithograph of Byron, after a bust by Bartolini made at Pisa in 1822 (" the best as well as latest Likeness of his Lordship "), was brought out.

Hazlitt, who wrote for the " Examiner " of July 11th, 1824, a character of George Canning, contributed once during 1825 (on " English and Foreign Manners.") Apart from that article, and the concluding " Wishing-Cap " papers, there is scarcely anything demanding to be specified in the 1825 volume. Leigh Hunt published, but did not sign, a poetical soliloquy expressing the possible feelings of the Italian singer Velluti, to whose appearance great objection was being expressed; a courageous act of sympathy, but it was almost the end of his " Examiner " writings. The dispute with John Hunt concerning the proprietorship of the newspaper had begun, and had quickly led to a severance of relations melancholy to reflect upon in the light of their previous admirable brotherhood of opinion and operation. It was destined to last a dozen years or so, John Hunt being as inflexible on a point of justice and right towards his idealistic Liberal brother as he would have been to the most hated and dishonourable Mock Constitutional sycophant.

What has been written is a sufficient epitaph from the present pen to the " Examiner." The ability and public spirit of the Hunts was the first chapter of a far-reaching series, but we can only refer to the later ones in a word or two. Albany Fonblanque, John Forster and others continued to uphold the dignity and intellectual excellence of the journal until 1881, and the contents of the later volumes are generally organised with greater skill and written in subtler journalistic tone than those which we have been looking over. But the dramatic directness, personality and transforming genius of the early years remained without eclipse.

Part II

SELECTIONS

Leigh Hunt's Criticisms of Keats, Shelley and Lamb;
Four Prose Papers and two Poems, ascribed to Lamb;
and other interesting Selections from the "Examiner,"
hitherto uncollected.

K

LEIGH HUNT
ON
YOUNG POETS

IN sitting down to this subject, we happen to be restricted by time to a much shorter notice, than we could wish : but we mean to take it up again shortly. Many of our readers however have perhaps observed for themselves, that there has been a new school of poetry rising of late, which promises to extinguish the French one that has prevailed among us since the time of Charles the 2d. It began with something excessive, like most revolutions, but this gradually wore away; and an evident aspiration after real nature and original fancy remained, which called to mind the finer times of the English Muse. In fact it is wrong to call it a new school, and still more so to represent it as one of innovation, its only object being to restore the same love of nature, and of *thinking* instead of mere *talking*, which formerly rendered us real poets, and not merely versifying wits, and bead-rollers of couplets.

We were delighted to see the departure of the old school acknowledged in the number of the *Edinburgh Review* just published, a candour the more generous and spirited, inasmuch as that work has hitherto been the greatest surviving ornament of the same school in prose and criticism, as it is now destined, we trust, to be still the leader in the new.

We also felt the same delight at the third canto of Lord Byron's *Child Harolde*, in which, to our conceptions at least, he has fairly renounced a certain leaven of the French style, and taken his place where we always said he would be found, among the poets who have a real feeling for numbers, and who go directly to Nature for inspiration. But more of this poem in our next.

The object of the present article is merely to notice three young writers, who appear to us to promise a considerable addition of strength to the new school. Of the first who came before us, we have, it is true, yet seen only one or two specimens, and these were no sooner sent us than we unfortunately mislaid them ; but we shall procure what he has published, and if the rest answer to what we have seen, we shall have no hesitation in announcing him for a very striking and original thinker. His name is Percy Bysshe Shelley, and he is the author of a poetical work entitled *Alastor, or the Spirit of Solitude.*

The next with whose name we became acquainted, was John Henry Reynolds, author of a tale called Safie, written, we believe, in imitation of Lord Byron, and more lately of a small set of poems published by Taylor and Hessey, the principal of which is called the *Naiad.* It opens thus :

> The gold sun went into the west,
> And soft airs sang him to his rest ;
> And yellow leaves all loose and dry
> Play'd on the branches listlessly ;
> The sky wax'd palely-blue, and high,
> A cloud seem'd touch'd upon the sky—
> A spot of cloud,—blue, thin and still,
> And silence bask'd on vale and hill.
> 'Twas autumn-tide,—the eve was sweet,
>   As mortal eye hath e'er beholden ;
> The grass look'd warm with sunny heat,—
> Perchance some fairy glowing feet
>   Had lightly touch'd—and left it golden ;
> A flower or two were shining yet ;
> The star of the daisy had not yet set,—
> It shone from the turf to greet the air,
> Which tenderly came breathing there ;
> And in a brook which lov'd to fret
>   O'er yellow sand and pebble blue,
>   The lily of the silvery hue
> All freshly dwelt, with white leaves wet.
> Away the sparkling water play'd,
>   Through bending grass, and blessed flower ;

Light, and delight seem'd all its dower ;
Away in merriment it strayed ;
Singing, and bearing, hour after hour,
Pale, lovely splendour to the shade.

We shall give another extract or two in a future number. The author's style is too artificial, though he is evidently an admirer of Mr. Wordsworth. Like all young poets too, properly so called, his love of detail is too overwrought and indiscriminate, but still he is a young poet, and only wants a still closer attention to things as opposed to the seduction of words, to realise all that he promises. His nature seems very true and amiable.

The last of these young aspirants whom we have met with, and who promise to help the new school to revive Nature and

"To put a spirit of youth in everything,"

is, we believe, the youngest of them all, and just of age. His name is John Keats. He has not yet published anything except in a newspaper ; but a set of his manuscripts was handed us the other day, and fairly surprised us with the truth of their ambition, and ardent grappling with Nature. In the following Sonnet there is one incorrect rhyme, which might be easily altered, but which shall serve in the meantime as a peace-offering to the rhyming critics. The rest of the composition, with the exception of a little vagueness in calling the regions of poetry " the realms of gold," we do not hesitate to pronounce excellent, especially the last six lines. The word *swims* is complete ; and the whole conclusion is equally powerful and quiet :

ON FIRST LOOKING INTO CHAPMAN'S HOMER

Much have I travel'd in the realms of Gold,
And many goodly States and Kingdoms seen ;
Round many western Islands have I been,
Which bards in fealty to Apollo hold ;

But of one wide expanse had I been told,
  That deep-brow'd Homer ruled as his demesne ;
  Yet could I never judge what men could mean,
Till I heard Chapman speak out loud and bold.
Then felt I like some watcher of the skies,
  When a new planet swims into his ken ;
Or like stout Cortez, when with eagle eyes
  He stared at the Pacific,—and all his men
Looked at each other with a wild surmise,—
  Silent, upon a peak in Darien.

JOHN KEATS.

Oct. 1816.

We have spoken with the less scruple of these poetical promises, because we really are not in the habit of lavishing praises and announcements, and because we have no fear of any pettier vanity on the part of young men, who promise to understand human nature so well.

[" Examiner," December 1st, 1816.]

LEIGH HUNT
ON
POEMS BY JOHN KEATS

THIS is the production of the young writer whom we had the pleasure of announcing to the public a short time since, and several of whose Sonnets have appeared meanwhile in the " Examiner " with the signature of J. K. From these and stronger evidences in the book itself, the readers will conclude that the author and his critic are personal friends ; and they are so— made however, in the first instance, by nothing but his poetry, and at no greater distance of time than the an- nouncement above-mentioned. We had published one of his Sonnets in our paper, without knowing more of him than any other anonymous correspondent ; but at the period in question, a friend brought us one morning some copies of verses, which he said were from the pen of a youth. We had not been led, generally speaking, by a good deal of experience in these matters, to expect pleasure from introductions of the kind, so much as pain ; but we had not read more than a dozen lines, when we recognised " a young poet indeed."

It is no longer a new observation, that poetry has of late years undergone a very great change, or rather, to speak properly, poetry has undergone no change, but something which was not poetry has made way for the return of something which is. The school which existed till lately since the restoration of Charles the 2d, was rather a school of wit and ethics in verse, than anything else ; nor was the verse, with the exception of Dryden's, of the best order. The authors, it is true, are to be held in great honour. Great wit there certainly was, excellent satire, excellent sense, pithy sayings ; and Pope distilled as much real poetry

as could be got from the drawing-room world in which the
art then lived,—from the flowers and luxuries of artificial
life,—into that exquisite little toilet-bottle of essence, the
Rape of the Lock. But there was little imagination, of a
higher order, no intense feeling of nature, no sentiment, no
real music or variety. Even the writers who gave evidences
meanwhile of a truer poetical faculty, Gray, Thomson,
Akenside, and Collins himself, were content with a great
deal of second-hand workmanship, and with false styles
made up of other languages and a certain kind of inverted
cant. It has been thought that Cowper was the first poet
who re-opened the true way to nature and a natural style ;
but we hold this to be a mistake, arising merely from certain
negations on the part of that amiable but by no means
powerful writer. Cowper's style is for the most part as
inverted and artificial as that of the others ; and we look
upon him to have been by nature not so great a poet as
Pope : but Pope, from certain infirmities on his part, was
thrown into the world, and thus had to get what he could
out of an artificial sphere : Cowper, from other and
distressing infirmities (which by the way the wretched
superstition that undertook to heal, only burnt in
upon him), was confined to a still smaller though more
natural sphere, and in truth did not much with it,
though quite as much perhaps as was to be expected
from an organisation too sore almost to come in contact
with any thing.

It was the Lake Poets in our opinion (however grudgingly
we say it, on some accounts) that were the first to revive a
true taste for nature ; and like most Revolutionists,
especially of the cast which they have since turned out to
be, they went to an extreme, calculated rather at first to
make the readers of poetry disgusted with originality and
adhere with contempt and resentment to their magazine
common-places. This had a bad effect also in the way of
re-action ; and none of those writers have ever since been
able to free themselves from certain stubborn affectations,

130

which having been ignorantly confounded by others with the better part of them, have been retained by their self-love with a still less pardonable want of wisdom. The greater part indeed of the poetry of Mr. Southey, a weak man in all respects, is really made up of little else. Mr. Coleridge still trifles with his poetical as he has done with his metaphysical talent. Mr. Lamb, in our opinion, has a more real tact of humanity, a modester, Shakespearean wisdom, than any of them; and had he written more, might have delivered the school victoriously from all its defects. But it is Mr. Wordsworth who has advanced it the most, and who in spite of some morbidities as well as mistaken theories in other respects, has opened upon us a fund of thinking and imagination, that ranks him as the successor of the true and abundant poets of the older time. Poetry, like Plenty, should be represented with a cornucopia, but it should be a real one; not swelled out and insidiously *optimized* at the top, like Mr. Southey's stale strawberry baskets, but fine and full to the depth, like a heap from the vintage. Yet from the time of Milton till lately, scarcely a tree had been planted that could be called a poet's own. People got shoots from France, that ended in nothing but a little barren wood, from which they made flutes for young gentlemen and fan-sticks for ladies. The rich and enchanted ground of real poetry, fertile with all that English succulence could produce, bright with all that Italian sunshine could lend, and haunted with exquisite humanities, had become invisible to mortal eyes like the garden of Eden:

" And from that time those Graces were not seen."

These Graces, however, are re-appearing; and one of the greatest evidences is the little volume before us; for the work is not one of mere imitation, or a compilation of ingenious and promising things that merely announce better, and that after all might only help to keep up a

131

bad system; but here is a young poet giving himself up to his own impressions, and revelling in real poetry for its own sake. He has had his advantages, because others have cleared the way into those happy bowers; but it shews the strength of his natural tendency, that he has not been turned aside by the lingering enticements of a former system, and by the self-love which interests others in enforcing them. We do not, of course, mean to say that Mr. Keats has as much talent as he will have ten years hence, or that there are no imitations in his book, or that he does not make mistakes common to inexperience; the reverse is inevitable at his time of life. In proportion to our ideas, or impressions of the images of things, must be our acquaintance with the things themselves. But our author has all the sensitiveness of temperament requisite to receive these impressions; and wherever he has turned hitherto, he has evidently felt them deeply.

The very faults indeed of Mr. Keats arise from a passion for beauties, and a young impatience to vindicate them; and as we have mentioned these, we shall refer to them at once. They may be comprised in two; first, a tendency to notice every thing too indiscriminately and without an eye to natural proportion and effect; and second, a sense of the proper variety of versification without a due consideration of its principles.

The former error is visible in several parts of the book, but chiefly though mixed with great beauties in the Epistles, and more between pages 28 and 47, where are collected the author's earliest pieces, some of which, we think, might have been omitted, especially the string of magistrate-interrogatories about a shell and a copy of verses. See also (p. 61) a comparison of wine poured out in heaven to the appearance of a falling star, and (p. 62) the sight of far-seen fountains in the same region to "silver streaks across a dolphin's fin." It was by thus giving way to every idea that came across him, that Marino, a man of real poetical fancy, but no judgment, corrupted the poetry

132

of Italy; a catastrophe, which however we by no means anticipate in our author, who with regard to this point is much more deficient in age than in good taste. We shall presently have to notice passages of a reverse nature, and these are by far the most numerous. But we warn him against a fault, which is the more tempting to a young writer of genius, inasmuch as it involves something so opposite to the contented commonplace and vague generalities of the late school of poetry. There is a superabundance of detail, which, though not so wanting, of course, in power of perception, is as faulty and unseasonable sometimes as common-place. It depends upon circumstances, whether we are to consider ourselves near enough, as it were, to the subject we are describing to grow microscopical upon it. A person basking in a landscape, for instance, and a person riding through it, are in two very different situations for the exercise of their eyesight; and even where the license is most allowable, care must be taken not to give to small things and great, to nice detail and to general feeling, the same proportion of effect. Errors of this kind in poetry answer to a want of perspective in painting, and of a due distribution of light and shade. To give an excessive instance in the former art, there was Denner, who copied faces to a nicety amounting to a horrible want of it, like Brobdingnagian visages encountered by Gulliver; and who, according to the facetious Peter Pindar,

> Made a bird's beak appear at twenty mile.

And the same kind of specimen is afforded in poetry by Darwin, a writer now almost forgotten and deservedly, but who did good in his time by making unconscious caricatures of all the poetical faults in vogue, and flattering himself that the sum total went to the account of his original genius. Darwin would describe a dragon-fly and a lion in the same terms of proportion. You did not know which he would have scrambled from the sooner. His

133

pictures were like the two-penny sheets which the little boys buy, and in which you see J Jackdaw and K King, both of the same dimensions.

Mr. Keats' other fault, the one in his versification, arises from a similar cause, that of contradicting over-zealously the fault on the opposite side. It is this which provokes him now and then into mere roughness and discords for their own sake, not for that of variety and contrasted harmony. We can manage, by substituting a greater feeling for a smaller, a line like the following :

I shall roll on the grass with two-fold ease;

but by no contrivance of any sort can we prevent this from jumping out of the heroic measure into mere rhythmicality,

How many bards gild the lapses of time!

We come now however to the beauties ; and the reader will easily perceive that they not only outnumber the faults a hundred fold, but that they are of a nature decidedly opposed to what is false and inharmonious. Their characteristics indeed are a fine ear, a fancy and imagination at will, and an intense feeling of external beauty in its most natural and least expressible simplicity.

We shall give some specimens of the least beauty first, and conclude with a noble extract or two that will shew the second, as well as the powers of our young poet in general. The harmony of his verses will appear throughout.

The first poem consists of a piece of luxury in a rural spot, ending with an allusion to the story of Endymion and to the origin of other lovely tales of mythology, on the ground suggested by Mr. Wordsworth in a beautiful passage of his *Excursion.* Here, and in the other largest poem, which closes the book, Mr. Keats is seen to his best advantage, and displays all that fertile power of association and imagery which constitutes the abstract poetical faculty as distinguished from every other. He wants age for a greater knowledge of humanity, but evidences of this also bud forth here and there. To come however to our specimens :

The first page of the book presents us with a fancy, founded, as all beautiful fancies are, on a strong sense of what really exists or occurs. He is speaking of

A GENTLE AIR IN SOLITUDE

There crept
A little noiseless noise among the leaves,
Born of the very sigh that silence heaves.

YOUNG TREES

There too should be
The frequent chequer of a youngling tree,
That with a score of light green brethren shoots
From the quaint mossiness of aged roots ;
Round which is heard a spring-head of clear waters.

Anybody who has seen a throng of young beeches, furnishing those natural clumpy seats at the root, must recognise the truth and grace of this description. The remainder of this part of the poem, especially from

Open afresh your round of starry folds,
Ye ardent marigolds !

down to the bottom of page 5, affords an exquisite proof of close observation of nature as well as the most luxuriant fancy.

THE MOON

Lifting her silver rim
Above a cloud, and with a gradual swim
Coming into the blue with all her light.

FIR TREES

Fir trees grow around,
Aye dropping their hard fruit upon the ground.

This last line is in the taste of the Greek simplicity.

A STARRY SKY

The dark silent blue
With all its diamonds trembling through and through.

SOUND OF A PIPE

And some are hearing eagerly the wild
Thrilling liquidity of dewy piping.

The *Specimen of an Induction to a Poem,* and the fragment of the Poem itself entitled *Calidore,* contain some very natural touches on the human side of things ; as when speaking of a lady who is anxiously looking out on the top of a tower for her defender, he describes her as one

Who cannot feel for cold her tender feet ;

and when Calidore has fallen into a fit of amorous abstraction, he says that

—The kind voice of good Sir Clerimond
Came to his ear, as something from beyond
His present being.

The Epistles, the Sonnets, and indeed the whole of the book, contain strong evidences of warm and social feelings, but particularly the Epistle to Charles Cowden Clarke, and the Sonnet to his own Brothers, in which the " faint cracklings " of the coal-fire are said to be

Like whispers of the household gods that keep
A gentle empire o'er fraternal souls.

The Epistle to Mr. Clarke is very amiable as well as poetical,

136

and equally honourable to both parties, to the young writer who can be so grateful towards his teacher, and to the teacher who had the sense to perceive his genius, and the qualities to call forth his affection. It consists chiefly of recollections of what his friend had pointed out to him in poetry and in general taste; and the lover of Spenser will readily judge of his preceptor's qualifications, even from a single triplet, in which he is described, with a deep feeling of simplicity, as one

> Who had beheld Belphoebe in a brook,
> And lovely Una in a leafy nook,
> And Archimago leaning o'er his book.

The Epistle thus concludes :

PICTURE OF COMPANIONSHIP

But many days have past—
Since I have walked with you through shady lanes,
That freshly terminate in open plains,
And revell'd in a chat that ceased not,
When at night-fall among your books we got ;
No, nor when supper came —nor after that,—
Nor when reluctantly I took my hat ;
No, nor till cordially you shook my hand
Midway between our homes :—your accents bland
Still sounded in my ears, when I no more
Could hear your footsteps touch the gravelly floor.
Sometimes I lost them, and then found again,
You changed the footpath for the grassy plain.
In those still moments I have wished you joys
That well you know to honour : " Life's very toys
With him," said I, " will take a pleasant charm ;
It cannot be that ought will work him harm."

And we can only add, without any disrespect to the graver warmth of our young poet, that if Ought attempted it, Ought would find he had stout work to do with more than one person.

The following passage in one of the Sonnets passes, with great happiness, from the mention of physical associations to mental; and concludes with a feeling which must have struck many a contemplative mind, that has found the sea-shore like a border, as it were, of existence. He is speaking of

THE OCEAN

The Ocean with its vastness, its blue green,
Its ships, its rocks, its caves,—its hopes, its fears,—
Its voice mysterious, which whoso hears
Must think on what will be, and what has been.

We have read somewhere the remark of a traveller, who said that when he was walking alone at night-time on the sea-shore, he felt conscious of the earth, not as the common everyday sphere it seems, but as one of the planets, rolling round with him in the mightiness of space. The same feeling is common to imaginations that are not in need of similar local excitements.

The best poem is certainly the last and longest, entitled *Sleep and Poetry*. It originated in sleeping in a room adorned with busts and pictures, and is a striking specimen of the restlessness of the young poetical appetite, obtaining its food by the very desire of it, and glancing for fit subjects of creation " from earth to heaven." Nor do we like it the less for an impatient, and as it may be thought by some irreverent assault upon the late French school of criticism and monotony, which has held poetry chained long enough to render it somewhat indignant when it got free.

The following ardent passage is highly imaginative:

AN ASPIRATION AFTER POETRY

[Quotation, beginning " O Poesy! for thee I grasp
my pen," and ending, " Wings to find out an immortality."]

Mr. Keats takes an opportunity, though with very different feelings towards the school than he has exhibited towards the one above-mentioned, to object to the morbidity that taints the productions of the Lake Poets. They might answer perhaps, generally, that they chuse to grapple with what is unavoidable, rather than pretend to be blind to it ; but the more smiling Muse may reply, that half of the evils alluded to are produced by brooding over them ; and that it is better to strike at as many *causes* of the rest as possible, than to pretend to be satisfied with them in the midst of the most evident dissatisfaction.

HAPPY POETRY PREFERRED

These things are doubtless : yet in truth we've had
Strange thunders from the potency of song ;
Mingled indeed with what is sweet and strong,
From majesty : but in clear truth the themes
Are ugly clubs, the Poets' Polyphemes
Disturbing the grand sea. A drainless shower
Of light is poesy ; 'tis the supreme of power ;
'Tis might half slumbering on its own right arm.
The very archings of her eye-lids charm
A thousand willing agents to obey.
And still she governs with the mildest sway :
But strength alone though of the Muses born
Is like a fallen angel ; trees uptorn,
Darkness, and worms, and shrouds, and sepulchres
Delight it ; for it feeds upon the burrs
And thorns of life ; forgetting the great end
Of poesy, that it should be a friend
To soothe the cares, and lift the thoughts of man.

We conclude with the beginning of the paragraph which follows this passage, and which contains an idea of as lovely and powerful a nature in embodying an abstraction, as we ever remember to have seen put into words :

Yet I rejoice : a myrtle fairer than
E'er grew in Paphos, from the bitter weeds
Lifts its sweet head into the air, *and feeds*
A silent space with ever sprouting green.

Upon the whole, Mr. Keats's book cannot be better described than in a couplet written by Milton when he too was young, and in which he evidently alludes to himself. It is a little luxuriant heap of

> Such sights as youthful poets dream
> On summer eves by haunted stream.

[" Examiner," July 6th and 13th, 1817.]

LEIGH HUNT

ON

THE STORIES OF LAMIA, THE POT OF BASIL, THE EVE OF ST. AGNES

AS TOLD BY MR. KEATS

IN laying before our readers an account of another new publication, it is fortunate that the nature of the work again falls in with the character of our miscellany; part of the object of which is to relate the stories of old times. We shall therefore abridge into prose the stories which Mr. Keats has told in poetry, only making up for it, as we go, by cutting some of the richest passages out of his verse, and fitting them in to our plainer narrative. They are such as would leaven a much greater lump. Their drops are rich and vital, the essence of a heap of fertile thoughts.

The first story, entitled Lamia, was suggested to our author by a passage in Burton's Anatomy of Melancholy, which he has extracted at the end of it. We will extract it here, at the beginning, that the readers may see how he has enriched it. Burton's relation is itself an improvement on the account in Philostratus. The old book-fighter with melancholy thoughts is speaking of the seductions of phantasmata.

"Philostratus, in his fourth book, 'De Vita Apollonii,' hath a memorable instance in this kind, which I may not omit, of one Menippus Lycius, a young man twenty-five years of age, that going betwixt Cenchreas and Corinth, met such a phantasm in the habit of a fair gentlewoman, which taking him by the hand, carried him home to her house, in the suburbs of Corinth, and told him she was a Phœnician by birth, and if he would tarry with her, he should hear her sing and play, and drink such wine as never

any drank, and no man should molest him ; but she, being
fair and lovely, would live and die with him, that was fair
and lovely to behold.   The young man, a philosopher,
otherwise staid and discreet, able to moderate his passions,
though not this of love, tarried with her awhile to his
great content, and at last married her, to whose wedding,
amongst other guests, came Apollonius ; who, by some
probable conjectures, found her out to be a serpent, a
lamia ; and that all her furniture was, like Tantalus' gold,
described by Homer, no substance but mere illusions.
When she saw herself descried, she wept, and desired
Apollonius to be silent, but he would not be moved, and
therefore she, plate, house, and all that was in it, vanished
in an instant : many thousands took notice of this fact,
for it was done in the midst of Greece."—Anatomy of
Melancholy, Part 3, Sect. 2.

According to our poet, Mercury had come down from
heaven, one day, in order to make love to a nymph, famous
for her beauty.   He could not find her ; and he was halting
among the woods uneasily, when he heard a lonely voice,
complaining.   It was

> A mournful voice,
> Such as once heard, in gentle heart, destroys
> All pain but pity : thus the lone voice spake.
> " When from this wreathed tomb shall I awake !
> " When move in a sweet body fit for life,
> " And love, and pleasure, and the ruddy strife
> " Of hearts and lips ! Ah, miserable me ! "

Mercury went looking about among the trees and grass,

> Until he found a palpitating snake,
> Bright, and cirque-couchant in a dusky brake.

The admiration, pity and horror, to be excited by humanity
in a brute shape, were never perhaps called upon by a
greater mixture of beauty and deformity than in the
picture of this creature.   Our pity and suspicions are begged

142

by the first word : the profuse and vital beauties with which she is covered seem proportioned to her misery and natural rights ; and lest we should lose sight of them in this gorgeousness, the " woman's mouth " fills us at once with shuddering and compassion.

> She was a gordian shape of dazzling hue,
> Vermilion-spotted, golden, green, and blue ;
> Striped like a zebra, freckled like a pard,
> Eyed like a peacock, and all crimson-barr'd ;
> And full of silver moons, that, as she breathed,
> Dissolv'd or brighter shone, or interwreathed
> Their lustries with the gloomier tapestries—
> So rainbow-sided, touch'd with miseries,
> She seem'd at once, some penanced lady elf,
> Some daemon's mistress, or the daemon's self.
> Upon her crest she wore a wannish fire,
> Sprinkled with stars, like Ariadne's tiar :
> Her head was serpent, but ah, bitter-sweet !
> She had a woman's mouth with all its pearls complete :
> And for her eyes : what could such eyes do there,
> But weep, and weep, that they were born so fair ?
> As Proserpine still weeps for her Sicilian air.

The serpent tells Mercury that she knows upon what quest he is bound, and asks him if he has succeeded. The god, with the usual eagerness of his species to have his will, falls into the trap ; and tells her that he will put her in possession of any wish she may have at heart, provided she can tell him where to find his nymph. As eagerly, she accepts his promise, making him ratify it by an oath, which he first pronounces with an earnest lightness, and afterwards with a deeper solemnity.

> Then once again the charmed God began
> An oath, and through the serpent's ears it ran
> Warm, tremulous, devout, psalterian.

The creature tells him that it was she who had rendered the nymph invisible, in order to preserve her from the importunities of the ruder wood gods. She adds, that

she was a woman herself, that she loves a youth of Corinth
and wishes to be a woman again, and that if he will let
her breathe upon his eyes, he shall see his invisible beauty.
The god sees, loves, and prevails. The serpent undergoes
a fierce and convulsive change, and flies towards Corinth.

A full-born beauty, new and exquisite, Lamia, whose
liability to painful metamorphosis was relieved by a supernatural imagination, had been attracted by the beauty of
Lycius, while pitching her mind among the enjoyments
of Corinth. By the same process, she knew that he was
to pass along, that evening, on the road from the sea-side
to Corinth ; and there accordingly she contrives to have
an interview, which ends in his being smitten with love,
and conducting her to her pretended home in that city.
She represents herself as a rich orphan, living " but half-
retired," and affects to wonder that he never saw her
before. As they enter Corinth, they pass the philosopher
Apollonius, who is Lycius's tutor, and from whom he
instinctively conceals his face. Lamia's hand shudders in
that of her lover ; but she says she is only wearied ; and
at the same moment, they stop at the entrance of a
magnificent house ;

> A pillar'd porch, with lofty portal door,
> Where hung a silver lamp, whose phosphor glow
> Reflected in the slabbed steps below,
> Mild as a star in water.

Here they lived for some time, undisturbed by the world,
in all the delight of a mutual passion. The house remained
invisible to all eyes, but those of Lycius. There were a
few Persian mutes, " seen that year about the markets " ;
and nobody knew whence they came ; but the most in-
quisitive were baffled in endeavouring to track them to
some place of abode.

But all this while, a god was every night in the house,
taking offence. Every night

LAMIA

With a terrific glare,
Love, jealous grown of so complete a pair,
Hovered and buzzed his wings with fearful roar
Above the lintel of their chamber door,
And down the passage cast a glow upon the floor.

Lycius, to the great distress of his mistress, who saw in
his vanity a great danger, persuaded her to have a public
wedding-feast. She only begged him not to invite Apollonius; and then, resolving to dress up her bridals with a
sort of despairing magnificence, equal to her apprehensions
of danger, she worked a fairy architecture in secret, served
only with the noise of wings and a restless sound of music—

A haunting music, sole perhaps and lone
Supportress of the faery-roof, made moan
Throughout, as fearful the whole charm might fade.

This is the very quintessence of the romantic. The walls
of the long vaulted room were covered with palms and
plantain-trees imitated in cedar-wood, and meeting over
head in the middle of the ceiling between the stems were
jasper pannels, from which "there burst forth creeping
imagery of slighter trees;" and before each of these "lucid
pannels

Fuming stood
A censer filled with myrrh and spiced wood,
Whose slender feet wide-swerv'd upon the soft
Wool-woofed carpets; fifty wreaths of smoke
From fifty censers their light voyage took
To the high roof, still mimick'd as they rose
Along the mirror'd walls by twin-clouds odorous.

Twelve tables stood in this room, set round with circular
couches, and on every table was a noble feast and the
statue of a god.

Lamia, regal drest,
Silently faced about, and as she went,
In pale contented sort of discontent,

Mission'd her viewless servants to enrich
The fretted splendour of each nook and niche.

*   *   *

Approving all, she faded at self-will,
And shut the chamber up, close, hush'd, and still,
Complete and ready for the revels rude,
When dreadful guests would come to spoil her solitude.

The guests came. They wondered and talked; but their gossiping would have ended well enough, when the wine prevailed, had not Apollonius, an unbidden guest, come with them. He sat right opposite the lovers, and

—Fixed his eye, without a twinkle or stir,
Full on the alarmed beauty of the bride,
Brow-beating her fair form, and troubling her sweet pride.

Lycius felt her hand grow alternately hot and cold, and wondered more and more both at her agitation and the conduct of his old tutor. He looked into her eyes, but they looked nothing in return; he spoke to her, but she made no answer: by degrees the music ceased, the flowers faded away, the pleasure all darkened, and

A deadly silence step by step increased,
Until it seemed a horrid presence there,
And not a man but felt the terror in his hair.

The bridegroom at last shrieked out her name; but it was only echoed back to him by the room. Lamia sat fixed, her face of a deadly white. He called in mixed agony and rage to the philosopher to take off his eyes; but Apollonius, refusing, asked him whether his old guide and instructor who had preserved him from all harm to that day, ought to see him made the prey of a serpent. A mortal faintness came into the breath of Lamia at this word; she motioned him, as well as she could, to be silent; but looking her stedfastly in the face, he repeated Serpent! and she vanished with a horrible scream. Upon the same

146

night, died Lycius, and was swathed for the funeral in his wedding-garments.

Mr. Keats has departed as much from common-place in the character and moral of this story, as he has in the poetry of it. He would see fair play to the serpent, and makes the power of the philosopher an ill-natured and disturbing thing. Lamia though liable to be turned into painful shapes had a soul of humanity; and the poet does not see why she should not have her pleasures accordingly, merely because a philosopher saw that she was not a mathematical truth. This is fine and good. It is vindicating the greater philosophy of poetry. At the same time, we wish that for the purpose of his story he had not appeared to give in to the common-place of supposing that Apollonius's sophistry must always prevail, and that modern experiment has done a deadly thing to poetry by discovering the nature of the rainbow, the air, etc.: that is to say, that the knowledge of natural history and physics, by shewing us the nature of things, does away the imaginations that once adorned them. This is a condescension to a learned vulgarism, which so excellent a poet as Mr. Keats ought not to have made. The world will always have fine poetry, as long as it has events, passions, affections, and a philosophy that sees deeper than this philosophy. There will be a poetry of the heart, as long as there are tears and smiles: there will be a poetry of the imagination, as long as the first causes of things remain a mystery. A man who is no poet, may think he is none, as soon as he finds out the physical cause of the rainbow; but he need not alarm himself; he was none before. The true poet will go deeper. He will ask himself what is the cause of that physical cause; whether truths to the senses are after all to be taken as truths to the imagination; and whether there is not room and mystery enough in the universe for the creation of infinite things, when the poor matter-of-fact philosopher has come to the end of his own vision. It is remarkable that an age of poetry has grown up with the progress of experiment; and that the very poets, who seem to countenance these notions, accompany them by some of their finest effusions. Even if there were nothing new to be created, if philosophy, with its line and rule, could even score the ground, and say to poetry " Thou shalt go no further," she would look back to the old world, and still find it inexhaustible. The crops from its fertility are endless. But these alarms are altogether idle. The essence of poetical enjoyment does not consist in belief, but in a voluntary power to imagine.

The next story, that of the Pot of Basil, is from Boccaccio. After the narrative of that great writer, we must make as short work of it as possible in prose. To turn one of his stories into verse, is another thing. It is like setting it to a more elaborate music. Mr. Keats is so struck with admiration of his author, that even while giving him this accompaniment, he breaks out into an apology to the great Italian, asking pardon for this

Echo of him in the north-wind sung.

We might waive a repetition of the narrative altogether, as the public have lately been familiarized with it in the Sicilian Story of Mr. Barry Cornwall: but we cannot help calling to mind that the hero and heroine were two young and happy lovers, who kept their love a secret from her rich brothers; that her brothers, getting knowledge of their intercourse, lured him into a solitary place, and murdered him; that Isabella, informed of it by a dreary vision of her lover, found out where he was buried, and with the assistance of her nurse, severed the head from the body that she might cherish even that ghastly memorial of him as a relic never to be parted with; that she buried the head in a pot of earth, and planting basil over it, watered the leaves with her continual tears till they grew into wonderful beauty and luxuriance; that her brothers, prying into her fondness for the Pot of Basil, which she

148

carried with her from place to place, contrived to steal it away; that she made such lamentations for it, as induced them to wonder what could be its value, upon which they dug into it, and discovered the head; that the amazement of that discovery struck back upon their hearts, so that after burying the head secretly, they left their native place, and went to live in another city; and that Isabella continued to cry and moan for her Pot of Basil, which she had not the power to cease wishing for; till, under the pressure of that weeping want, she died.

Our author can pass to the most striking imagination from the most delicate and airy fancy. He says of the lovers in their happiness,

> Parting they seemed to tread upon the air,
>   Twin roses by the zephyrs blown apart
> Only to meet again more close, and share
>   The inward fragrance of each other's heart.

These pictures of their intercourse terribly aggravate the gloom of what follows. Lorrenzo when lured away to be killed, is taken unknowingly out of his joys, like a lamb out of the pasture. The following masterly anticipation of his end, conveyed in a single word, has been justly admired:

> So the two brothers and their *murder'd* man
> Rode past fair Florence, to where Arno's stream
> Gurgles through straitened banks.
>   They passed the water
> Into a forest quiet for the slaughter.

When Mr. Keats errs in his poetry, it is from the ill management of a good thing—exuberance of ideas. Once or twice, he does so in a taste positively bad, like Marino or Cowley, as in a line in his Ode to Psyche

> At tender eye-dawn of aurorean love;

but it is once or twice only, in his present volume. Nor has he erred much in it in a nobler way. What we allude

149

to is one or two passages in which he over-informs the
occasion or the speaker ; as where the brothers, for instance,
whom he describes as a couple of mere " money-bags,"
are gifted with the power of uttering the following exquisite
metaphor :

> " To day we purpose, ay, this hour we mount
>   To spur three leagues towards the Apennine :
> Come down, we pray thee, ere the hot sun count
>   His dewy rosary on the eglantine."

But to return to the core of the story.   Observe the fervid
misery of the following :

> She gaz'd into the fresh-thrown mould, as though
>   One glance did fully all its secrets tell ;
> Clearly she saw, as other eyes would know
>   Pale limbs at bottom of a crystal well ;
> Upon the murderous spot she seem'd to grow,
>   Like to a native lily of the dell :
> Then with her knife, all sudden, she began
> To dig more fervently than misers can.
>
> Soon she turn'd up a soiled glove, whereon
>   Her silk had play'd in purple phantasies,
> She kissed it with a lip more chill than stone
>   And put it in her bosom, where it dries
> And freezes utterly unto the bone
>   Those dainties made to still an infant's cries :
> Then 'gan she work again ; nor stay'd her care,
> But to throw back at times her veiling hair.
>
> That old nurse stood beside her wondering,
>   Until her heart felt pity to the core
> At sight of such a dismal labouring,
>   And so she kneeled, with her locks all hoar,
> And put her lean hands to the horrid thing ;
>   Three hours they labour'd at this travail sore ;
> At last they felt the kernel of the grave,
> And Isabella did not stamp and rave.

It is curious to see how the simple pathos of Boccaccio,
or (which is the same thing) the simple intensity of the

heroine's feelings, suffices our author more and more, as he gets to the end of his story. And he has related it as happily as if he had never written any poetry but that of the heart. The passage about the tone of her voice—the poor lost-witted coaxing—the "chuckle" in which she asks after her Pilgrim and her Basil—is as true and touching an instance of the effect of a happy familiar word, as any in all poetry. The poet bids his imagination depart,

> For Isabel, sweet Isabel, will die ;
> Will die a death too lone and incomplete,
> Now they have ta'en away her Basil sweet.
>
> Piteous she look'd on dead and senseless things,
>   Asking for her lost Basil amorously ;
> And with melodious chuckle in the strings
>   Of her lorn voice, she oftentimes would cry
> After the Pilgrim in his wanderings,
>   To ask him where her Basil was ; and why
> 'Twas hid from her ; " For cruel 'tis," said she,
> " To steal my Basil-pot away from me."
>
> And so she pined, and so she died forlorn,
>   Imploring for her Basil to the last.
> No heart was there in Florence but did mourn
>   In pity of her love, so overcast.
> And a sad ditty of this story born
>   From mouth to mouth through all the country pass'd :
> Still is the burthen sung—" O cruelty,
> " To steal my Basil-pot away from me ! "

The Eve of St. Agnes, which is rather a picture than a story, may be analysed in a few words. It is an account of a young beauty, who going to bed on the eve in question to dream of her lover, while her rich kinsmen, the opposers of his love, are keeping holiday in the rest of the house, finds herself waked by him in the night, and in the hurry of the moment agrees to elope with him. The portrait of the heroine, preparing to go to bed, is remarkable for its union of extreme richness and good taste ; not that

those two properties of description are naturally distinct ;
but that they are too often separated by very good poets,
and that the passage affords a striking specimen of the
sudden and strong maturity of the author's genius. When
he wrote Endymion he could not have resisted doing too
much. To the description before us, it would be a great
injury either to add or diminish. It falls at once gorgeously
and delicately upon us, like the colours of the painted glass.
Nor is Madeline hurt by all her encrusting jewelry and
rustling silks. Her gentle, unsophisticated heart is in the
midst, and turns them into so many ministrants to her
loveliness.

[Quotation beginning

> A casement high and triple-arch'd there was,

and ending

> As though a rose should shut, and be a bud again.]

Is not this perfectly beautiful ?

*   *   *   *   *

As a specimen of the Poems, which are all lyrical, we
must indulge ourselves in quoting entire the Ode to a
Nightingale. There is that mixture in it of real melancholy
and imaginative relief, which poetry alone presents us in
her " charmed cup," and which some over-rational critics
have undertaken to find wrong because it is not true. It
does not follow that what is not true to them, is not true
to others. If the relief is real, the mixture is good and
sufficing. A poet finds refreshment in his imaginary wine,
as other men do in their real ; nor have we the least doubt,
that Milton found his grief for the loss of his friend King,
more solaced by the allegorical recollections of Lycidas,
(which were exercises of his mind, and recollections of a
friend who would have admired them) than if he could
have anticipated Dr. Johnson's objections, and mourned in

nothing but broadcloth and matter of fact. He yearned after the poetical as well as social part of his friend's nature; and had as much right to fancy it straying, in the wilds and oceans of romance, where it had strayed, as in the avenues of Christ's College where his body had walked. In the same spirit the imagination of Mr. Keats betakes itself, like the wind, "where it listeth," and is as truly there, as if his feet could follow it. The poem will be the more striking to the reader, when he understands what we take a friend's liberty in telling him, that the author's powerful mind has for some time past been inhabiting a sickened and shaken body, and that in the mean while it has had to contend with feelings that make a fine nature ache for its species, even when it would disdain to do so for itself; we mean, critical malignity, that unhappy envy, which would wreak its own tortures upon others, especially upon those that really feel for it already.

[Here follows the *Ode to a Nightingale*.]

The Hyperion is a fragment—a gigantic one, like a ruin in the desert, or the bones of the mastodon. It is truly of a piece with its subject, which is the downfall of the elder gods. It opens with Saturn, dethroned, sitting in a deep and solitary valley, benumbed in spite of his huge powers with the amazement of the change.

[Quotation beginning,

> Deep in the shady sadness of a vale

and ending,

> Was with its stored thunder labouring up.]

By degrees, the Titans meet in one spot, to consult how they may regain their lost empire; but Clymene the gentlest, and Oceanus the most reflective of those earlier deities, tell them that it is irrecoverable. A very grand and deep-thoughted cause is assigned for this by the latter.

Intellect, he gives them to understand, was inevitably displacing a more brute power,

> Great Saturn, thou
> Hast sifted well the atom universe ;
> But for this reason, that thou art the King,
> And only blind from sheer supremacy,
> One avenue was shaded from thine eyes,
> Through which I wandered to eternal truth.
> And first, as thou wast not the first of powers,
> So thou art not the last ; it cannot be ;
> Thou art not the beginning nor the end.
>
> * * *
>
> Now comes the pain of truth, to whom 'tis pain ;
> O folly ! for to bear all naked truths,
> And to envisage circumstance, all calm,
> That is the top of sovereignty.　Mark well !
> As Heaven and Earth are fairer, fairer far
> Than Chaos and blank Darkness, though once chiefs ;
> And as we show beyond that Heaven and Earth
> In form and shape compact and beautiful,
> In will, in action free, companionship,
> And thousand other signs of purer life ;
> So on our heels a fresh perfection treads,
> A power more strong in beauty, born of us
> And fated to excel us, as we pass
> In glory that old Darkness.

The more imaginative parts of the poem are worthy of this sublime moral. Hyperion, the God of the Sun, is the last to give away ; but horror begins to visit his old beatitude with new and dread sensations. The living beauty of his palace, whose portals open like a rose, the awful phænomena that announce a change in heaven, and his inability to bid the day break as he was accustomed— all this part, in short, which is the core and inner diamond of the poem, we must enjoy with the reader.

> [He quotes the long passage beginning "His palace bright " and ending, " He stretched himself in grief and radiance faint."]

154

LAMIA

The other Titans, lying half lifeless in their valley of despair, are happily compared to

> A dismal cirque
> Of Druid stones, upon a forlorn moor,
> When the chill rain begins at shut of eve,
> In dull November, and their chancel vault,
> The Heaven itself, is blinded throughout night.

The fragment ends with the deification of Apollo. It strikes us that there is something too effeminate and human in the way in which Apollo receives the exaltation which his wisdom is giving him. He weeps and wonders somewhat too fondly; but his powers gather nobly on him as he proceeds. He exclaims to Mnemosyne, the Goddess of Memory,

> Knowledge enormous makes a God of me,
> Names, deeds, gray legends, dire events, rebellions,
> Majesties, sovran voices, agonies,
> Creations and destroyings, all at once
> Pour into the wide hollows of my brain,
> And deify me, as if some blithe wine
> Or bright elixir peerless I had drunk,
> And so become immortal.

After this speech, he is seized with a glow of aspiration, and an intensity of pain, proportioned to the causes that are changing him; Mnemosyne upholds her arms, as one who prophesied; and

> At length
> Apollo shrieked; and lo! from all his limbs
> Celestial

Here the poem ceases, to the great impatience of the poetical reader.

If any living poet could finish this fragment, we believe it is the author himself. But perhaps he feels that he ought not. A story which involves passion, almost of necessity involves speech; and though we may well enough describe beings greater than ourselves by comparison,

M

unfortunately we cannot make them speak by comparison.
Mr. Keats, when he first introduces Thea consoling Saturn,
says that she spoke

> Some mourning words, which in our feeble tongue
> Would come in these like accents ; O how frail
> To that large utterance of the early Gods !

This grand confession of want of grandeur is all that he
could do for them. Milton could do no more. Nay, he
did less, when according to Pope he made

> God the father turn a school divine.

The moment the God speaks, we forget that they did not
speak like ourselves. The fact is, they feel like ourselves ;
and the poet would have to make them feel otherwise,
even if he could make them speak otherwise, which he
cannot, unless he venture upon an obscurity which would
destroy our sympathy : and what is sympathy with a God,
but turning him into a man ? We allow, that superiority
and inferiority are, after all, human terms, and imply
something not so truly fine and noble as the levelling of a
great sympathy and love ; but poems of the present nature,
like Paradise Lost, assume a different principle ; and
fortunately perhaps, it is one which it is impossible to
reconcile with the other.

We have now to conclude the surprise of the reader,
who has seen what solid stuff these poems are made of,
with informing him of what the book has not mentioned—
that they were almost all written four years ago, when the
author was but twenty. Ay, indeed ! cries a critic, rubbing
his hands delighted (if indeed even criticism can do so,
any longer) ; " then that accounts for the lines you speak
of, written in the taste of Marino." It does so ; but,
sage Sir, after settling the merits of those one or two lines
you speak of, what accounts, pray, for a small matter which
you leave unnoticed, namely, all the rest ? The truth is,
we rather mention this circumstance as a matter of ordinary

curiosity, than anything else; for great faculties have great privileges, and leap over time as well as other obstacles. Time itself, and its continents, are things yet to be discovered. There is no knowing even how much duration one man may crowd into a few years, while others drag out their slender lines. There are circular roads full of hurry and scenery, and straight roads full of listlessness and barrenness; and travellers may arrive by both, at the same hour. The Miltons, who begin intellectually old, and still intellectual, end physically old, are indeed Methusalems; and may such be our author, their son.

Mr. Keats's versification sometimes reminds us of Milton in his blank verse, and sometimes of Chapman both in his blank verse and rhyme; but his faculties, essentially speaking, though partaking of the unearthly aspirations and abstract yearnings of both these poets, are altogether his own. They are ambitious, but less directly so. They are more social, and in the finer sense of the word, sensual than either. They are more coloured by the modern philosophy of sympathy and natural justice. Endymion, with all its extraordinary powers, partook of the faults of youth, though the best ones; but the reader of Hyperion and these other stories would never guess that they were written at twenty. The author's versification is now perfected, the exuberances of his imagination restrained, and a calm power, the surest and loftiest of all power, takes place of the impatient workings of the younger god within him. The character of his genius is that of energy and voluptuousness, each able at will to take leave of the other, and possessing, in their union, a high feeling of humanity not common to the best authors who can less combine them. Mr. Keats undoubtedly takes his seat with the oldest and best of our living poets.

[*Indicator*, August 2nd and 9th, 1820; included here because the *Indicator* served Hunt as the literary supplement to the " Examiner " when that newspaper's treatment of politics crowded out other topics.]

LEIGH HUNT'S
ADIEU TO KEATS

AH, dear friend, as valued a one as thou art a poet, John Keats, we cannot, after all, find it in our hearts to be glad, now thou art gone away with the swallows to seek a kindlier clime. The rains began to fall heavily, the moment thou wast to go; we do not say, poet-like, for thy departure. One tear in an honest eye is more precious to thy sight, than all the metaphorical weepings in the universe; and thou didst leave many starting to think how many months it would be till they saw thee again. And yet thou didst love metaphorical tears too, in their way; and couldst always liken every thing in nature to something great or small; and the rains that beat against thy cabin window will set, we fear, thy over-working wits upon many comparisons that ought to be much more painful to others than thyself—Heaven mend their envious and ignorant numskulls. But thou hast " a mighty soul in a little body ; " and the kind cares of the former for all about thee shall no longer subject the latter to the chance of impressions which it scorns ; and the soft skies of Italy shall breathe balm upon it ; and thou shalt return with thy friend the nightingale, and make all thy other friends as happy with thy voice as they are sorrowful to miss it. The little cage thou didst sometime share with us, looks as deficient without thee, as thy present one may do without us ; but—farewell for awhile : thy heart is in our fields : and thou wilt soon be back to rejoin it.

[*Indicator*, September 20th, 1820, following a humorously written paper " The Return of Autumn " ; it seems appropriate and worth while to append it to the other pieces on Keats given here.]

LEIGH HUNT

ON

THE REVOLT OF ISLAM, A POEM

BY PERCY BYSSHE SHELLEY

THIS is an extraordinary production. The ignorant will not understand it; the idle will not take the pains to get acquainted with it; even the intelligent will be startled at first with its air of mysticism and wildness; the livelier man of the world will shake his head at it good-naturedly; the sulkier one will cry out against it, the bigot will be shocked, terrified, and enraged, and fall to proving all that is said against himself; the negatively virtuous will resent the little quarter that is given to mere custom; the slaves of bad customs or bad passions of any sort will either seize their weapons against it, trembling with rage or conscious worthlessness, or hope to let it quietly pass by, as an enthusiasm that must end in air; finally, the hopeless, if they are ill-tempered, will envy its hopefulness; if good tempered, will sorrowfully anticipate its disappointment; both from self-love, though two different sorts; but we will venture to say, that the intelligent and the good, who are yet healthy-minded, and who have not been so far blinded by fear and self love as to confound superstition with desert, anger and hatred with firmness, or despondency with knowledge, will find themselves amply repaid by breaking through the outer shell of this production, even if it be with the single reflection, that so much ardour for the happy virtues, and so much power to recommend them, have united in the same person. To will them with hope indeed is to create them; and to extend that will is the object of the writer before us.

The "EXAMINER" EXAMINED

The story of the "Revolt of Islam" is this. The poet, rising from "visions of despair" occasioned by the late triumphs over the progress of mankind, goes meditating by the sea-shore, and after an awful and prophetic tempest suddenly sees in the air the extraordinary spectacle of a combat between a serpent and an eagle:

> The Serpent's mailed and many-coloured skin
> Shone through the plumes its coils were twined within
> By many a swollen and knotted fold; and high
> And far, the neck, receding light and thin,
> Sustained a crested head, which warily
> Shifted and glanced before the Eagle's stedfast eye.

The Serpent is defeated, and falls into the sea, from whence he is received into the bosom of a beautiful woman who sits lamenting upon the shore. She invites the poet to go somewhere across the sea with them in a boat. He consents, more in fear for her than for himself; and in the course of the voyage she tells him that the Serpent and the Eagle are the Powers of Good and Evil, who combat with each other at intervals, that the Serpent or Power of Good has again been defeated; and that she herself is his selected companion, whom in his more radiant shape he appeared to once at night, and announced his having fallen in love with. The Serpent all this while lies still, recovering from the effects of the combat; and at last the voyagers come to a magnificent temple beyond the polar ocean, in which

> —There sat on many a sapphire throne
> The Great, who had departed from mankind,
> A mighty Senate; some, whose white hair shone
> Like mountain snow, mild, beautiful, and blind;
> Some female forms, whose gestures beamed with mind;
> And ardent youths—and children bright and fair;
> And some had lyres, whose strings were intertwined
> With pale and clinging flames, which ever there
> Waked faint yet thrilling sounds that pierced the chrystal air.

160

A magic and obscure circumstance then takes place, the result of which is, that the woman and serpent are seen no more, but that a cloud opens asunder, and a bright and beautiful shape, which seems compounded of both, is beheld sitting on a throne, a circumstance apparently imitated from Milton :

> Wonder and joy a passing faintness threw
> Over my brow—a hand supported me,
> Whose touch was magic strength : *an eye of blue*
> Looked into mine—Thou must a listener be
> This day—two mighty Spirits now return,
> Like birds of calm from the world's raging sea ;
> They pour fresh light from Hope's immortal urn,
> A tale of human power—despair not—list and learn !
>
> I looked, and lo ! one stood forth eloquently ;
> His eyes were dark and deep, and the clear brow
> Which shadowed them was like the mourning sky,
> The cloudless Heaven of Spring, when in their flow
> Through the bright air, the soft winds as they blow,
> *Wake the green world.*
>
> Beneath the darkness of his outspread hair,
> He stood thus beautiful : but there was one
> Who sate beside him like his shadow there,
> And held his hand—*far lovelier—she was known*
> *To be thus fair by the few lines alone*
> *Which through her floating locks and gathered cloak,*
> *Glances of soul-dissolving glory, shone.*

This is a fine Grecian feeling of what may be called the sentiment of shape. The two strangers are the hero and heroine of the poem : and here the more human part of the story commences. *Laon, the hero*, relates it. He was an ardent and speculative youth, born in modern Greece ; grew up with great admiration of the beauties and kindness of external nature, and a great horror of the superstitions and other oppressions with which his country and mankind in general were afflicted. A beautiful female orphan under

161

the care of his parents shared these feelings with him; and
mutual love was the consequences. She even speculated
upon taking some extraordinary though gentle step to
deliver the world from its thraldom; when she was torn
away from him by some slaves of the Grand Turk's Seraglio;
and he himself, for endeavouring to rescue her, and for
taking that opportunity of proclaiming freedom, was shut
up in a prison in a rock, where his senses forsook him. The
effect of the circumstance however is not lost. He is
delivered from his dungeon by an old man, and after a
second but milder insanity, is informed by his preserver,
that the people had been awakened to new ideas, and that
there was a maiden who went about exciting them to a
bloodless freedom. It was his love Cythna, after having
been likewise imprisoned, and robbed of her senses. A
considerable interval elapses while Laon recovers his reason,
but on so doing, and hearing of the exploits of her whom he
justly supposed to be his lovely friend, he takes leave of
the old man, and journeys for Constantinople or the Golden
City, where he finds the people risen, the tyrant fallen,
and Cythna the predominant spirit of the change. He
goes with others to the palace, and sees the " sceptered
wretch " sitting silent and sullen on the footstool of his
throne,

> Alone, but for one child, who led before him
> A graceful dance: weeping and murmuring
> 'Mid her sad task of unregarded love
> That to no smiles it might his speechless sadness move.

She clasps the tyrant's feet, and then stands up when the
strangers come nigh;

> Her lips and cheeks seemed very pale and wan,
> But on her forehead, and within her eye
> Lay beauty, which makes hearts that feed thereon
> Sick with excess of sweetness; on the throne
> She leaned; the king, with gathered brow and lips
> Wreathed by long scorn, did inly sneer and frown

> With hue like that when some great painter dips
> His pencil in the gloom of earthquake and eclipse.

Laon saves his life from the fury of the crowd; a festival
is held at which Cythna presides like a visible angel, and
every thing seems happiness and security. The Revolters
however are suddenly assailed by the allies of the tyrant;
and the fortune of the contest is changed. Cythna reaches
Laon through the lost battle on a huge black Tartarian
horse, "whose path makes a solitude;" and they fly to a
distance through a desolate village, in the dwellings of
which the flames and human beings were now dead;

> But the wide sky,
> Flooded with lightening, *was ribbed overhead*
> By the black rafters; and around did lie
> Women, and babes, and men, slaughtered confusedly.

The only survivor is a female, who has gone mad, and
fancies herself the Plague. The description of her desperate
laughter and actions is appalling, though not without a
tendency, we think, to something overwrought and artificial. When the travellers arrive at a place of rest, Cythna
tells Laon her adventures. They have been briefly alluded
to, and include a finely-fancied and pathetic account of a
child which she had in her dungeon, and which was taken
from her. Laon goes out from the retreat occasionally
to get food and intelligence, and finds that Revenge, and
subsequently Pestilence and Famine, have been making
terrible havoc in the city. The tyrant and his slaves, in
their terror, make frightened addresses to heaven, and a
priest advises them to expiate its "vengeance" by sacrificing Laon and Cythna. He accordingly dispatches
numbers to hunt them out; upon which Laon comes
forward disguised, and offers to give up the man provided
the woman be spared. They take an oath to do so, and
he declares himself; but it is then declared impious to
have made the oath; and at last, Cythna comes voluntarily

forward, and shares the funeral pyre with her beloved friend, from which they find themselves suddenly sailing on a beautiful sea to the Paradise in which the Spirit of Good resides, where Cythna meets with her child who had died of the plague; and the poem concludes.

*   *   *   *   *

We have given the story of this extraordinary book, and some extracts by which the reader can easily judge of its general merits. We have some remarks however to make on the particular qualities of its poetry, and on the deep social interests upon which it speculates; but as we are much pressed for room now the Parliament are sitting, and yet do not wish to pass over the work lightly, we had better occupy our present article at once with some extracts we intended to make from the author's preface. He explains in them the general object of his poem, and touches in a masterly manner upon the great political point of it, and indeed of the age in which we live.

"The poem," says he, "which I now present to the world is an attempt from which I scarcely dare to expect success, and in which a writer of established fame might fail without disgrace.

"It is an experiment on the temper of the public mind, as to how far a thirst for a happier condition of moral and political society survives, among the enlightened and refined, the tempests which have shaken the age in which we live. I have sought to enlist the harmony of metrical language, the ethereal combinations of the fancy, the rapid and subtle transitions of human passion, all those elements which essentially compose a Poem, in the cause of a liberal and comprehensive morality, and in the view of kindling, within the bosoms of my readers, a virtuous enthusiasm, for those doctrines of liberty and justice, *that faith and hope in something good,* which neither violence, nor misrepresentation, nor prejudice, can ever totally extinguish among mankind."

After dilating a little more on the subjects of his poem,

164

Mr. Shelley, with the feeling that ever seems to be at the bottom of his warmth, gives the following placid and easy solution of a difficulty, which the world, we believe, is also instinctively solving, but which, as he says, has been the "moral ruin" of some eminent spirits among us. If the Lake School, as they are called, were not as dogmatic in their despair as they used to be in their hope, we should earnestly recommend the passage to their attention. They might see in it, at any rate, how it becomes an antagonist to talk; and how charitable and consistent the mind can be, that really inquires into the philosophical causes of things. Mr. Shelley does not say that Mr. Southey is "no better than a house-breaker," nor does he exclaim with Mr. Wordsworth, in the ill-concealed melancholy of a strange piety, which would be still stranger if it were really chearful, that "Carnage is God's daughter." He is not in the habit, evidently, of begging the question against the low and uneducated; nor has he the least respect for that very sweeping lady, Miss Theodosia Carnage: —but stop! we must not be violating the charity of his philosophy.

"The panic," says our author, "which, like an epidemic transport, seized upon all classes of men during the excesses consequent upon the French Revolution, is gradually giving place to sanity. It has ceased to be believed, that whole generations of mankind ought to consign themselves to a hopeless inheritance of ignorance and misery, *because* a nation of men who had been dupes and slaves for centuries were incapable of conducting themselves with the wisdom and tranquility of freemen, as soon as some of their fetters were partially loosened. That their conduct could not have been marked by any other characters than ferocity and thoughtlessness, is *the historical fact* from which liberty derives all its deformity. There is a reflux in the tide of human things, which bears the shipwrecked hopes of men into a secure haven after the storms are past. Methinks, those who now live have survived an age of despair."

" The French Revolution may be considered as one of those manifestations of a general state of feeling among civilized mankind, produced by a defect of correspondence between the knowledge existing in society and the improvement, or gradual abolition of political institutions. The year 1788 may be assumed as the epoch of one of the most important crises produced by this feeling. The sympathies connected with that event extended to every bosom. The most generous and amiable natures were those which participated the most extensively in these sympathies. But such a degree of unmingled good was expected, as it was impossible to realize. *If the Revolution had been in every respect prosperous,* then misrule *and superstition would lose half their claims to our abhorrence,* as fetters *which the captive can unlock with the slightest motion of his fingers, and which do not eat with poisonous rust into the soul.* The revulsion occasioned by the atrocities of the demagogues, and the re-establishment of successive tyrannies in France, was terrible, and felt in the remotest corner of the civilized world. Could they listen to the plea of reason, who had groaned under the calamities of a social state, according to the provisions of which, one man riots in luxury, while another famishes for want of bread ? Can he who the day before was a trampled slave, suddenly become liberal-minded, forbearing, and independent ? This is the consequence of the habits of a state of society to be produced by resolute perseverance and indefatigable hope, and long suffering, and long believing courage, and the systematic efforts of generations of men of intellect and virtue. Such is the lesson which experience teaches now. But on the first reverses of hope in the progress of French liberty, the sanguine eagerness for good overleaped the solution of those questions, and for a time extinguished itself in the unexpectedness of their result. Thus many of the most ardent and tender-hearted of the worshippers of public good have been *morally ruined,* by what a partial glimpse of the events they deplored appeared to show as the melancholy desolation of all their cherished hopes. Hence gloom and misanthropy have become the characteristics of the age in which we live, the solace of a disappointment that unconsciously finds relief only in the wilful exaggeration of its own despair. This influence has tainted the literature of the age with the hopelessness of the minds from which it flows. Metaphysics, and inquiries into moral and polical science, have become little else than vain attempts to revive exploded superstitions, or sophisms like those of Mr. Malthus, calculated to lull the oppressors of mankind into a security of everlasting triumph. Our works of fiction and poetry have been overshadowed by the same infectious gloom. But mankind appear to me to be emerging from their trance. I am aware, methinks, of a slow, gradual, silent change. In that belief I have composed the following poem."

*   *   *   *   *

The reader has seen the fable as well as some passages of this poem, and heard the author's own account of his intentions in extracts from the preface. It remains for me to give a general criticism upon it, interspersed with a few more specimens; and as the object of the work is decidedly philosophical, we shall begin with the philosophy.

Mr. Shelley is of opinion with many others that the world is a very beautiful one externally, but wants a good deal of mending with respect to its mind and habits; and for this purpose he would quash as many cold and selfish passions as possible, and rouse up the gentle element of Love, till it set our earth rolling more harmoniously. The answer made to a writer, who sets out with endeavours like these, is that he is idly aiming at perfection; but Mr. Shelley has no such aim, neither have nine hundred and ninety-nine out of a thousand of the persons, who have ever been taunted with it. Such a charge, in truth, is only the first answer which egotism makes to any one who thinks he can go beyond its own ideas of the possible. If this however be done away, the next answer is, that you

167

are attempting something wild and romantic, that you will get disliked for it as well as lose your trouble, and that you had better coquet, or rather play the prude, with things as they are. The worldly sceptic smiles, and says " Hah ! "—the dull rogues wonder, or laugh out—the disappointed egotist gives you a sneering admonition, having made up his mind about all these things because he and his friends could not alter them ; the hypocrite affects to be shocked ; the bigot anticipates the punishment that awaits you for daring to say that God's creation is not a vile world, nor his creatures bound to be miserable, and even the more amiable compromiser with superstition expresses alarm for you—does not know what you may be hazarding, though he believes nevertheless that God is all good and just—refers you to the fate of Adam to show you that because he introduced the knowledge of evil, you must not attempt to do it away again—and finally, advises you to comfort yourself with *faith*, and to secure a life in the next world because *this* is a bad business, and *that*, of course, you may find a worse. It seems forgotten all this while, that Jesus Christ himself recommended Love as the great law that was to supersede others ; and recommended it too to an extreme, which has been held impracticable. How far it has been found impracticable, in consequence of his doctrines having been mixed up with contradictions and threatening dogmas, and with a system of after-life which contradicts all its principles, may be left to the consideration. Will theologians never discover, that men, in order to be good and just to each other, must either think well of a Divine Being, really and not pretendingly, or not think of him at all ? That they must worship Goodness and a total absence of the revengeful and malignant passions, if not Omnipotence ? or else that they must act upon this quality for themselves, and agree with a devout and amiable Pagan, that " it were better men should say there was no such being as Plutarch, than that there was one Plutarch who eat his own children ? "

Instead of the alarms about searches after happiness being wise and salutary, when the world is confessedly discordant, they would seem, if we believed in such things, the most fatal and ingenious invention of an enemy of mankind. But it is only so much begging of the question, fatal indeed as far as it goes, and refusing in the strangest manner to look after good, because there is a necessity for it. And as to the Eastern apologue of Adam and Eve (for so many Christians as well as others have thought it), it would be merely shocking to humanity and to a sense of justice in any other light ; but it is, in fact, a very deep though not wisely arranged allegory, deprecating the folly of mankind in losing their simplicity and enjoyment, and in taking to those very mistakes about vice and virtue, which it is the object of such authors as the one before us to do away again. Faith ! It is the very object they have in view ; not indeed faiths in endless terrors and contradictions, but " a faith and hope," as Mr. Shelley says, " in something good," that faith in the power of men to be kinder and happier, which other faiths take so much pains, and professed pains, to render unbelievable even while they recommend it ! " Have faith," says the theologian, " and bear your wretchedness, and escape the wrath to come." " Have faith," says the philosopher, " and begin to be happier now, and do not attribute odious qualities to any one."

People get into more inconsistencies in opposing the hopes and efforts of a philosophical enthusiasm than on any other subject. They say, " use your reason, instead of your expectations ; " and yet this is the reverse of what they do in their own beliefs. They say, take care how you contradict custom ; yet Milton, whom they admire, set about ridiculing it, and paying his addresses to another woman in his wife's life-time, till the latter treated him better. They say it is impossible the world should alter ; and yet it has often altered. They say it is impossible, at any rate, it should mend ; yet people are no longer burnt at the stake. They say, but it is too old to alter to any

great purpose of happiness, that all its experience goes
to the contrary ; and yet they talk at other times of the
brief life and shortsighted knowledge of man, and of the
nothingness of " a thousand years." The experience of
a man and an ephemeris are in fact just on a par in all that
regards the impossibility of change. But one man—
they say—what can one man do ? Let a glorious living
person answer, let Clarkson answer ; who sitting down
in his youth by a roadside, thought upon the horrors of the
Slave Trade, and vowed he would dedicate his life to
endeavour at overthrowing it. He was laughed at ; he
was violently opposed ; he was called presumptuous and
even irreligious ; he was thought out of his senses ; he
made a noble sacrifice of his own health and strength, and
he has lived to see the Slave Trade, aye, even the slavery
of the descendants of the " cursed " Ham, made a Felony.

We have taken up so much room in noticing these
objections, that we have left ourselves none for entering
into a further account of Mr. Shelley's views than he
himself has given ; and we have missed any more quotations
at last. But we are sure that he will be much better
pleased to see obstructions cleared away from the progress
of such opinions as his, than the most minute account
given of them in particular. It may be briefly repeated,
that they are at war with injustice, violence, and selfishness of every species, however disguised ; that they
represent, in a very striking light, the folly and misery of
systems, either practical or theoretical, which go upon
penal and resentful grounds, and add " pain to pain ; "
and that they would have men, instead of worshipping
tyrannies and terrors of any sort, worship goodness and
gladness, diminish the vices and sorrows made by custom
only, encourage the virtues and enjoyments which mutual
benevolence may realize ; and in short, make the best and
utmost of this world, as well as hope for another.

The beauties of the poem consist in depth of sentiment,
in grandeur of imagery, and a versification remarkably

sweet, various, and noble, like the placid playing of a great organ. If the author's genius reminds us of any other poets, it is of two very opposite ones, Lucretius and Dante. The former he resembles in the Daedalian part of it, in the boldness of his speculations, and in his love of virtue, of external nature, and of love itself. It is his gloomier or more imaginative passages that sometimes remind us of Dante. This sort of supernatural architecture in which he delights has in particular the grandeur as well as obscurity of that great genius, to whom however he presents this remarkable and instructive contrast, that superstition and pain and injustice go hand in hand even in the pleasantest parts of Dante, like the three Furies, while philosophy, pleasure, and justice, smile through the most painful passages of our author, like the three Graces.

Mr. Shelley's defects as a poet are obscurity, inartificial and yet not natural economy, violation of costume, and too great a sameness and gratuitousness of image and metaphor, too drawn from the elements, particularly the sea. The book is full of humanity; and yet it certainly does not go the best way to work for appealing to it, because it does not appeal to it through the medium of its common knowledges. It is for this reason that we must say something, which we would willingly leave unsaid, both from admiration of Mr. Shelley's genius and love of his benevolence; and this is, that the work cannot possibly become popular. It may set others thinking and writing, and we have no doubt will do so; and those who can understand and relish it, will relish it exceedingly; but the author must forget his metaphysics and sea-sides a little more in his future works, and give full effect to that nice knowledge of men and things which he otherwise really possesses to an extraordinary degree. We have no doubt he is destined to be one of the leading spirits of his age, and indeed has already fallen into his place as such; but however resolute as to his object, he will only be doing it justice to take the most effectual means in his power to forward it.

We have only to observe in conclusion, as another hint to the hopeless, that although the art of printing is not new, yet the Press in any great and true sense of the word is a modern engine in the comparison, and the changeful times of society have never yet been accompanied with so mighty a one. *Books* did what was done before ; they have now a million times the range and power ; and the Press, which has got hold of Superstition and given it some irrecoverable wounds already, will, we hope and believe, finally draw it in altogether, and crush it as a steam-engine would a great serpent.

[" Examiner," 1818.]

LEIGH HUNT

ON

THE QUARTERLY REVIEW, AND THE REVOLT OF ISLAM

SINCE our last paper, we have met with the *Quarterly Review*; and we shall beg our reader's disgust at that publication to be patient a little, while we say something upon its present number. *The Quarterly Review itself* (for there are one or two deeper articles in it, this time, than usual) ought to be ashamed of the one it has written upon Mr. Shelley. Heavy, and swelling, and soft with venom, it creeps through the middle of it like a skulking toad. The Editor, and the other more malignant writers in this Review, (for we know too much of such publications to confound all the writers together) have grown a little more cunning in their mode of attack. They only missed their aim, and pitched themselves headlong, with their blind fury, in such articles as that on the *Story of Rimini*. They have since undertaken to be more candid and acknowledging; and accordingly, by a ludicrous effort of virtue, they now make a point of praising some one thing, or rather giving some *one* extract, which they find rather praiseworthy than otherwise; and then they set to, sharper than ever, and reward their new morals with a double draught of malignity.

They are always too impatient, however, not to betray themselves at the outset. They begin their article on Mr. Shelley's *Revolt of Islam* by referring to the same book under another title, which that gentleman suppressed. He suppressed it by the advice of his friends, because in the ardour of his sincerity he had carried one of his theories to an excess which they thought would injure the perusal of it. Perhaps but two or three copies of that first impression were sold. The public at large certainly knew nothing of it. And yet the *Quarterly Reviewers*, who think these theories so pernicious, drag forth the impression, in order to abuse what he has not used. If on the other hand, he had not suppressed it, then the cry would have been— Surely he ought at least to have suppressed this ; and he would have been reproached for what he did use.

We are not going to nauseate the reader with all the half-sighted and whole-clawed meanness of the article in question. It is, in truth, a dull as well as a malicious endeavour ; and to any body acquainted with the speculations which it undertakes to handle, talks quite as much against itself as for. We will content ourselves with a short specimen or two. Mr. Shelley, in endeavouring to shew the per-niciousness of superstition in general, from which the perniciousness of its family members is to be deduced, lays the scene of his philosophical poem among the Mahometans : —upon which the Reviewer after blessing himself upon our present happy government, and expressing his own infinite content with it (which we have no doubt is great) calls upon the author to witness his triumph in the following manner :

" The laws and government on which Mr. Shelley's reasoning proceeds, are the Turkish, and ministered by a lawless despot ; his religion is the Mohammedan, main-tained by servile hypocrites ; and his scene for their joint operation Greece, the land full beyond all others of recollections of former glory and independence, now covered with shame and sunk in slavery. We are English-men, Christians, free, and independent ; we ask Mr. Shelley how his case applies to us ? Or what *we* learn from it to the prejudice of our own constitution ? " The Reviewer might as well ask what we learnt from any other fiction, which was to apply without being literal. Mr. Shelley is not bound to answer for his critic's stupidity. The reader of Gulliver's Travels might as well ask how the big or little men applied to *him*, he being neither as tall

as a church nor as short as a mole-hill. The Editor of the
Review himself, for instance, might as well ask how Mr.
Hazlitt's appellation of Grildrig applied to him, his
name being not Grildrig, but Gifford; and he never
having stood in the hand of an enormous prince, though
he has licked the feet of petty ones, and thrown stones at
their discarded mistresses' crutches.

Another, and we have done with specimens. Mr.
Shelley, says the Reviewer, "speaks of his school as ' a
world of woes,' of his masters as ' tyrants,' of his school-
fellows as ' enemies.' Alas! what is this but to bear
evidence against himself? Every one who knows what a
public school ordinarily must be, can only trace in these
lines the language of an insubordinate, a vain, a mortified
spirit."

Now, Reader, take the following lines :

—Public schools 'tis public folly feeds
The slaves of custom and established mode,
With pack horse constancy we keep the road,
Crooked or strait, through quags or thorny dells,
True to the jingling of our leader's bells.
To follow foolish precedents, and wink
With both our eyes, is easier than to drink.

Speaking of the worldly views with which even future
priests are sent to these schools, the Poet says :

Egregious purpose worthily begun,
In barb'rous prostitution of your son ;
Press'd on his part by means, that would disgrace
A scriv'ner's clerk, or footman out of place ;
And ending, if at last its end be gain'd,
In sacrilege, in God's own house profan'd.

*   *   *

The royal letters are a thing of course ;
A King, that would, might recommend his horse ;
And Deans, no doubt, and Chapters with one voice,
As bound in duty, would confirm the choice.

And lastly :

> Would you your son should be a sot or dunce,
> Lascivious, headstrong, or all these at once ;
> That in good time the stripling's finished taste
> For loose expense, and fashionable waste,
> Should prove your ruin, and his own at last,
> Train him in public with a mob of boys.

Reader, these are not the profane Mr. Shelley's verses, but the pious Cowper's ; Cowper, the all-applauded as well as the deserving, who in these lines, according to the Quarterly Reviewer, " bears evidence against himself," and proves that there is nothing to be traced in them but the " language of an insubordinate, a vain, a mortified spirit ; " Cowper in short, the independent, the good, and the sensitive, who, because he had not callousness enough to reconcile his faith in the dreadful dogmas of the Church to his notions of the Supreme Goodness, like these reviewing worshippers of power, nor courage enough to wage war with them, like Mr. Shelley, finally lost his senses ; and withered away in the very imagination of " blasts from hell," like a child on the altar of Moloch.

*   *   *   *   *

Our reviewing Scribes and Pharisees beg the question against Mr. Shelley's theories because he does not believe in their own creed. As if they had any creed but that which is established, and the better spirit of which they and men like them, have ever prevented from appearing ! They cannot affect meekness itself, but out of hostility. In the course of an article, full of anger, scandal, and bigotry, they put on little pale-lipped airs of serenity like a vixenish woman ; and during one of these they say they would recommend Mr. Shelley to read the Bible, only it is " a sealed book to a proud spirit." We will undertake to say that Mr. Shelley knows more of the Bible, than all the priests who have any thing to do with the Review, or its writers. He does not abjure " the pomps and vanities of

176

this wicked world " only to put them on with the greater relish. To them, undoubtedly, the Bible is not a sealed book, in one sense. They open it to good profit enough. But in the sense which the Reviewer means, they contrive to have it sealed wherever the doctrines are inconvenient. What do they say to the injunctions against " judging others that ye be not judged," against revenge, against tale-bearing, against lying, hypocrisy, " partiality," riches, pomps and vanities, swearing, perjury (videlicet, Nolo-Episcopation) Pharisaical scorn, and every species of worldliness and malignity ? Was Mr. Canning (the parodist) a worthy follower of him who denounced Scribes, Pharisees, and "devourers of widows' houses," when he swallowed up all those widows' pensions ! Was Mr. Gifford a worthy follower of him who was the forgiver and friend of Mary Magdalen, when he ridiculed the very lameness and crutches of a Prince's discarded mistress ! Men of this description are incapable of their own religion. If Christianity is compatible with all that they do and write, it is a precious thing. But if it means something much better—which we really believe it does mean, in spite both of such men and of much more reverenced and ancient authorities, then is the spirit of it to be found in the aspiration of the very philosophies which they are most likely to ill treat. The Reviewer for instance quotes, with horrified Italics, such lines as these

> Nor hate another's crime, nor loathe thine own.
> And love of joy can make the foulest breast
> A paradise of flowers, where peace might build her nest.

What is this first passage but the story of the woman taken in adultery ? And what the second, but the story of Mary Magdalen, " out of whom went seven devils," and who was forgiven because " she loved much ? " Mr. Shelley may think that the sexual intercourse might be altered much for the better, so as to diminish the dreadful evils to which it is now subject. His opinions on that matter, however denounced or misrepresented, he shares in common with some of the best and wisest names in philosophy, from Plato down to Condorcet. It has been doubted by Doctors of the Church, whether Christ himself thought on these matters as the Jews did. But be this as it may, it does not hurt the parallel spirit of the passages. The Jews were told " not to hate another's crime." The woman was not told to loathe her sin, but simply not to repeat it ; and was dismissed gently with these remarkable words, " Has any man condemned thee ? No, Lord. Neither do I condemn thee." Meaning, on the most impartial construction, that if no man had brought her before a judge to be condemned, neither would he be the judge to condemn her. She sinned, because she violated the conventional ideas of virtue, and thus hazarded unhappiness to others, who had not been educated in a different opinion ; but the goodness of the opinion itself is left doubtful. It is to the spirit of Christ's actions and theories that we look, and not to the comments or contradictions even of apostles. It was a very general spirit, if it was any thing, going upon the sympathetic excess, instead of the anti-pathetic, notoriously opposed to existing establishments, and reviled with every term of opprobrium by the Scribes and Pharisees then flourishing. If Mr. Shelley's theological notions run counter to those which have been built upon the supposed notions of Christ, we have no hesitation in saying that the moral spirit of his philosophy approaches infinitely nearer to that Christian benevolence, so much preached and so little practised, than any the most orthodox dogmas ever published. The Reviewers with their usual anti-Christian falsehood say that he recommends people to " hate no crime " and " abstain from no gratification." In the Christian sense he *does* tell them to " hate no crime " ; and in a sense as benevolent, he does tell them to " abstain from no gratification." But a world of gratification is shut out from his code, which the Reviewer would hate to be debarred from ; and which he instinctively hates him for denouncing already. Hear the end of the Preface to the *Revolt of Islam.* " I have avoided all *flattery* to those violent and malignant passions of our nature, which are ever on the watch to mingle with and to alloy the most beneficial innovations. There is no quarter given to *Revenge, Envy,* or *Prejudice.* Love is celebrated everywhere as the sole law which should govern the moral world." Now, if Envy is rather tormenting to ye, Messieurs Reviewers, there is some little gratification, is there not, in Revenge ? and some little gratifying profit or so in Prejudice ? " Speak, Grildrig."

*   *   *   *   *

Failing in the attempt to refute Mr. Shelley's philosophy, the Reviewers attack his private life. What is the argument of this ? or what right have they to know any thing of the private life of an author ? or how would they like to have the same argument used against themselves ? Mr. Shelley is now seven and twenty years of age. He entered life about 17 ; and everybody knows, and every candid person will allow, that a young man at that time of life, upon the very strength of a warm and trusting nature, especially with theories to which the world are not accustomed, may render himself liable to the misrepresentations of the worldly. But what have the Quarterly Reviewers to do with this ? What is Mr. Shelley's private life to the *Quarterly Review,* any more than Mr. Gifford's, or Mr. Croker's, or any other Quarterly Reviewer's private life is to the " Examiner," or the *Morning Chronicle,* or to the *Edinburgh Review*—a work, by the bye, as superior to the Quarterly, in all the humanities of social intercourse, as in the liberality of its opinions in general. The Reviewer talks of what he " now " knows of Mr. Shelley. What does this pretended *judge* and actual male-gossip, this willing listener to scandal, this minister to the petty wants of excitement, now know more than he ever knew, of an absent man, whose own side of whatever stories have been told him he has never heard ? Suppose the opponents of the *Quarterly Review* were to listen to all the scandals that have been reported of writers in it, and to proclaim this man by name as a pimp, another as a scamp, and another as a place or pulpit hunting slave made out of a school-boy tyrant ? If the use of private matters in public criticism is not to be incompatible with the decencies and charities of life, let it be proved so ; and we know who would be the sufferers. We have experienced, in our own persons, what monstrous misrepresentations can be given of a man, even with regard to the most difficult and unselfish actions of his life, and solely because others just knew enough of delicacy, to avail themselves of the inflexible love of it in others.

We shall therefore respect the silence hitherto observed publicly by Mr. Shelley respecting such matters, leaving him when he returns to England to take such notice or otherwise of his calumniators as may seem best to him. But we cannot resist the impulse to speak of one particular calumny of this Reviewer, the falsehood of which is doubly impressed upon us in consequence of our own personal and repeated knowledge of the reverse. He says Mr. Shelley "is shamefully dissolute in his conduct." We laugh the scandal-monger to scorn. Mr. Shelley has theories, as we have said before, with regard to the regulation of society, very different certainly from those of the Quarterly Reviewers, and very like opinions which have been held by some of the greatest and best men, ancient and modern. And be it observed that all the greatest and best men who have ever attempted to alter the condition of sexual intercourse at all have been calumniated as profligates, the devout Milton not excepted. A man should undoubtedly carry these theories into practice with caution, as well as any other new ones, however good, which tend to hurt the artificial notions of virtue, before reasoning and education have prepared them. We differ with Mr. Shelley in some particulars of his theory, but we agree in all the spirit of it; and the consequence has partly been to us, what it has been to him: those who have only a belief, or an acquiescence, and no real principle at all; or who prefer being rigid theorists and lax practisers, with the zest of hypocrisy first and penitence afterwards; or who love to confound conventional agreements and reputations with all that is to be wished for in human nature, and hate, and persecute, and delight to scandalize anybody, who, with the kindest intentions, would win them out of the hard crust of their egotism, however wretched, or lastly, those who, having acted with the most abominable selfishness and unfeelingness themselves, rejoice in the least opportunity of making a case out to the world against those they have injured— these, and such persons as these, have chosen to assume from our theories all which they think the world would least like in point of practice; and because we disdained to notice them, or chose to spare not only the best feelings of others, whom they should have been the last to wound, but even their own bad, false, and malignant ones, would have continued to turn that merciful silence against us, had they not unfortunately run beyond their mark, and shown their own fear and horror at being called upon to come forward. But to return to Mr. Shelley. The Reviewer asserts that he " is shamefully dissolute in his conduct." We heard of similar assertions, when we resided in the same house with Mr. Shelley for nearly three months; and how was he living all that time? As much like Plato himself, as any of his theories resemble Plato—or rather still more like a Pythagorean. This was the round of his daily life: He was up early; breakfasted sparingly; wrote this *Revolt of Islam* all the morning; went out in his boat or into the woods with some Greek author or the Bible in his hands; came home to a dinner of vegetables (for he took neither meat nor wine); visited (if necessary) " *the sick and the fatherless*," whom others gave Bibles to and no help; wrote or studied again, or read to his wife and friends the whole evening; took a crust of bread or a glass of whey for his supper; and went early to bed. This is literally the whole of the life he led, or that we believe he now leads in Italy; nor have we ever known him, in spite of the malignant and ludicrous exaggerations on this point, deviate, notwithstanding his theories, even into a single action which those who differ with him might think blameable. We do not say, that he would always square his conduct by their opinions as a matter of principle: we only say, that he acted just as if he did so square them. We forbear, out of regard for the very bloom of their beauty, to touch upon numberless other charities and generosities which we have known him exercise; but this we must say is general, that we never lived with a man who gave so complete an idea of an ardent and principled aspirant in philosophy as Percy Shelley; and that we believe him, from the bottom of our hearts, to be one of the noblest hearts as well as heads which the world has seen for a long time. We never met in short with a being who came nearer, perhaps so near, to that height of humanity mentioned in the conclusion of an essay of Lord Bacon's, where he speaks of excess of Charity and of its not being in the power of " man or angel to come in danger by it."

" If a man be gracious and courteous to strangers," continues this wise man of the world, in opening the final organ-stop of his high worship of a greater and diviner wisdom,—" If a man be gracious towards strangers it shows he is a citizen of the world, and that his heart is no island cut off from other lands, but a continent that joins to them. If he be compassionate towards the afflictions of others, it shows that his heart is like the noble tree that is wounded itself when it gives the balm. If he be thankful for small benefits, it shows that he weighs men's minds, and not their trash. But, above all, if he have St. Paul's perfection, that he would wish to be an anathema from Christ, for the salvation of his brethren, it shows

182

much of a divine nature, and a kind of conformity with Christ himself."

We could talk, after this, of the manner in which natures of this kind are ever destined to be treated by the Scribes, Pharisees, and Hypocrites of all times and nations ; but what room can we have for further indignation, when the ideas of benevolence and wisdom unite to fill one's imagination ?   Blessings be upon thee, friend ; and a part of the spirit which ye profess to serve, upon ye, enemies.

[" Examiner," September–October, 1819.]

LEIGH HUNT

ON

ROSALIND AND HELEN, A MODERN ECLOGUE; WITH OTHER POEMS

BY PERCY BYSSHE SHELLEY

THIS is another poem in behalf of liberality of sentiment and the deification of love, by the author of the *Revolt of Islam*. It is "not an attempt," says the writer, "in the highest style of poetry. It is in no degree calculated to excite profound meditation; and if, by interesting the affections and amusing the imagination, it awakens a certain ideal melancholy favourable to the reception of more important impressions, it will produce in the reader all that the writer experienced in the composition. I resigned myself, as I wrote, to the impulse of the feelings which moulded the conception of the story; and this impulse determined the pauses of a measure, which only pretends to be regular inasmuch as it corresponds with, and expresses, the irregularity of the imaginations which inspired it."

Mr. Shelley has eminently succeeded in all that he thus wished to do. The speakers, who tell each other their stories, are two fine-hearted women, who have been unhappy in their loves, the one having seen her partner in life die of a disappointed sympathy with mankind in consequence of the late great polical changes; and the other having for the sake of her reduced family accepted a hard, cold-blooded man for her husband, after she had been on the eve of marrying a beloved friend, who turned out at the altar to be her brother. The father

> —Came from a distant sky
> And with a loud and fearful cry

184

Rushed between us suddenly.
I saw the stream of his thin grey hair,
I saw his lean and lifted hand,
And heard his words—and live ! Oh God !
Wherefore do I live ?—" Hold, hold ! "
He cried, " I tell thee 'tis her brother ! "

The couplet marked in Italics, especially the first line, is very striking and fearful. He comes between them like a spirit grown old. There is something very beautiful in the way in which the two heroines meet. It is in Italy, whither they have both gone, like solitary birds of passage, from a climate every way colder ; and *Rosalind*, who it seems is a legitimate widow, turns away from her old friend, who had adopted Mary Woolstonecraft's opinion, in those matters. This fortune however, coming in aid of her former tenderness, melted her heart ; and it again ran into that of *Helen* with tears. They unite their fortunes, and have the pleasure of seeing their children, a girl and boy, grow up in love with each other, till in their union they saw,

The shadow of the peace denied to them.

This little publication, in form and appearance resembling the one we criticised last week, presents a curious contrast with it in every other respect. It is in as finer a moral taste, as *Rosalind and Helen* are pleasanter names than *Peter Bell.* The object of Mr. Wordsworth's administrations of melancholy is to make men timid, servile, and (considering his religion) selfish ; that of Mr. Shelley's, to render them fearless, independent, affectionate, infinitely social. You might be made to worship a devil by the process of Mr. Wordsworth's philosophy ; by that of Mr. Shelley, you might re-seat a dethroned goodness. The Poet of the Lakes, always carries his egotism and " saving knowledge " about with him, and unless he has the settlement of the matter, will go in a pet and plant himself by the side of the oldest tyrannies and slaveries ; our

Cosmopolite-Poet would evidently die with pleasure to all personal identity, could he but see his fellow-creatures reasonable and happy. He has no sort of respect, real or sullen, for mere power and success. It does not affect him in its most powerful shapes ; and he is inclined to come to no compromise with it ; he wants others happy, not himself privileged. But comparisons are never so odious, as when they serve to contrast two spirits who ought to have agreed. Mr. Wordsworth has become hopeless of this world, and therefore would make everybody else so ; Mr. Shelley is superior to hopelessness itself, and does not see why all happiness and all strength is to be bounded by what he himself can feel or can effect.

But we shall again be tempted to transgress the limits of our Literary Notices. We must give some further specimens of the poetry. The following is a passage which will go to every true woman's heart :

> When flowers were dead, and grass was green
> Upon my mother's grave,—that mother
> Whom to outlive, and cheer, and make
> My wan eyes glitter for her sake,
> Was my vowed task, the single care
> Which once gave life to my despair,—
> When she was a thing that did not stir,
> And the crawling worms were cradling her
> To a sleep more deep and so more sweet
> Than a baby's rocked on its nurse's knee,
> I lived ; a living pulse then beat
> Beneath my heart that awakened me.
> What was this pulse so warm and free ?
> Alas ! I knew it could not be
> My own dull blood ; 'twas like a thought
> Of liquid love, that spread and wrought
> Under my bosom and in my brain,
> And crept with the blood through every vein ?
> And hour by hour, day after day,
> The wonder could not charm away,
> But laid in sleep my wakeful pain,
> Until I knew it was a child,

And then I wept. For long, long years
These frozen eyes had shed no tears;
But now—'twas the season fair and mild
When April has wept itself to May:
I sate through the sweet sunny day
By my window bowered round with leaves,
And down my cheeks the quiet tears ran
Like twinkling rain drops from the eaves,
When warm spring showers are passing o'er:
O Helen, none can ever tell
The joy it was to weep once more!

Of Helen's lover Lionel, in his happier times, it is said that

A winged band
Of bright persuasions, which had fed
On his sweet lips and liquid eyes,
Kept their swift pinions half outspread
To do on men his least command.

The gentle noise arising from the earth during a still
summer evening is thus delightfully described: but we
must go back, and make a larger extract than we intended.
Lionel comes out of a prison, into which he had been cast
for his opinions ; and so, says his fond survivor :

We travelled on
By woods, and fields, of yellow flowers,
And towns, and villages, and towers,
Day after day of happy hours.
It was the azure time of June,
When the skies are deep in the stainless noon,
And the warm and fitful breezes shake
The fresh green leaves of the hedge-row briar,
And there were odours then to make
The very breath we did respire
A liquid element, whereon
Our spirits, like delighted things
That walk the air on subtle wings,
Floated and mingled far away,
'Mid the warm winds of the sunny day.
And when the evening star came forth
Above the curve of the newbent moon,

o

And light and sound ebbed from the earth,
Like the tide of the full and weary sea
To the depths of its tranquillity,
Our natures to its own repose
Did the earth's breathless sleep attune;
Like flowers, which on each other close
Their languid leaves when day-light's gone.

A picture follows, which we were going to say would be appreciated by none but the most delicate-minded; but Mr. Shelley can make his infinite earnestness and sincerity understood even by critics of a very different cast, who happen to have no personal pique with him; though we understand also that they take care to abuse him enough, in order to shew the time-serving bigotry of their opinions in general.

To the chief poem succeeds a smaller one entitled " Lines written among the Euganean Hills." Some of them are among the grandest if not the deepest that Mr. Shelley has produced, with a stately stepping in the measure. But we have not space to quote any, not even a noble compliment which he introduces to his friend Lord Byron. We must also abstain from many other passages which tempt us in the poem we have criticised.

Upon the whole, with all our admiration of the *Revolt of Islam,* we think that *Rosalind and Helen* contains, for the size, a still finer and more various, as well as a more popular style of poetry. The humanity is brought nearer to us, while the abstractions remain as lofty and noble. Mr. Shelley seems to look at Nature with such an earnest and intense love, that at last if she does not break her ancient silence, she returns him look for look. She seems to say to him, " You know me, if others do not." For him, if for any poet that ever lived, the beauty of the external world has an answering heart, and the very whispers of the wind a meaning. Things, with mankind in general, are mere words: they have only a few paltry common places about them, and see only the surface of those. To Mr. Shelley, all that exists, exists indeed—colour, sound, motion, thought, sentiment, the lofty and the humble, great and small, detail and generality—from the beauties of a blade of grass or the most evanescent tint of a cloud, to the heart of a man which he would elevate, and the mysterious spirit of the universe which he would seat above worship itself.

[" Examiner," 1819.]

LEIGH HUNT

ON

THE DESTRUCTION OF THE CENCI FAMILY, AND TRAGEDY ON THAT SUBJECT

"THE highest moral purpose aimed at in the highest species of the drama, is the teaching the human heart, through its sympathies and antipathies, the knowledge of itself; in proportion to the possession of which knowledge, every human being is wise, just, sincere, tolerant, and kind. If dogmas can do more, it is well: but a drama is no fit place for the enforcement of them. Undoubtedly, no person can be truly dishonoured by the act of another; and the fit return to make to the most enormous injuries is kindness and forbearance, and a resolution to convert the injurer from his dark passions by love and peace. Revenge, retaliation, atonement, are pernicious mistakes. If Beatrice had thought in this manner, she would have been wiser and better; but she would never have been a tragic character: the few whom such an exhibition would have interested, could never have been sufficiently interested for a domestic purpose, from the want of finding sympathy in their interest among the mass who surround them. It is in the restless and anatomizing casuistry with which men seek the justification of Beatrice, yet feel that she has done what needs justification; it is in the superstitious horror with which they contemplate alike her wrongs and revenge; that the dramatic character of what she did and suffered, consists."

Thus speaks Mr. Shelley, in the preface to his tragedy of the Cenci, a preface beautiful for the majestic sweetness of its diction, and still more lovely for the sentiments that flow forth with it. There is no living author, who writes

190

a preface like Mr. Shelley. The intense interest which he takes in his subject, the consciousness he has upon him nevertheless of the interests of the surrounding world, and the natural dignity with which a poet and philosopher, sure of his own motives, presents himself to the chance of being doubted by those whom he would benefit, casts about it an inexpressible air of amiableness and power. To be able to read such a preface, and differ with it, is not easy; but to be able to read it, and then go and abuse the author's intentions, shews a deplorable habit of being in the wrong.

* * * * *

The beauties of a dramatic poem, of all others, are best appreciated by a survey of the whole work itself, and of the manner in which it is composed and hangs together. We shall content ourselves therefore, in this place, with pointing out some detached beauties; and we will begin, as in the grounds of an old castle, with an account of a rocky chasm on the road to Petrella:

> *Lucrezia.* To-morrow before dawn
> Cenci will take us to that lonely rock,
> Petrella, in the Apulian Apennines.
> If he arrive there—
> *Beatrice.* He must not arrive.
> *Orsino.* Will it be dark before you reach the tower?
> *Lucr.* The sun will scarce be set.
> *Beatr.* But I remember
> Two miles on this side of the fort, the road
> Crosses a deep ravine; 'tis rough and narrow,
> And winds with short turns down the precipice,
> And in its depth there is a mighty rock,
> Which has, from unimaginable years,
> Sustained itself with terror and with toil
> Over a gulph, and with the agony
> With which it clings, seems slowly coming down;
> Even as a wretched soul, hour after hour,
> Clings to the mass of life; yet clinging, leans;
> And leaning, makes more dark the dread abyss
> In which it fears to fall: beneath this crag

> Huge as despair, as if in weariness,
> The melancholy mountain yawns : below
> You hear but see not an impetuous torrent
> Raging among the caverns, and a bridge
> Crosses the chasm, and high above there grow,
> With intersecting trunks, from crag to crag,
> Cedars, and yews, and pines, whose tangled hair
> Is matted in one solid roof of shade
> By the dark ivy's twine. At noon-day there
> 'Tis twilight, and at sunset blackest night.

With what a generous and dignified sincerity does Beatrice shew at once her own character and that of the prelate her lover.

> As I have said, speak not to me of love.
> Had you a dispensation, I have not :
> Nor will I leave this home of misery,
> Whilst my poor Bernard, and that gentle lady
> To whom I owe life and these virtuous thoughts,
> Must suffer what I still have strength to share.
> Alas, Orsino! All the love that once
> I felt for you, is turned to bitter pain.
> Ours was a youthful contract, which you first
> Broke, by assuming vows no Pope will loose.
> And yet I love you still, but holily,
> Even as a sister or a spirit might ;
> And so I swear a cold fidelity.
> And it is well perhaps we should not marry.
> You have a sly, equivocating vein,
> That suits me not.

The following is one of the gravest and grandest lines we ever read. It is the sum total of completeness. Orsino says, while he is meditating Cenci's murder, and its consequences,

> I see, as from a tower, the end of all.

The terrible imaginations which Beatrice pours forth during her frenzy, are only to be read in connection with the outrage that produced them. Yet take the following,

192

where the excess of the agony is softened to us by the wild and striking excuse which it brings for the guilt.

> What hideous thought was that I had even now ?
> 'Tis gone ; and yet its burthen remains still
> O'er these dull eyes—upon this weary heart.
> O, world ! O, life ! O, day ! O, misery !
> *Lucr.*   What ails thee, my poor child ?
>   She answers not ;
> Her spirit apprehends the sense of pain,
> But not its cause : Suffering has dried away
> The source from which it sprung.
> *Beatr.* (frantically).   Like Parricide,
> *Misery has killed its father.*

When she recovers, she " approaches solemnly " Orsino, who comes in, and announces to him, with an aweful obscurity, the wrong she has endured.   Observe the last line.

>   Welcome, friend !
> I have to tell you, that since last we met,
> I have endured a wrong so great and strange
> That neither life nor death can give me rest.
> Ask me not what it is, for there are deeds
> Which have no form, sufferings which have no tongue.
> *Ors.*   And what is he that has thus injured you ?
> *Beatr.*   The man they call my father ; a dread name.

The line of exclamations in the previous extract is in the taste of the Greek dramatists ; from whom Mr. Shelley, who is a scholar, has caught also his happy feeling for compounds, such as " the all-communicating air," the " mercy-winged lightning," " sin-chastising dreams," " wind-walking pestilence," the " palace-walking devil, gold," etc.   Gold in another place, is finely called " the old man's sword."

Cenci's angry description of the glare of day is very striking.

> The all-beholding sun yet shines : I hear
> A busy stir of men about the streets ;
> I see the bright sky through the window panes :
> It is a garish, broad, and peering day ;

Loud, light, suspicious, full of eyes and ears,
And every little corner, nook and hole
Is penetrated with the insolent light.
Come darkness !

The following is edifying :

The eldest son of a rich nobleman
Is heir to all his incapacities ;
He has wide wants, and narrow powers.

We are aware of no passage in the modern or ancient drama, in which the effect of bodily torture is expressed in a more brief, comprehensive, imaginative manner, than in an observation made by a judge to one of the assasins. The pleasure belonging to the original image renders it intensely painful.

Marzio.   My God ! I did not kill him ;
                                        I know nothing :
Olimpio sold the robe to me, from which
You would infer my guilt.
2d. Judge.   Away with him !
1st Judge.   Dare you, with lips yet white from the rack's kiss,
Speak false ?

Beatrice's thoughts upon what she might and might not find in the other world are very terrible ; but we prefer concluding our extracts with the close of the play, which is deliciously patient and affectionate. How triumphant is the gentleness of virtue in its most mortal defeats !

Enter Camillo and Guards.
Bernarde.   They come ! Let me
Kiss those warm lips, before their crimson leaves
Are blighted—white—cold. Say farewell, before
Death chokes that gentle voice ! O, let me hear
You speak !
Beatr.   Farewell, my tender brother. Think
Of our sad fate with gentleness, as now :
And let mild, pitying thoughts lighten for thee
Thy sorrow's load. Err not in harsh despair,

But tears and patience. One thing more, my child ;
For thine own sake, be constant to the love
Thou bearest us ; and to the faith that I,
Tho' wrapt in a strange cloud of crime and shame,
Lived ever holy and unstained. And tho'
Ill tongue shall wound me, and our common name
Be as a mark stamped on thine innocent brow
For men to point at as they pass, do thou
Forbear, and never think a thought unkind
Of those, who perhaps love thee in their graves.
So mayest thou die as I do ; fear and pain
Being subdued. Farewell ! Farewell ! Farewell !
Bern.   I cannot say, farewell !
Cam.   O, lady Beatrice !
Beatr.   Give yourself no unnecessary pain,
My dear Lord Cardinal. Here, mother, tie
My girdle for me, and bind up this hair
In any simple knot ; aye, that does well.
And yours, I see, is coming down. How often
Have we done this for one another : now
We shall not do it any more. My Lord,
We are quite ready. Well, 'tis very well.
Exeunt.

Mr. Shelley, in this work, reminds us of some of the most strenuous and daring of our old dramatists, not by any means as an imitator, though he has studied them, but as a bold, elemental imagination, and a framer of "mighty lines." He possesses also however, what those to whom we more particularly allude did not possess, great sweetness of nature, and enthusiasm for good ; and his style is, as it ought to be, the offspring of this high mixture. It disproves the adage of the Latin poet. Majesty and Love do sit on one throne in the lofty buildings of his poetry ; and they will be found there, at a late and we trust a happier day, on a seat immortal as themselves.

[The *Indicator*, July 26th, 1820.]

LEIGH HUNT

ON

MR. SHELLEY'S NEW POEM
ENTITLED ADONAIS

SINCE I left London, Mr. Shelley's *Adonais, or Elegy on the Death of Mr. Keats,* has, I find, made its appearance. I have not seen the London edition; but I have an Italian one printed at Pisa, with which I must content myself at present. The other was to have had notes. It is not a poem calculated to be popular, any more than the *Prometheus Unbound*; it is of too abstract and subtle a nature for that purpose; but it will delight the few, to whom Mr. Shelley is accustomed to address himself. Spenser would be pleased with it if he were living. A mere town reader and a Quarterly Reviewer will find it *caviare. Adonais,* in short, is such an elegy as poet might be expected to write upon poet. The author has had before him his recollections of Lycidas, of Moschus and Bion, and of the doctrines of Plato; and in the stanza of the most poetical of poets, Spenser, has brought his own genius, in all its etherial beauty, to lead a pomp of Loves, Graces, and Intelligences, in honour of the departed.

Nor is the Elegy to be considered less sincere, because it is full of poetical abstractions. Dr. Johnson would have us believe, that *Lycidas* is not " the effusion of real passion." " Passion," says he, in his usual conclusive tone (as if the force of critic could no further go) " plucks no berries from the myrtle and ivy; nor calls upon Arethuse and Mincius, nor tells of rough Satyrs and Fauns with cloven heel. Where there is leisure for fiction, there is little grief." This is only a more genteel commonplace, brought in to put down a vulgar one. Dr. Johnson, like most critics, had no imag-

196

ination; and because he found nothing natural to his own
impulses in the associations of poetry, and saw them so often
abused by the practice of versifiers inferior to himself, he was
willing to conclude, that on natural occasions they were
always improper. But a poet's world is as real to him as
the more palpable one to people in general. He spends his
time in it as truly as Dr. Johnson did his in Fleet-street or
at the club. Milton felt that the happiest hours he had
passed with his friend had been passed in the regions of
poetry. He had been accustomed to be transported with
him " beyond the visible diurnal sphere " of his fire-side
and supper-table, things which he could record nevertheless
with a due relish. (See the *Epitaphium Damonis*.) The
next step was to fancy himself again among them, missing the
dear companion of his walks; and then it is that the rivers
murmur complainingly, and the flowers hang their heads—
which to a truly poetical habit of mind, though to no other,
they may literally be said to do, because such is the aspect
which they present to an afflicted imagination. " I see
nothing in the world but melancholy," is a common phrase
with persons who are suffering under a great loss. With
ordinary minds in this condition the phrase implies a vague
feeling, but still an actual one. The poet, as in other
instances, gives it a life and particularity. The practice has
doubtless been abused; so much so, that even some imaginative minds may find it difficult at first to fall in with it,
however beautifully managed. But the very abuse shews
that it is founded in a principle in nature. And a great
deal depends upon the character of the poet. What is
mere frigidity and affectation in common magazine rhymers,
or men of wit and fashion about town, becomes another
thing in minds accustomed to live in the sphere I spoke of.
It was as unreasonable in Dr. Johnson to sneer at Milton's
grief in *Lycidas*, as it was reasonable in him to laugh at Prior
and Congreve for comparing Chloe to Venus and Diana, and
pastoralizing about Queen Mary. Neither the turn of
their genius, nor their habits of life, included this sort of

ground. We feel that Prior should have stuck to his tuckers and boddices, and Congreve appeared in his proper Court-mourning.

Milton perhaps overdid the matter a little when he personified the poetical enjoyments of his friend and himself under the character of actual shepherds. Mr. Shelley is the more natural in this respect, inasmuch as he is entirely abstract and imaginative, and recalls his lamented acquaintance to mind in no other shape than one strictly poetical. I say acquaintance, because such Mr. Keats was ; and it happens, singularly enough, that the few hours which he and Mr. Shelley passed together were almost entirely of a poetical character. I recollect one evening in particular, which they spent with the writer of these letters in composing verses on a given subject. But it is not as a mere acquaintance, however poetical, that Mr. Shelley records him. It is as the intimate acquaintance of all lovely and lofty thoughts, as the nursling of the Muse, the hope of her coming days, the creator of additional Beauties and Intelligences for the adornment and the inhabitation of the material world. The poet commences with calling upon Urania to weep for her favourite ; and in a most beautiful stanza, the termination of which is in the depths of the human heart, informs us where he is lying. You are aware that Mr. Keats died at Rome :

> To that high Capital, where kingly Death
> Keeps his pale court in beauty and decay,
> He came ; and bought, with price of purest breath,
> A grave among the eternal—Come away !
> Haste, while the vault of blue Italian day
> Is yet his fitting charnel-roof ! while still
> He lies, as if in dewy sleep he lay ;
> Awake him not, surely he takes his fill
> Of deep and liquid rest, forgetful of all ill.

" The forms of things unseen," which Mr. Keats's imagination had turned into shape, the " airy nothings " to which it is the high prerogative of the poet to give " a local habitation and a name," are then represented, in a most fanciful manner, as crowding about his lips and body, and lamenting him who called them into being :

> And others came . . . Desires and Adorations,
> Winged Persuasions and veiled Destinies,
> Splendours, and glooms, and glimmering Incarnations
> Of hopes and fears, and twilight Phantasies ;
> And Sorrow, with her family of sighs ;
> And Pleasure, blind with tears, led by the gleam
> Of her own dying smile instead of eyes.
> All he had loved, and moulded into thought,
> From shape, and hue, and odour, and sweet sound,
> Lamented Adonais.

A phrase in the first line of the following passage would make an admirable motto for that part of the *Literary Pocket Book*, in which the usual lists of kings and other passing dominations are superseded by a list of Eminent Men :

> And he is gathered to *the kings of thought*,
> Who waged contention with their time's decay,
> And of the past are all that cannot pass away.

The spot in which Mr. Keats lies buried is thus finely pointed out. The two similes at the close are among the happiest we recollect, especially the second :

> Go thou to Rome—at once the Paradise,
> The grave, the city, and the wilderness ;
> And where its wrecks like shattered mountains rise,
> And flowering weeds, and fragrant copses dress
> The bones of Desolation's nakedness,
> Pass, till the Spirit of the spot shall lead
> Thy footsteps to a slope of green access,
> Where, like an infant's smile, over the dead,
> A light of laughing flowers along the grass is spread.
> And gray walls moulder round, on which dull Time
> Feeds, like slow fire upon a hoary brand.

In the course of the poem some living writers are introduced, among whom Lord Byron is designated as

The "EXAMINER" EXAMINED

> The Pilgrim of Eternity, whose fame
> Over his living head like Heaven is bent
> An early but enduring monument!

The poet of Ireland is called, with equal brevity and felicity,

> The sweetest lyrist of her saddest wrong:

And among "others of less note," is modestly put one, the description of whom is strikingly calculated to excite a mixture of sympathy and admiration. The use of the Pagan mythology is supposed to have worn it out, never wore it all. See to what a natural and noble purpose a true scholar can turn it:

> He, as I guess,
> Had gazed on Nature's naked loveliness,
> Actaeon-like, and now he fled astray
> With feeble steps o'er the world's wilderness,
> And his own thoughts, along that rugged way,
> Pursued, like raging hounds, their father and their prey.
>
> A pard-like Spirit, beautiful and swift—
> A Love in desolation masked; a Power
> Girt round with weakness; it can scarce uplift
> The weight of the superincumbent hour;
> It is a dying lamp, a falling shower,
> A breaking billow; even while we speak
> Is it not broken? On the withering flower
> The killing sun smiles brightly: on a cheek
> The life can burn in blood, even while the heart may break.

> Ah! te meae si partem animae rapit
> Maturior vis!——

But the poet is here, I trust, as little of a prophet, as affection and a beautiful climate, and the extraordinary and most vital energy of his spirit, can make him. The singular termination of this description, and the useful reflections it is calculated to excite, I shall reserve for another subject in my next. But how is it, that even that termination could not tempt the malignant common-place of the Quarterly

Reviewers to become unblind to the obvious beauty of this poem, and venture upon laying some of its noble stanzas before their readers ?   How is it that in their late specimens of Mr. Shelley's powers they said nothing of the style and versification of the majestic tragedy of the *Cenci*, which would have been equally intelligible to the lowest, and instructive to the highest, of their readers ?   How is it that they have not even hinted at the existence of this *Elegy on the death of Mr. Keats*, though immediately after the arrival of copies of it from Italy they thought proper to give a pretended review of a poem which appeared to them the least calculated for their reader's understandings ? And finally, how happens it, that Mr. Gifford has never taken any notice of Mr. Keats's *last* publication, the beautiful volume containing *Lamia*, the Story from Boccaccio and that magnificent fragment *Hyperion* ?   Perhaps the following passage of the Elegy will explain :

> Our Adonais has drunk poison !—Oh,
> What deaf and viperous murderer could crown
> Life's early cup with such a draught of woe ?
> The nameless worm would now itself disown :
> It felt, yet could escape the magic tone
> Whose prelude held all envy, hate, and wrong,
> But what was howling in one breast alone
> Silent with expectation of the song,
> Whose master's hand is cold, whose silver lyre unstrung.
>
> Live thou, whose infamy is not thy fame !
> Live ! fear no heavier chastisement from me,
> Thou noteless blot on a remembered name !
> But be thyself, and know thyself to be !
> And ever at thy season be thou free
> To spill the venom when thy fangs o'erflow :
> Remorse and Self-Contempt shall cling to thee ;
> Hot shame shall burn upon thy secret brow,
> And like a beaten hound tremble thou shalt—as now.

This, one would think, would not have been " unintelligible " to the dullest *Quarterly* peruser, who had read the review of

Mr. Keats's *Endymion.* Nor would the following perhaps have been quite obscure:

> Nor let us weep that our delight is fled
> Far from these carrion kites that scream below;
> He wakes or sleeps with the enduring dead;
> Thou canst not soar where he is sitting now.
> Dust unto dust! but the pure spirit shall flow
> Back to the burning fountain whence it came,
> A portion of the Eternal, which must glow
> Through time and change, unquenchably the same,
> While thy cold embers choke the sordid hearth of shame.

However, if further explanation had been wanted, the Preface to the Elegy furnishes it in an abundance, which even the meanest admirers of Mr. Gifford could have no excuse for not understanding. Why then did he not quote this? Why could he not venture, once in his life, to try and look a little fair and handsome; and instead of making all sorts of misrepresentations of his opponents, lay before his readers something of what his opponents say of him? He only ventures to allude, in convulsive fits and starts, and then not by name, to the *Feast of the Poets.* He dares not even allude to Mr. Hazlitt's epistolary dissection of him. And now he, or some worthy coadjutor for him, would pretend that he knows nothing of Mr. Shelley's denouncement of him, but criticises his other works out of pure zeal for religion and morality! Oh these modern " Scribes, Pharisees, and Hypocrites!" How exactly do they resemble their prototypes of old!

" It may well be said," observes Mr. Shelley's Preface, " that these wretched men know not what they do. They scatter their insults and their slanders without heed as to whether the poisoned shaft lights on a heart made callous by many blows, or one, like Keats's, composed of more penetrable stuff. One of their associates is, to my knowledge, a most base and unprincipled calumniator. As to " Endymion," was it a poem, whatever might be its defects, to be treated contemptuously by those who had

celebrated with various degrees of complacency and panegyric, 'Paris,' and 'Woman,' and a 'Syrian Tale,' and
Mrs. Lefanu, and Mr. Barrett, and Mr. Howard Payne,
and a long list of the illustrious obscure? Are these the
men, who in their venal good-nature, presumed to draw a
parallel between the Rev. Mr. Milman and Lord Byron?
What gnat did they strain at here, after having swallowed all
those camels? Against what woman taken in adultery,
dares the foremost of these literary prostitutes to cast his
opprobrious stone? Miserable man! you, one of the
meanest, have wantonly defaced one of the noblest specimens of the workmanship of God. Nor shall it be your
excuse, that murderer as you are, you have spoken daggers
but used none."

Let us take the taste of the Gifford out of one's mouth
with the remainder of the Preface, which is like a sweet nut
after one with a worm in it.

"The circumstances of the closing scene of poor Keats's
life were not made known to me until the Elegy was ready
for the press. I am given to understand that the wound
which his sensitive spirit had received from the criticism
of 'Endymion,' was exasperated by the bitter sense of
unrequited benefits; the poor fellow seems to have been
hooted from the stage of life, no less by those on whom
he had wasted the promise of his genius, than those on whom
he had lavished his fortune and his care. He was accompanied to Rome, and attended in his last illness by Mr.
Severn, a young artist of the highest promise, who, I have
been informed, 'almost risked his own life, and sacrificed
every prospect to unwearied attendance upon his dying
friend.' Had I known these circumstances before the
completion of my poem, I should have been tempted to
add my feeble tribute of applause to the more solid recom-
pense which the virtuous man finds in the recollection of
his own motives. Mr. Severn can dispense with a reward
from 'such stuff as dreams are made of.' His conduct is a
golden augury of the success of his future career—may the

unextinguished Spirit of his illustrious friend animate the creations of his pencil, and plead against oblivion for his name ! "

Amen ! says one who knew the poet, and who knows the painter.

[" Examiner," 1822.]

LEIGH HUNT

ON

PROMETHEUS UNBOUND

A S a conclusive proof of Mr. Shelley's nonsense, the Reviewer selects one of his passages which most require attention, separates it from its proper context, and turns it into prose : after which he triumphantly informs the reader that this prose is not prose, but "the conclusion of the third act of Prometheus verbatim et literatim." Now poetry has often a language as well as music of its own, so distinct from prose, and so universally allowed a right to the distinction (which none are better aware of than the versifiers in the Quarterly Review), that secretly to decompose a poetical passage into prose, and then call for a criticism of a reader upon it, is like depriving a body of its distinguishing properties, or confounding their rights and necessities, and then asking where they are. Again, to take a passage abruptly from its context, especially when a context is more than usually necessary to its illustration, is like cutting out a piece of shade from a picture, and reproaching it for want of light. And finally, to select an obscure passage or two from an author, or even to show that he is often obscure, and then to pretend from these specimens, that he is nothing but obscurity and nonsense, is mere dishonesty.

For instance, Dante is a great genius who is often obscure ; but suppose a critic were to pick out one of his obscurest passages, and assert that Dante was a mere writer of jargon. Suppose he were to select one of the metaphysical odes from his *Amoroso Convivio* ; or to take a passage from Mr. Cary's translation of his great poem, and turn it into prose for the better mystification of the reader. Here is a specimen :

"Every orb, corporeal, doth proportion its extent unto

the virtue through its parts diffused. The greater blessed-
ness preserves the more. The greater is the body (if all
parts share equally) the more is to preserve. Therefore the
circle, whose swift course enwheels the universal frame,
answers to that, which is supreme in knowledge and in
love. Thus by the virtue, not the seeming breadth of
substance, measuring, thou shalt see the heavens, each to
the intelligence that ruleth it, greater to more, and smaller
unto less, suited in strict and wondrous harmony."—
Paradiso, Canto 28.

The lines in question from Mr. Shelley's poem are as
follow. A spirit is describing a mighty change that has just
taken place on earth. It is the consummation of a state of
things, for which all the preceeding part of the poem has
been yearning:

> The painted veil, by those who were, called life,
> Which mimicked, as with colours idly spread,
> All men believed and hoped, is torn aside;
> The loathsome mask is fallen, the man remains
> Sceptreless, free, uncircumscribed, but man
> Equal, unclassed, tribeless, and nationless,
> Exempt from awe, worship, degree, the king
> Over himself; just gentle, wise; but man
> Passionless; no, yet free from guilt or pain,
> Which were, for his will made or suffered them;
> Nor yet exempt, tho' ruling them like slaves;
> From chance, and death and mutability,
> The clogs of that which else might oversoar
> The loftiest star of unascended heaven,
> Pinnacled dim in the intense inane.

That is to say, the veil or superficial state of things, which
was called life by those who lived before us, and which had
nothing but an idle resemblance to that proper state of
things, which we would fain have thought it, is no longer
existing. The loathsome mask is fallen; and the being
who was compelled to wear it, is now what he ought to be,
one of a great family who are their own rulers, just, gentle,
wise and passionless; no, not passionless, though free from

206

guilt or pain, which were only the consequences of their
former wilful mistakes ; nor are they exempt, though they
turn them to the best and most philosophical account, from
chance, and death, and mutability ; things, which are the
clogs of that lofty spirit of humanity, which else might rise
beyond all that we can conceive of the highest and happiest
star of heaven, pinnacled, like an almost viewless atom, in
the space of the universe. *The intense inane* implies excess
of emptiness, and is a phrase of Miltonian construction,
like " the palpable obscure " and " the vast abrupt." Where
is the unintelligible nonsense of all this ? and where is the
want of " grammar," with which the " pride " of the
Reviewer, as Mr. Looney M'Twoulter says, would " come
over " him ?

Mr. Shelley has written a great deal of poetry equally
unmetaphysical and beautiful. The whole of the tragedy
of the Cenci, which the Reviewers do not think it to their
interest to notice, is written in a style equally plain and
noble. But we need not go farther than the volume
before us, though, according to the Reviewer, the " whole,"
of it does not contain " one original image of nature, *one*
simple expression of human feeling, or *one* new association
of the appearances of the moral with those of the material
world." We really must apologize to all intelligent readers
who know anything of Mr. Shelley's genius, for appearing
to give more notice to these absurdities than they are
worth ; but there are good reasons why they ought to be
exposed. The *Prometheus* has already spoken for itself.
Now take the following *Ode* to a *Skylark*, of which I will
venture to say, that there is not in the whole circle of lyric
poetry a piece more *full* of " original images of nature, of
simple expressions of human feeling, and of the associations
of the appearances of the moral with those of the material
world." You shall have it entire, for it is as fitting for the
season, as it is true to the musical and ethereal beauty of
its subject.

*   *   *   *   *

I know of nothing more beautiful than this—more
choice of tones, more natural in words, more abundant in
exquisite, cordial, and most poetical associations one gets
the stanzas by heart unawares, and repeats them like
"snatches of old tunes." To say that nobody who writes
in the *Quarterly Review* could produce anything half as
good (unless Mr. Wordsworth writes in it, which I do not
believe he does) would be sorry praise. When Mr. Gifford
"sings" as the phrase is, one is reminded of nothing but
snarling. Mr. Southey, though the gods have made him
more poetical than Mr. Gifford, is always affecting something original, and tiring one to death with common-place.
"Croker," as Goldsmith says, "rhymes to joker;" and as
to the chorus of priests and virgins, of scribes and pharisees,
which make up the poetical undersong of the Review,
it is worthy of the discordant mixture of worldliness and
religion, of faith and bad practice, of Christianity and
malignity, which finds in it something ordinary enough to
merit its approbation.

One passage more from this immoral and anti-christian
volume, that contains, "not one simple expression of
human feeling," and I will close my letter. It is part of
"*An Ode, written October* 1819, *before the Spaniards* had
recovered their liberty" :

> Glory, glory, glory,
> To those who have greatly suffered and done !
> Never name in story
> Was greater than that which ye shall have won.
> Conquerors have conquered their foes alone,
> Whose revenge, pride, and power they have overthrown :
> *Ride ye, more victorious, over your own.*

Hear that, ye reverend and pugnacious Christians of the
Quarterly !

> Bind, bind every brow
> With crownals of violet, ivy and pine :
> Hide the blood-stains now
> With hues which sweet nature has made divine ;

Green strength, azure hope, and eternity ;
But let not the pansy among them be ;
Ye were injured, and that means memory.

How well the Spaniards have acted up to this infidel in-
junction is well known to the whole of wondering Christen-
dom, and affords one of the happiest presages to the growth
of true freedom and philosophy. Why did not the Reviewer
quote such passages as these by way of specimens of the
author's powers and moral feeling ? Why did his boasted
Christianity lead him to conceal these, as well as to omit
what was necessary to the one quoted in my last ? You
pretty well understand why by this time ; but I have still
further elucidations to give, which are more curious than
any we have had yet, and which you shall see in my next.
I shake your hands.

[" Examiner," July, 1822.]

LEIGH HUNT

ON

THE WORKS OF CHARLES LAMB

WE must fairly sit down to these delightful volumes to say what shall come first to us, or we find we shall never criticize them at all. We fear indeed, that by everybody but the author, we have been thought culpably negligent, in not noticing them before; but will credit be given to us when we say, (we! who have been hardy critics for a number of years, man and boy), that we felt diffident in writing upon the subject? Yes; those will believe us, who know, that great liking is often as hesitating a thing as delay itself; and that there are subjects, before which the stoutest encounterer of all the rougher topics of life, feels himself taken with a bland and enjoying stillness, which he is almost afraid to break by expressing his sense of it.

If these are refinements, they are such as the work before us is well calculated to produce. There is a spirit in Mr. Lamb's productions, which is in itself so *anti-critical*, and tends so much to reconcile us to all that is in the world, that the effect is almost neutralizing to every thing but complacency and a quiet admiration. We must even plainly confess, that one thing which gave a Laputan flap to our recollections on this occasion, was the meeting with a flimsy criticism in an orthodox review, which mistook the exquisite simplicity and apprehensiveness of Mr. Lamb's genius for want of power; and went vainly brushing away at some of the solidest things in his work, under the notion of its being chaff.

That the poetical part of Mr. Lamb's volumes (and as this comes first, we will make the first half of our criticism upon it) is not so striking as the critical, we allow. And there are several reasons for it: first, because criticism inevitably explains itself more to the reader; whereas poetry, especially such as Mr. Lamb's, often gives him too much credit for the apprehensiveness in which it deals itself; second, because Mr. Lamb's criticism is obviously of a most original cast, and directly informs the reader of a number of things which he did not know before; whereas the poetry, for the reason just mentioned, leaves him rather to gather them; third, because the author's genius, though in fact of an anti-critical nature (his very criticisms chiefly tending to overthrow the critical spirit) is also less busied with creating new things, which is the business of poetry, than with inculcating a charitable and patient content with old, which is a part of humanity; fourth and last, because from an excess of this content, of love for the old poets, and of diffidence in recommending to others what has such infinite recommendations of its own, he has really, in three or four instances, written pure common-places on subjects deeply seated in our common humanity, such as the recollections of childhood (vol. I. p. 71.), the poem that follows it, and one or two of the sonnets. But he who cannot see, that the extreme old simplicity of style in *The Three Friends* is a part and constituent recommendation of the very virtue of the subject; that the homely versification of the *Ballad noticing the Difference of Rich and Poor* has the same spirit of inward reference; that the little Robert Burton-like effusion, called *Hypochondriacus*, has all the quick mixture of jest and earnest belonging to such melancholy, and that the *Farewell to Tobacco* is a piece of exuberant pleasantry, equally witty and poetical, in which the style of the old poets becomes proper to a wit overflowing as theirs; such a man may be fit enough to set up for a critic once a month, but we are sure he has not an idea in his head once a quarter.

From this last poem, which is an old friend of ours, and passages of which used to be, and are still, often in our mouth like a favourite tune, we must indulge ourselves in a few extracts. It opens in this pleasant manner, agitato :

> May the Babylonish curse
> Strait confound my stammering verse,
> If I can a passage see
> In this word-perplexity,
> Or a fit expression find,
> Or a language to my mind,
> (Still the phrase is wide or scant)
> To take leave of thee, GREAT PLANT !
> Or in any terms relate
> Half my love, or half my hate :
> For I hate, yet love, thee so,
> That, whichever thing I shew,
> The plain truth will seem to be
> A constrain'd hyperbole,
> And the passion to proceed
> More from a mistress than a weed.

Mr. Lamb, we see, has altered a couple of rhymes here from what they were in the *Reflector*. There is something, we allow, of a thunder-like vastness of admiration in the words " Great Plant," which are very properly set forth in capitals ; but still we prefer the old straightforward carelessness of

> Still the phrase is wide an acre
> To take leave of thee, Tobacco.

There was a royal disdain of the rhyme in it, befitting a vegetable superior to all considerations.

*   *   *   *   *

There is something very touching as well as vivid in the poem that stands first, entitled *Hester*. The object of it is a female Quaker who died young, and who appears to have been of a spirit that broke through the cold shell of her sect. She was of a nature so sprightly and strong, that the poet, for some time, says he could not

By force be led
To think upon the wormy bed,
And her together.

*   *   *

My sprightly neighbour, gone before
To that unknown and silent shore,
Shall we not meet, as heretofore,
Some summer morning.

When from thy chearful eyes a ray
Hath struck a bliss upon the day,
A bliss that would not go away,
A sweet fore-warning ?

If the Quakers appear to be the only real Christians extant, they are such only in a negative sense. We allude to them, of course, in general. They deny themselves a good deal, but they allow others little ; and this, we suspect, is Christianity wrong side outwards. A Quaker will not be outrageous, and will not get drunk ; he will also prevent his wife from copying the beauties of God's creation in the colours of her dress ; and God's gift of music he holds to be very small ; but next to a hypocrite (and we by no means intend to confound the two), he would be the last man in the world to forgive a woman taken in adultery, or to be present at an avowed feast, or to refer a money-getter to " the lilies of the valley which toil not," or to patronize the waste of a box of precious ointment for the sake of a sentiment. If a true Christian means anything, it means, we suspect, something which would startle all the commonly received notions and establishments out of their wits ; and is made up of a mixture of Platonism in speculation, and a community of good in practice, equally calculated to baffle the despisers of the ancient world, and the sharers of the present. When a Quaker, or a Methodist, or an indifferent Churchman, talks of Christianity, we see in it nothing but vain negation, or fanaticism, or worldliness. All these men send those who differ with them to the devil, and know no more about the finer aspirations of one's nature than any bad passion or selfishness can. It is difficult, from his works, to collect whether Mr. Lamb is a professed Christian or not. The Calvinist would surely pronounce against him, because he decries eternal punishment ; the Quaker, because he finds out something more than pardonable in the vehement passions ; and all other Protestants, because at the sight of a picture by Leonardo da Vinci, he wishes to be a Catholic, that he may worship the Madonna. All this must be *caviare* to the Christian multitude. It is another version of the sentiment about the box of ointment. Yet the less Christian he may be thought to be in these matters, the finer spirit of religious feeling is there in the following lines on the same picture. They are a recognition, not of Catholic bigotry, but of the diviner aspirations of our being, under whatever devout shape they appear, and which always appear finest and most probable when connected with ideas of childlike innocence and joy. Filicaia or Tasso might have been proud of writing them ; and, by the way, it would have done both Filicaia and Tasso good, and made them less perturbed Christians, had they possessed what they would have called the Anti-Christian tolerance in the rest of our Author's works :

LINES ON THE CELEBRATED PICTURE BY LEONARDO DA VINCI, CALLED THE VIRGIN OF THE ROCKS

While young John runs to greet
The greater Infant's feet,
The Mother standing by, with trembling passion
Of devout admiration,
Beholds the engaging mystic play, and pretty adoration ;
Nor knows as yet the full event
Of those so low beginnings,
From whence we date our winnings,
But wonders at the intent
Of those new rites, and what that strange child-worship meant.
But at her side
An angel doth abide,

With such a perfect joy
As no dim doubts alloy,
An intuition,
A glory, an amenity,
Passing the dark condition
Of blind humanity,
As if he surely knew
All the blest wonders should ensue,
Or he had lately left the upper sphere,
And had read all the sovran schemes and divine riddles there.

The tragedy of John Woodvil, which we think liable in some measure to Mr. Coleridge's objection mentioned in the Dedication, of its being a little too over-antique in the style, gave rise, partly on that account, to less fortunate objection from the critics on its first appearance. People were not acquainted then as they are now with the older dramatists ; and the critics, finding it a new production which was like none of their select commonplaces, confounded the oldness of the style and the manly and womanly simplicity of the sentiments with something hitherto unheard of, equally barbarous and mawkish. They have since learnt better, partly, perhaps chiefly, from the information of this very author ; and it is doubtless a good deal owing to this circumstance, that some of them chose to abstain from noticing this publication, the better natured from a feeling of awkwardness, and the malignant from having since turned commentators on old plays themselves. The tragedy of John Woodvil has this peculiarity, that it is founded on a frailty of a very unheroic nature, and ends with no punishments to the offender but repentance. Yet so finely and humanly is it managed, with such attractions of pleasantry and of pathos, that these circumstances become distinguishing features of its excellence ; and the reader begins to regret that other poets have not known how to reconcile moral lessons, so familiar and useful, with the dignity of dramatic poetry. Sir Walter Woodvil, a gentleman of an ancient family, who had taken part against Charles the First, is obliged to hide himself at the Restoration. His son, left in possession of the family mansion, grows in the meantime riotous and dissipated, after the court fashion; and partly from his natural frankness, is excited during the fever of drunkenness to intrust the secret of his father's hiding-place with one *Lovel*, a bottle-companion and supposed friend. Sir Walter is in consequence sought out in Sherwood Forest by Lovel and another drinking associate, and during a violent parley between the two intruders and his faithful younger son *Simon, breaks his heart without a word.* This is as true a piece of pathos as we remember in tragedy. John Woodvil, after great wretchedness of mind, leaves the reader to suppose that he is restored to comparative peace, partly by the force of repentance, and partly by the attentions of *Margaret*, an orphan ward of his late father, and a most noble creature, whose character alone would serve to show the generous delicacy of the author's genius. During his unhappy and noisy prosperity, John, though avowedly her lover, treats her with unceasing neglect, and under the peculiar circumstances of her situation she thinks it becoming a proper pride in her to go and seek out Sir Walter, and to unite her helping fortunes with him and his younger son. She does so, and only shews that *John* has treated her unhandsomely by turning away with a tear when the question is asked for, and then resuming her kindly aspect of society. After the catastrophe which happens to Sir Walter, she excuses *John* as well as she may, resolves at all events not

> ——to join the clamour of the world
> Against her friend,

and again appears before him to show him that sympathy in adversity, which he refuses to cultivate in her during prosperity. The best passages in this play are the pathetic ones; but as these depend a good deal on the context, and are more pervading than the others, we must content ourselves with selecting some lines of beautiful description.

The story of Rosamund Gray, which very properly stands at the head of the prose part of Mr. Lamb's Works, is one of the most painful yet delightful in the world. There is one part of it, in which, to be sure, the pain greatly predominates; but this is told very briefly, and with something beyond delicacy: and we have here to make a remark which has often struck us; namely, that in the most painful, most humiliating, and even most overwhelming and stupifying death of a virtuous person, there is a something still which conquers the conqueror. The mere fact that the virtue, the good-heartedness, the sentiment (in whatever shape it may be) of the sufferer survives to the last, leaves the happy-making faculty victorious over the temporary misfortune, however dreadful; so that goodness in its most passive shape is greater and more powerful than vice is in its most active. *Rosamund*, like *Clarissa Harlowe*, is violated; but good God! what a difference in the management of the two stories. Mr. Lamb need not be alarmed: we are not going to say that Richardson is not a very extraordinary person. He was the more extraordinary inasmuch as he writes the most affecting books, in a spirit which to us at least appears one of the most unfeeling imaginable. He writes seven or eight thick volumes on the tortures of a young woman; and seems at the end as if he could have written seven or eight more, had it been politic as a matter of trade. There is wonderful ability in his books, wonderful knowledge of all sorts of petty proceedings, wonderful variety of character; and with all this one cannot help being interested at a first reading. But in all the finer as well as larger meanings of the word, he wants humanity. He neither knows what vice nor what virtue is, properly speaking. He even, not unfrequently, makes them change ideas, his vice being occupied at any rate in some kind of sympathy with others, while his virtue at bottom thinks of nothing but itself.

He does not, like the author before us, hurry over an agonizing incident, or touch it with some sweet, unaffected, unconscious superiority to its situation, like a dying flower ; neither does he, like Shakespeare, bring about it all the redeeming graces of poetry and humanity, like so many winged and deep-thoughted angels ; but there is a pettiness and detail of preparation, a pedantry and ostentation of virtue, even in its retirements, and a cool never-ending surgical anatomy of suffering, equally destructive, in our minds, of the real dignity of the subject, and the respectability of the writer. He put forth his thorns and burrs, with as vegetable an indifference as a thistle. He wrote like a sentimental familiar of the Inquisition. He resembled one of his own printing presses, furnished with formal layers of literal knowledge, squeezing and grinding it down with a wooden and metallic want of remorse, and giving off so many sheets an hour with as little wear and tear as a mangle.

But to return. *Rosamund Gray* is the story of a lovely young girl, a perfect picture of intelligent innocence, whose family have been brought low in the world, and who grows up with a blind old grandmother, that doats and rests all her being upon her. There grows a love between her and a fine frank-hearted youth, *Allan Clare,* which is described or rather constantly implied and felt, with a world of delicacy and young devotedness. *Allan* had a sister, who learnt to love *Rosamund* as he did ; and one night, after the two friends had had a happy long walk about the fields and green places near the village, *Rosamund,* unable to get out of her head the scenes which were now endeared to her by *Allan's* sister as well as himself, played her grandmother for the first time in her life a little trick, and in the irresponsible and innocent enthusiasm of her heart stole out of the cottage to go over them again. *Matravis,* a villain, met her—" Late at night he met her, a lonely unprotected virgin—no friend at hand—no place near of refuge "—We thank the author for making this

218

scoundrel sallow and ugly. It looks as if his physical faculties were perturbed and bad by nature, like a mistake; and that these had infected the humanity common to us all. Rosamund " polluted and disgraced, wandered, an abandoned thing, about the fields and meadows till day-break." She then did not go home, but laid herself down stupified at *Elinor Clare's* gate; and in her friend's house she soon died, having first heard that her grandmother had died in the meanwhile. The blind old woman—her death is thus related:

An old man that lay sick in a small house adjoining to Margaret's, testified the next morning, that he had plainly heard the old creature calling for her grand-daughter. All the night long she made her moan, and ceased not to call upon the name of Rosamund. But no Rosamund was there—*the voice died away, but not till near day-break.*

When the neighbours came to search in the morning, Margaret was missing! She had struggled out of bed, and made her way into Rosamund's room—worn out with fatigue and fright, when she found the girl not there, she had laid herself down to die—and, it is thought, she died *praying*, for she was discovered in a kneeling posture, her arms and face extended on the pillow, where Rosamund has slept the night before—a smile was on her face in death.

As to *Rosamund*, she scarcely uttered a word thence-forward. " She expired in the arms of *Elinor*—quiet, gentle, as she lived—thankful, that she died not among strangers—and expressing by signs rather than words, a gratitude for the most trifling services, the common offices of humanity. She died uncomplaining."

Allan's sister, to whom Matravis had once paid his addresses though *in vain*, dies of a frenzy-fever; and the young blighted lover himself is missed for a long while afterwards, till recognized sitting on his sister's tombstone in the village by his friend the surgeon, who is the supposed author of the book. His goodness, his sympathy with his

Q

fellow-creatures had survived his happiness; and he was still the same gentle yet manly creature as ever. His great enjoyment, his "wayward pleasure, *for he refused to name it a virtue*," was in visiting hospitals, and unostentatiously contriving to do personal and pecuniary services to the most wretched. The surgeon was called one night to attend the dying bed of a man of the name of *Matravis*. *Allan* went with him, to give the miserable wretch what comfort he could; but he talked deliriously, bidding them "not tell *Allan Clare*," who stood shedding over him his long-repressed tears. The paper before us glimmers through our own.

The piece that follows (but we find we have got into the long criticism we were afraid of, and must take care òf our hedomadal pen) is entitled *Recollections of Christ's Hospital*, and is a favourite with us on many accounts, not the least of which is, that we had the honour of being brought up in that excellent foundation as well as Mr. Lamb himself. Our *Recollections* of the school were some-what later than his; but with the exception of a little less gratitude to one individual, and of a single character-istic, which his friend Mr. Coleridge had the chief hand, we suspect, in altering, (and we trust not essentially or for the worse), we can give cordial testimony, up to that later period, of the fidelity of his descriptions. We know not how completely or otherwise they may remain; but from what we see of the Christ Hospital boys in the streets, especially of the older and more learned part of them, and from the share which some of our old school-fellows have in the present tuition, we should guess that they still apply.

*   *.   *   *   *

In coming to the *Essays* and their masterly criticism, we must repress our tendency to make extracts, or we shall never have done We must content ourselves with but one noble passage; and with expressing our firm con-viction, that to these *Essays*, including remarks on the performance of Shakespeare's tragedies, and the little notice of his contemporaries originally published in the well-known *Specimens of the Old English Dramatists*, the public are originally indebted for that keener perception and more poetical apprehension of the genius of those illustrious men, which has become so distinguishing a feature among the literary opinions of the day. There was a relish of it in *Seward*, but a small one, nor did his contemporaries sympathise even with that. The French revolution, which for a time took away attention from everything but politics, had a great and new effect in rousing up the thinking faculties in every respect, and the mind, strengthened by unusual action, soon pierced through the flimsy common-places of the last half century. By degrees, they were all broken up ; and though some lively critics, who saw only the more eccentric part of the new genius and confounded it with the genius itself, re-edified them, they were too late, as now begins to be pretty generally felt. Mr. Lamb, whose resemblance to the old poets in his tragedy was ludicrously taken for imbecility, had sown his criticisms as well as his example against a genial day ; it came ; and lo and behold ! the very critics, who cried out the most disdainfully against him, adopted these very criticisms, most of them, we are ashamed to say, without any acknowledgment. But he is now beginning to receive his proper praise, after waiting for it in the most quiet and unassuming manner perhaps of any writer living. The following is the passage we alluded to ;

So to see Lear acted—

*   *   *

With the Letters under assumed signatures, some of which are in an exquisite taste of humour and wisdom united, many of our readers are acquainted through the medium of the *Reflector*. Some of the pleasantries are among what may be called our *prose tunes*—things which we repeat almost involuntarily when we are in the humour—

as the one for instance about the coffin handles " with wrought gripes," and the drawn battle between Death and the ornamental drops, at p. 145, vol. 2.

The undramatic mistake of the *Farce* at the conclusion of the volume is, that the humour is really too entertaining and the interest too much excited not to lead to inevitable disappointment, when the mysterious Mr. H—, who has such a genteel horror of disclosing his name, turns out to have no worse a patronymic than *Hogsflesh*. It is too desperate an appeal to the normal infirmities common to great numbers of people. Had it been Mr. Horridface, or Mr. Hangman, or Mr. Highwayman, or Mr. Hornowl, Hag-laugh, or Mr. Hellish, it might have been a little better ; but then these would not have been so natural ; in short, nothing would have done to meet so much expectation.

If we were to make a summary of Mr. Lamb's merits as a writer, we should say that there was not a deeper or more charitable observer existing. He has none of the abhorrent self loves that belong to lesser understandings. He takes little, and grants much. He sees through all the causes or circumstances that modify the human character ; and while he likes from sympathy, he dislikes with generosity and sincerity, and offers rather than pretends to be better. If there is anything indeed that looks like affectation in the most sincere and unaffected temper of his writings, it arises partly from the excess of his sympathy with his species, and partly from a wish to make the best of all which they do or suffer ; and it leads him into the only inconsistency that we can trace to him. As an admirer for instance of Christianity, and perhaps as a Christian himself in the truest sense of the world, he sympathizes exceedingly with patience and gentleness and the forgive-ness of wrongs. This also appears to be his own temper ; but then he seems fearful lest this should be construed into a weakness instead of a strength ; and so from turning his sympathy to another side of human nature, he palliates some of the most vehement and doubtful passions, and has a good word to say now and then in behalf of revenge itself. The consequence of this exceeding wish to make the best of things as they are (we do not speak politely, but philosophically), is, that his writings tend rather to prepare others for doing good wisely, than to help the progress of the species themselves. It is this sympathy also, which tends to give his criticism a more prominent effect, than his poetry. He seems to think that poetry as well as prose has done enough, when it reconciles men to each other as they are; and that after Shakespeare and others, it is useless to say much on this subject; so that he deals little in the abstractions of fancy and imagination. He desires no better Arcadia than Fleet-street; or at least pretends as much, for fear of not finding it. Mr. Lamb's style is sound, idiomatic English, equally free from the foreign invasions of the pedantic, and the freaks of us prose coiners, who dabble in a light mint of our own for lawless purposes. It is variously adapted to the occasion. If he is somewhat too antiquated in his verse, he is familiar, short, and striking in his more passionate prose narrative; and in his criticisms, flowing and eloquent.

Among the poems we ought not to forget two or three by the author's sister, who is the main writer, if we mistake not, in some excellent little publications for schools. There is a delightful family likeness in the turn of her genius. One of these little pieces in particular, (*on a Picture of Two Females by Leonardo da Vinci*) looks like an epitome of his whole philosophy; full of sympathies with this world, yet with a thoughtful eye to the world unknown. It sets out in a fine stately moving manner, like the noble young beauty of which it speaks. Mr. Lamb has addressed a sonnet to his sister, full of a charming deference and gratitude.

["Examiner," March, 1819.]

LEIGH HUNT
VELLUTI TO HIS REVILERS

[Velluti, an Italian singer, was received with
great hostility on his appearance in London.]

VELLUTI, the lorn heart, the sexless voice,
To those who can insult a fate without a choice.

You wrong your manhood, critics, and degrade
Your just disdain of an inhuman trade,
When, in your zeal for what a man should be,
You wreak your shuddering epithets on me.
Scorn, as you will, the trade; you cannot err;
But why with curses load the sufferer?
Was I the cause of what I mourn?   Did I
Unmake myself, and hug deformity?
Did I, a smiling and a trusting child,
See the curst blow, to which I was beguil'd?
Call for the knife? and not resist in vain,
With shrieks convulsive and a fiery pain,
That second baptism, bloody and profane?

O fate! what was I then?   A rosy boy,
Trusting in all things, radiant at a toy.
What am I now?   A shadow with lorn eyes;
A toy myself, to hear and to despise.

I own I felt a reverential fear
Of English thoughts, when I was venturing here.
In Italy, my friends know well, it took
Strong hold upon me, nor in France forsook:
But most I felt it, when I cross'd the sea,
That awful sphere of English mastery.
The skies were misty; and there hung in air
Behemoth shapes, and phantoms with huge hair;
Antediluvian things, as though they stood

Once more alive, and guarded the old flood.
Wonder not at these thoughts in me : I've read
Old bards ; and mine has been a suffering head.
As I look'd round upon the awful shows,
While the rains bicker'd, and mad winds arose,
And the sea dealt us its disdainful blows,
I felt my soul look grave, and said—Are these
The gods and playmates of the British seas ?
And have I, venturing with my little store,
A song to please the lords of such a shore ?
I know not :—but I whisper'd—Manly thought
Stands by me still, and serves me as it ought.
I can behold these waves, with awe, 'tis true,
But yet with something of th' exulting too.
Not mean have I been held, not void of soul ;
No hollow friend, nor servile o'er the bowl.
Free songs have I bestow'd, best quitted then ;
Free pleasures have exchang'd with nobler men ;
And in my song, when manly verses come,
The thought, no stranger, finds my heart at home.
I scorn not praise, I own ; what can I scorn,
That makes this heart a little less forlorn ?
I dare the public eye : my very shame
Would fly for refuge in the arms of fame.
But witness, all my friends, how cheap I hold
What makes the powerless powerful, even gold.
I waste it not ; but 'tis not in my thought :
Twice has my purse to its last weight been brought ;
And were it not for a brave servant (nay,
Call him my friend) were pennyless this day.
Not pow'r I seek, but prouder sympathy :
A song and a sweet smile are all to me.
If I came hither not for fame alone,
Let honest natures judge me by their own.
Liberal and rich may still be found in one :
In English ground the glorious mixtures run.
England, my patrons told me, is a place
Where honest men soon know each other's face ;
Where to be just, is all ; and a wrong blow
Must light on none, and least on the laid low.
There, said my friends with exultation, there
The men are manly, as the fair are fair :

There you will find true knowledge : there a mind
Made to partake all good with all mankind.
If England warn you from the public view,
'Twill be to shame your lot, not injure you.
Go then, Velluti, no ungenerous name,
And get what happiness you can, with fame.
I came : I stood not in the public eye :
I needed urging, e'en for company :
I said, I will not, in a land so kind,
Risk a wrong wonder in the public mind ;
I will not hurt one humbler innocence ;
I'll stay where I am known, and bar offence.
I did so. Manly were the men indeed,
And fair the fair, that bade my song proceed :
And yet the storm broke in upon me there,
And with amazement bow'd me, and despair.

What have I done ? Could not these men have shown
Kindly my fault, and let my soul alone ?
Perhaps 'twas wrong to venture my disgrace,
However spared, in any crowded place.
Fame may be food unlawful for my sect,
An odious caste whom no one may protect ;
Doom'd to withdraw their being from remark ;
And shut, were tears the deluge, from the ark.
Perhaps 'twas wrong ; but why not warn me off
With kindly signs, at least without a scoff ?
Why not have said,—Velluti, you will find
Too great a pity for a generous mind ;
Hearts, moved too much to hear that hapless tone,
And doubting, e'en by praise, to please your own.
With tears I would have thank'd them ; yes, with tears
Used to my eyes, and not unworthy theirs.
But they mistake. I'm not the veriest stain
On manhood ; nor are they the perfect men.
External men, and statues cold and void,
Never had eye like theirs a look that was enjoyed.
They share their honours with the inferior kind :
My sex is human still, and of the mind.
Go, sorrier tramplers of a sorry frame ;
Boast of your prowess to the lovely dame ;
Say (for you can say) how, with your high frown

And manly parts, you put the warbler down ;
And want the noblest in a woman's eye,
The best, and manliest, generosity.

O woman, by thy nature kind and good ;
With bosom for the bird, howe'er pursued ;
Whom I must love, unduly as I may ;
Whom I must thank, whate'er the world may say ;
O lost (not all, for thou hast tears) to me,
Let them not, pitying sweetness, unsex *thee !*
Women are never ignorant as men,
For more or less they surely taste of pain :
Of pain they taste, and bashful secrecy,
And thus they learn to pity one like me.
My censurers say, they play a shameful part :
I say, they're right, and they rejoice my heart.
If in their pity some ideas intrude
That force a thought of joy, 'tis fair and good :
No tear of mine shall wish the comfort less ;
Love put the knowledge there, and grief shall bless.

A dim desire, a sweetness hard to bear,
Hangs ever on me, like a charmed air.
'Tis beauteous ; 'tis a woe. My languid eyes
Look dimly through, and mourn their destinies.
Yet what is on the other side, I know
But faintly ; only a sweet voice, and low ;
A woman's form ; a beating heart like mine ;
The rest runs off in tears, and even they're divine.
Oh God of heav'n ! what is this thought, and this,
Made up of weak and strong, of anguish and of bliss ?
Tears can shine sweetly, looking on a smile ;
Not so, when what we look on mourns the while.
How often have I wept the dreadful wrong,
Told by the poet in as pale a song,
Which the poor bigot did himself, who spoke
Such piteous passion when his reason woke !—
To the sea-shore he came, and look'd across,
Mourning his land and miserable loss.—†
Oh worse than wits that never must return,
To act with madness, and with reason mourn !

† Atys, in Catullus.

I see him, hear him ; I myself am he,
Cut off from thy sweet shores, Humanity !
A great gulf rolls between. Winds, with a start,
Rise like my rage, and fall like my poor heart ;
Despair is in the pause, and says " We never part."
'Twas asked me once (that day was a black day)
To take this scene, and sing it in a play !
Great God ! I think I hear the music swell,
The moaning bass, the treble's gibbering yell ;
Cymbals and drums a shatter'd roar prolong,
Like drunken woe defying its own song :
I join my woman's cry ; it turns my brain ;
The wilder'd people rise, and chase me with disdain !

    O let me still some little seeming know,
Some fancied pride : my life is but a show.
Something should pay me for what fate has done ;
Some little lustre for my darken'd sun ;
Some gift unenvied (none can envy me)
Wherewith to solace my heart's poverty.
And something surely 'tis, on some great stage,
When overtures have read their fiery page,
While taste and wit quicken the sparkling rounds,
And beauty sits expecting beauteous sounds,
Something it is, to issue on that scene,
With clapping hands receiv'd, and shouts between,
And lose myself, and live in the charm'd ear
Around me, in some generous character.
Something it surely is, to give and take
That pleasure and that pride : to keep awake
Beauty's bright eye ; to fill it with sweet fears,
Tears glad as smiles, and smiles as soft as tears ;
To make the Graces vocal ; to rejoice
Through the round raptures of an easy voice,
Uttering such meaning, far beyond the verse,
As was the speech in Eden, and occurs
Now only in the depth of poet's books,
Or failing language when it flies to looks.
Then win I up my way, like lark to heaven,
With happy shudders, quivering, quick and even,
Catching at every strain a nicer height
Of cordial subtlety and rare delight.

VELLUTI TO HIS REVILERS

While yearning eyes, and words cut short, below,
Witness delicious wonder, as I go ;
Till, with the passion pierc'd as with a dart,
I feel the headlong impulse at my heart,
And struck at once, down sliding, more than dove,
Drop in the bosom of the general love.

O music, solace made for the bereav'd ;
Giver of gentle answers to the griev'd ;
To labour, rest ; to tiresome wealth, employ ;
Companion whom the loneliest may enjoy,
Ev'n if with nothing left him to rejoice
His sorrow with but his own sorrowing voice ;
Whate'er is graceful in calamity,
And wise above disdain, finds balm in thee ;
And all whose wretchedness would fain divide
Their aching thought with some sweet thought beside.
The dark'ning King sat on his throne, and felt
At thy caress his fiery eyeballs melt.
With thee the Bard in his blind orbs withdrew ;
The winds of Paradise his organ blew,
And rais'd him to the angelic choirs, to hear
Heav'n's homage trav'lling to the eternal ear.
He too, in nature kindred as in wrong,
The master of the earthly heav'n of song,
While in the public gaze he sat, and led
The poet's wail for Samson's rayless head,
Felt thy soft touch on his benighted eyes,
And wept with his deploring harmonies.
Benignant art ! and must I blush to join
One genius more from thy own land and mine ?
O blow to redden priestly dust with shame !
From the curst rack with injur'd hands he came ;
With injur'd hands the starry Seer, whose eyes
Had left their sacred vision in the skies.
From the pale villany he came, and found
His generous lute, and tried a feeble sound :
A shake of his grey head confess'd the unholy wound.

I blush again, thinking of men like these,
To name with theirs my very miseries :
And yet I know not : few and stout were theirs ;

Their name a blessing, mine a mockery wears ;
Nay, and there's dignity in desperate cares.
Alas ! 'tis slavery to excuse thee so :
Arise, my heart, and claim no second place in woe.

I talk of triumphs in the theatre :
The rottenest part of all the core is there.
How, when admir'd on the resounding stage,
My pulses high, my song in all its rage,
When the proud notes, demanding a rich death,
Ran down my voice, and lavish'd glorious breath,
How often when they thought, ears, arms and sight
Drew to my heart one deluge of delight,
Was the most lofty triumph of the air
But its own mockery and a high despair !
No soul, thought I, in all this ample round,
Weighs me for more than what I am, a sound :
No soul regards me, loves me, is my own,
Will look me in the face, when these are gone ;
And say, and fold me to her dancing breast,
" Dearest, 'tis late, and all our birds at nest."
And yet (would I continue) here, e'en here,
Some one may sit, that might have held me dear ;
Here may she sit, fair, gentle, wise, apart,
A pleasurable eye, a pilgrim's heart ;
One that perhaps may know no fitting lot
Of wedded sweetness, because I must not :
Oh ! how I turn'd, as if to wipe that tear,
And sung, and sacrificed my soul to her !

Alone ! alone ! no cheek of love for me,
No wish to be wherever I may be
(For that is love) : no helpmate ; no defence
From this one, mortal, undivided sense
Of my own self, wand'ring in aching space ;
No youth, no manhood, no reviving race ;
No little braving playmate, who belies
The ruffling gibe in his proud father's eyes ;
No gentler voice—a smaller one—her own—
No—nothing.   'Tis a dream that I have known
Come often at mid-day.—I waked, and was alone.

Not on the stage, not amidst heaps of eyes—
Half kind—half scornful, my true comfort lies ;
But where 'tis humblest of humilities.
Lo ! in the church the pomps of this world meet
To lay their service at the sufferer's feet :
Prostrate they bend : all love the meek distress :
The draperied pomps adore that nakedness :
Thither the odour breathes, the tear aspires,
And seraph tapers waste with yearning fires.
Then stirs the organ, and with gusty roar
Sweeps like a storm from some etherial shore ;
And through the sphery volume and stern noise
Takes its meek way the imploring human voice.
Is it a voice most meek, most full of wants,—
One, that the ear with strange compassion haunts ?
'Tis mine.   Mine also is that voice of tears,
When the dark casket of the grave appears,
A diamond in it.   See—she came—she's gone—
The only bride for me ; and I am still alone.
O death too hard !   Yet O still harder death,
Borne by the virgin with no dying breath,
When in their veils the living ghosts come round,
And gather one soul more, and void her place is found.
Once at that sacrifice I sat apart,
And seem'd in weltering tears to weep away my heart.

Go forth, my thoughts.   Breathe me a little ease,
Ye blowing airs ; and take me, noble trees,
To your old arms, out of the crowd, and let
My lonely soul taste of a pleasure yet.
Alas ! my heart goes with me.   I am not
What I would fain become, a point, a mote,
A thought or intuition, a blind air
Gathering some faint sensation here and there ;
Much less the calm superiority
Of some angelic, intellectual eye,
Looking on all, and loving all, but still
Out of the pale of passion and weak will.
I sit sometimes within the woods, and feign
A spirit comes to soothe me in my pain ;
Nymph more than spirit, and of mortal birth ;
Something of shapely warmth, 'twixt heav'n and earth.

I clasp her hand at meeting, and embrace;
The day before us dances in her face;
And we sit down, and read, and play on lutes
Past thinking of, and feed on rosy fruits,
And wander by untrodden paths, and lead—
Oh, such a life! No young Elysian mead
Ever held sweeter; no poetic nest
Took disappointment to a balmier breast.
Yet when our bliss is greatest, when the sense
Of one another's hearts is most intense,
When each grows wild to vent its gratitude
For love so high, so graceful, and so good,
And in the depths of our commingling eyes
We see, upcoming, the dark ecstasies,—
Sudden the landscape fades; my wits forlorn
Deal her, instead of love, some dreadful scorn;
And her poor lover, torn with self-rebuke,
Dies of the pardoning sweetness of her look.

Oh curst be (not my parents, for they knew
Surely no better, yet they lov'd me too!)
But curst be their effeminate souls, who first
Found out the way to make their betters curst.
What tasks they put them to, what impious cares,
How Tantalus's fate was heav'n to theirs,
Better be told by any pen but mine:
My headlong soul would burst along the line.
Once and away the slave has sprung, and rid
His scorners' necks, as dire Eutropius did;
Once and away has won a glorious name,
Like Narses, by outstripping manly fame,
And saving Rome her very self from shame;
But mostly, blighted in the stirring bud,
The wheel undone that whirls the strenuous blood,
Shorn of his strength for sweetness or for strife,
The quavering eunuch is a child for life:
In all a child, as in his beardless chin;
In all but the warm heart, that grows within.
Darkling it grows, and wonders, and in vain
Calls for the cup that should have eased its pain,
And so with tears and infant gentleness,
Gathers meek patience for its great distress.

VELLUTI TO HIS REVILERS

Nature will find some comfort, first or last ;
The wither'd warbler weeps not for the past ;
But young in age, as he in youth was old,
Dies like a singing child, and quits his gentle hold.

   Peace with the critics.   What must be, must be :
One common gift is mine, mortality ;
And 'twixt my grave and this, pardon, ye sounds
Of peace and love, and in your wonted rounds
Take me again, and be to me whate'er
Love would have been, and peace, and honourable care.
I lean my cheek against ye, though ye be
But air ; for 'tis supporting air to me,
My world, my wings, my rest, my shore at even,
From which I launch my thoughts, and dream, and glide to
     heaven.
Oh ! though denied my birthright, and shut up
In my own heart and with this thirsting cup ;
Though bound for life, and the sweet drink denied,
Which glad and loud makes every heart beside ;
Yet as the bird who, in his prison born,
Never knew tree, or drank the dewy morn,
Still feels a native sweetness at his tongue,
And tow'rds his woodland shakes a glittering song ;
So the sweet share of nature left in me
Yearns for the rest, but yearns with harmony ;
And through the bars and sorrows of his fate
Hails his free nest, and his intended mate.
Love's poorest voice shall loving still be found,
Though far it strays and weeps,—a solitary sound.

           [" Examiner," August 7, 1825.]

LEIGH HUNT
HIS LAST ARTICLE IN THE "EXAMINER"

HAYMARKET

READERS of the "Examiner" of some fourteen or fifteen years standing will recognize the "hand" of an old acquaintance at the bottom of this article; and its owner does not affect to think that they will be sorry to see it. His appearance (to speak theatrically) is "for this night only;" so, for old acquaintance sake, he reckons upon being made much of, like a friend who has come from a distance, and is obliged to return the next morning. An old friend's sudden and brief appearance has privileges :

"Like *sailors'* visits, few and far between."

The visitor is to be considered meritorious, though he does little but sit and be looked at, and is "dry as the remainder biscuit." But we have pleasant things to talk of, and other old friends, and a capital new one.

Customary playgoers are apt to lose sight of the advantages they possess in easy boxes, snug pits, and the having a trim stage before them, full of coming wonders or jokes, with lively actors, pretty women, &c., and a whole world of humanity round about them. They like it all, and miss it when lost; but they too often grow more nice than wise—critical and fastidious—and are satisfied with nothing unless it be very new or very fine. Sometimes they go so far in their aberrations from the wise ignorance and rich content of their *playhood*, as to get acquainted behind the scenes, where they learn that pleasant actors can have

234

cares, and get mixed up with jealousies ; to say nothing of
face paintings, and oceans of tin ; of

" Snows of paper, and fierce hail of pease ; "

hich is *cutting up their drum*, and making the front of
the curtain a totally different thing from what it was
before. Now we (innocent youth !) never did get acquainted
behind the scenes, nor were privy to the manufacture of
" Mediterraneans," so that our drum, for that matter,
remains for us in proper boylike condition ; and as to the
rest, we have been so long studying the blessed art of
making everything yield as much as it can, that when we
found ourselves, after an absence of several years from all
theatres, sitting the other night at the Haymarket, pit,
boxes, and galleries verily seemed to embrace us, as if in
reward for those philosophies.

What recollections did not go through our mind as we
sat looking at the curtain before it rose ! What cares,
what joys, what *time*, what losses of dear friends, what
losses of actors, also dear—though we never knew them but
in their stage-home ! There Lewis played to and fro—
the feather of the stage ; there Munden developed a thousand
faces ; there you loved the laugh of Mrs. Jordan, before
she bounded from behind the scenes ; there stood the
heartiness of Bannister, the earnestness of Elliston, the
chuckling quaintness of Suett, the meanness of little
Simmons (in *Filch* and *Beau Mordecai*) ; there the dignity
of Kemble, the regal passion of Mrs. Siddons, the malignity
of Cooke, the quarterdeck *balladry* of Incledon, the simple
song of dear, plain, swarthy, little Mrs. Bland ; the finer
one, and gentlest womanhood of Miss Stephens ; the
Proteus humour of Mathews ; the passion of fine-eyed
Kean, elegant in despite of a blackguard education, and
knowing how to repose on Shakespeare's most golden lines.
There also glowed the affectionate eyes of Miss Murray
(afterwards Mrs. Henry Siddons) ; and there came dancing
the elegance of Miss Searle (who married a brother of Sir

R

Gilbert Heathcote), and the plump little activity of pretty black-haired Lupino (Mrs. Noble); with all of whom, we beg to say, we were in love, and did often take to our heart, though we had an orchestra and three benches between us.

But why speak of fine actors and charming women? An actor is so good for his own sake, and becomes so touching in mere connection with a theatre, that we were reminded the other night of an old theory of ours, which we have often thought of putting to paper—to wit, that your bad actor is the only true one; and that all others depend for their attraction upon something common to other geniuses, and to poor human nature in general—to passions and affections, and all that. We doubt whether we are not of Partridge's mind when he sat at the representation of *Hamlet* with his friend Tom Jones, and said, "The *King* for my money. Any body can tell that *he's* an actor. As to that little fellow who was so frightened (Garrick at sight of the *Ghost*), I should have been just as frightened myself, and shook and trembled in the same manner." Yes; those sort of geniuses, the Garricks and Keans, cannot help themselves; Nature makes them; Nature makes the paternity of Macready, the humour of Liston, &c., whereas your bad actor (we do not mean an actor unbearable, but such as nature-demanding critics *think* bad, and unsophisticated galleries love—a regular strutting king, like the late Mr. Barrymore, or melancholy gentleman in a black suit and white handkerchief, like Mr. Powell, just deceased) *he* is made by himself and his good will, and becomes as proper to the theatre as a box-keeper, or one of its stone pillars. This is one of the reasons why you see him haunting the play-house door at noon-day. To perfect the idea of him, he ought to have a sense of the dignity of his profession, to possess a little library of plays and play-bills, and to shake his head at the irregularities of " Mr. Kean." We have long had a more than sneaking kindness for such a man. and shall now out with it. He partakes of our own love of the optimizing and ideal. He makes the best of himself

and his position, and has a world of his own, not contra-
dictory, after all, to nature (for nature includes Tomkins),
but apart from her other uncommon productions, and
sufficient to itself. He has four different readings for one
line (careless of the poor matter-of-fact truth, that there
can only be a single right one). He reverences the tradi-
tional readings and post-humous wigs of his predecessors.
He thinks that the critics pass him over, because they are
not "up to the true thing;" and that A or B is praised
purely because he is personally acquainted with them;
whereas, if he lights upon a similar luck himself, it is all
right, and his friend the Editor is the only impartial man
going; though apt to be too sparing of his eulogy, and not
sufficiently deferential to professional knowledge. He is
always identified in one's mind with a bye-gone generation,—
with a certain mortal formality, or quaint retrospective
humour; and as the greatest misery you can inflict upon
him is to call him "respectable," so the height of his
ambition (next to being able to convince the great theatres
that he can act *Richard*) is to see himself in one of the
frontpieces to some series of plays, and to be invited by
some staid friends to meet old Mr. Smith or Mr. Higson
at dinner, a "great admirer of his," and one that "recollects
Mossop."

But the curtain draws up, and the mournful beauty of
Ion commences. What a different play from the *Roman
Fathers* and *Grecian Daughters*, and other misnomers of
the Murphys and Whiteheads of the last generation,
intended to remind us of the heroical days of antiquity!
Our friend, the actor just mentioned, would have just
done for those; here, we fear, we must have nature
again, and poetry. Here, to be sure, are the golden helmets
and white vests of his youth, and the beard of his old age—
the only things we think of in those Enfield-Speakers of
plays; but the helmets have brains in them, and the vests
are full of heart, and we forget both helmet and vest in
their contents. So much has been said of *Ion*, in this as

well as in other periodicals, that we have no right to repeat criticisms and quotations with which the reader has become familiar. We must content ourselves with giving a general summary of our feelings about it, and adding one or two remarks suggested by that fullness of reputation, which objection, as in all such cases, has completed. When the tragedy first appeared, we were too ill to go to the theatre ; but we had read it ; and never shall we forget the unaccustomed and (perhaps the reader will forgive a care-worn though not uncheerful reformer for adding) the long-wanted flood of tears, which poured down our cheeks at reading the victorious afflictions of this young embodiment of old hope and endeavour, from the pen of a successful lawyer ! For the agony is not merely Greek, or the result of a bye-gone superstition : it is Christian also ; it is human ; it is the old and gradually increasing instinct of the superiority of the much over the little, and the many to the few, taking its stand at last as the habitual admission of all good and graceful minds, and of conventionality itself ; for the author of *Ion*, besides having a good and graceful mind, is of a profession supposed to be of the very worldliest sort ; and this author, at once ideal and conventional, puts forth his tragedy to an age remarkable for its love of the practical, and finds it as heartily responded to by the general understanding as by the particular. Formerly, scholars only would have admired such a subject, or it would have been approved as being classical ; and the approbation would have been cold as the writing. Now the universality, and gentler personal considerateness of the Christian charities, instinctively mingle themselves with the Greek patriotism ; Modern Philosophy itself (Christianity's unconscious daughter), claims the creed as its own ; and the lawyer himself, with the approbation of his fellows, steps forth, and embodies it in a Græco-Christian shape. These reflections, and an undoubting anticipation of the tragedy's success, passed delightedly through our mind, when it first came before us : we

238

thought of all the struggles of the world, some too reverend to be more than alluded to; we thought of a beloved friend, himself an _Ion_ in his worn heart; we thought even of our own worship of such aspirations, and of what we had endured for them; and it seemed to us, at the moment, as if we had a right to take pity on our very selves, by virtue of the contrast between the weakness of our endeavours and the beauty and the victoriousness of what we admired; and hence the refreshment of those tears. When we saw it in the theatre the other night, they were renewed, though not in the plentifulness of that first outpouring; for between one's own feelings and those of the author stood the habits of the stage; and though Miss Ellen Tree was very sweet and graceful in _Ion_, and pitched her voice to the music of a mournful doom, and though Miss Taylor was earnest and impressive, and Mr. Vandenhoff surprised us with passages of such emotion as ought to have made him a greater actor throughout, yet when was fine tragedy ever fitly represented to the height of its argument? We never knew an instance; though we have had at times a solitary character or so, nearly as good as the poet's—an _Othello_ or a _William Tell_.

Have we no objections, then, to make to the tragedy? Yes; we think that the speeches have a tendency to be too long, and to criticise their own feelings, even after the curtailments made in the representation; and we miss, in a play with conspiracy and violence in it, some of that short quick dialogue, for which Beaumont and Fletcher are remarkable, and which, to say the truth, has been wanting to almost all our drama, old and new, till it was restored by the author of _Dramatic Scenes_ and _Mirandola_; who always appeared to us to be a bit of the soul of Fletcher. Even the heartiness of Knowles is deficient in it—another genuine countryman of the old dramatists. We cannot help thinking (with due awe at making the objection) that Shakespeare himself would have been the better for more of it; though he so fills the mind with feelings and ideas, that one cares for nothing else at the time. In other respects *Ion* is worthy of its subject throughout. It has poetry, passion, action; delicatest love-making, grandest faith. The complete and unhalting sufficingness of the action even surprised us, when we saw it represented; but the author had made some judicious changes from his first edition; and if some greater evidence of struggle and wretchedness might have been looked for on the part of the hero, when thinking of the mistress and the existence he was going to give up (as in that affecting farewell to life of Alcestis in the Greek poet), or if some critics have objected that the general effect of the play should have been rather on the side of an overwhelming than a soothing emotion—of (apparent) strength rather than gentleness— it is to be recollected that it is by the very force of a gentle nature that *Ion* can do what he does; that if he could not concentrate his thoughts and purposes in that sweet and considerate fashion, he would not have been the being to execute them; and that he retreats from a love that would have distracted him (much more a coarser and apparently stronger mind) and diverted him from those purposes into another that includes its very self while appearing to forget it. The author, in the preface to his tragedy, has shown himself quite aware of this possible point of objection, and avowedly anticipated it in a beautiful description of his hero's character; and we may add, that it was of the very essence of his moral and its ability to set up this noble gentleness above this imaginary strength; for the fault and misfortune (or untaught vigour) of the world, and the cause of all which its strength is strong to complain of and get angry about, is that very setting up of a strong and selfish sensation above a considerate and self-sacrificing one, which it is the object of all martyrdoms, and all preferences of the many to the few, to reduce to its proper level.

Among the evidences of social advancement which *Ion* has been a means of affording, none of the least interesting, next to the fact of its having been written by a lawyer, is that of its having been written by a very industrious and successful one. There is another though less public example to the same effect, in a gentleman at the bar, with whose tragedy we are unfortunately unacquainted; and the translations of Faust, by Messrs. Hayward and Anster, ought not to be forgotten. Blackstone, therefore, and others who have thought proper to bid "farewell to the Muses" on entering the legal profession, have shown that they were in the wrong; or at least, that if they themselves were not in the wrong, but took a just measure of the powers of their muse, others may take no such farewell and yet be in the right. It is a blessed discovery, and will turn to account in many more ways than the production even of good poems. The whole poetry of life will profit by it. The belief in the good and true, as well as the cultivation of it, will be found compatible with what has hitherto been thought its contradiction; and the poetry of honourably earned leisure go hand in hand with the prose of business and profit. They must go together, however, throughout. Nobody must suppose he will be able to say to himself that he will be a poet at the eleventh hour, after being a mere proser all the ten, much less a misbelieving or a scornful one. Together with the acquired knowledge of his manhood, he must retain the wisdom, and faith in nature, of the child. And what hearty and fine minds will it not require to do this! Aye, such as are akin to Shakespeare's itself, which at the close of all his experience of the world, could produce the good-natured and romantic play of *Twelfth-Night*—the last of his productions.

[" Examiner," 1836.]

ROBERT HUNT

ON

MRS. HUNT'S OUTLINE PRINT OF
LORD BYRON

ONE of the most earnest features of curiosity is a desire to know the personal appearance of distinguished individuals. As a means of indulging this curiosity, the value of engraving is much increased, in consequence of his multiplying their portraits after the original works done from the life. Of this we have just had new experience, in looking at an Outline Print, from a Cutting in Paper, by a Lady, who has associated with Lord Byron, and who is remarkable for conveying by such simple means the form and air of the person represented. The print —(which is an outline strongly thrown out from a black ground, and thus reversed to most silhouettes, whose outlines are filled up with black, and relieved by a white ground)—shows that she possesses three main qualities of portraiture—a correct eye—a strong apprehensiveness of the represented object—and the power of visibly communicating it. Though the species of Outline here given is but the general boundary of the many interior outlines of the figure, and thus little more than the general air is seen, yet the portrait is in a moment acknowledged as that of Lord Byron by all who have seen him in Italy, differing as it does from all the portraits executed in England, for he had much altered in Italy. The remark of Sir J. REYNOLDS is thus corroborated, that, " in portraits, the grace, and we may add, the *likeness*, consists more in taking the *general air*, than in observing the exact similitude of every feature." The following interesting statement respecting the look and demeanour of Lord Byron is annexed to the portrait :

242

"LORD BYRON AS HE APPEARED AFTER HIS DAILY RIDE AT PISA AND GENOA.

"He used to sit in this manner out of doors with the back of the chair for an arm ; his body indolently bent, and his face turned gently upwards ; often with an expression of doubt and disdain about the mouth. His riding dress was a mazarine blue camlet frock with a cape, a velvet cap of the same colour, lined with green with a gold band and tassel, and black shade, and trowsers, waistcoat, and gaiters, all white, and of one material. The cap had something of the look of a coronet, and was a little pulled forward over the shade. His lame foot (the left) but slightly affected his general appearance. It was a shrunken, not a club foot, was turned a little on one side, and hurt him if much walked upon, but as he lounged about a room the defect was hardly observable. The rest of his person, till he grew fat, was eminently handsome : so were his mouth and chin—fit for a bust of Apollo. The fault of the face was, that the jaws were too wide compared with the temples, and the eyes too near one another. Latterly he grew thin again as he was in England. His hair had been thick and curling, but was rapidly falling off. The above likeness is believed to be the only genuine one of the noble Poet ever taken at full length. It was recognised by those who knew his Lordship in Italy, with that laughter of delight common upon seeing the expression as well as features happily caught. And it is but justice to the able engraver (who was kind enough to undertake a work apparently very easy, but in reality far from it) to say, that he has been equally happy in transferring it to the copper."

[" Examiner," November 5th, 1826 : the description of Byron is by L. H.]

CHARLES LAMB

ON

POOR GENTLEMEN

MR. EDITOR,—I am one of that unfortunate class of persons who once was enabled, tolerably well, to support the character and appearance of a gentleman ; but now, through the almost insupportable pressure of increasing taxes, and the unnecessary imposition on every article necessary to form a decent appearance in the world, I am reduced to the situation, and insulted with the appellation, of a distressed buck. 'Tis now almost four years since my body was graced with a new suit, which you must think has long shewn its age ; like the wearer it has experienced many changes, being under the necessity of mounting a new set of buttons with every changing fashion, besides the frequent sprinkling with a little table beer, before I dare venture to walk with the sun at my back. As I have paced the streets on a summer's afternoon, I have heard it said respecting me, what a miserable shadow of respectability ! while others more severe have declared that my boots had felt the shock of many an engagement. I must confess, that beside new bottoming, they have received so many additions, that it would be hardly possible to find the original workmanship. Nor does my hat and gloves pass unnoticed, the former of which I purchased from a gentleman's butler for three shillings. Thus, Sir, like some monster, I am driven by distress from the society of those who once associated with me, and am obliged to fly through all the courts and alleys of the metropolis, to avoid the insults of the merciless and ignorant. With the sum of twenty-five shillings per week, the usual income of a collecting clerk, I some years ago could dine at a respectable ordinary more than twice a week; but now I dare not venture near an eating house on a Sunday, lest my re-elbowed coat and my greasy pantaloons, or my more eloquently distressed appetite, should proclaim my privations, and purchase more insult; so that now I am compelled to carry a cheap half-dressed bone, or a small portion of bread and cheese, in my pocket, to the most retired public-house I can find, where I have frequently been obliged to hear the most flagrant outrages offered to common sense, by the boorish puns and vulgar jests of town carters and inn porters, whose leisure hours are employed in the exercise of tap-room eloquence. Thus, after passing a day of anxious care, I am compelled to retire to my apartment, which is a lofty attic, to contemplate my misery, without the most distant prospect of a termination thereof. If, Mr. Examiner, you have any regard for insulted human nature, I conjure you to cry aloud against the abominably disgraceful extent of our public burthens, which if not speedily removed must sink not only you and me as individuals, but the Nation and Government itself, into the bottomless abyss of destruction. Sir, I remain your very distressed, but most obedient humble servant,

THE WRECK OF A GENTLEMAN.

["Examiner," May 20th, 1810. Attributed to Lamb on the style of characterisation and writing, the liking for humorous dilemma, with the typical pen-name: it has a family likeness to several known letters of the kind from his pen in Hunt's *Reflector* and elsewhere.]

CHARLES LAMB
ON
WHO WAS JUNIUS?

M R. EDITOR,—At length I am enabled to set the
world right as to the real name of that mysterious
and extraordinary personage, whose letters, under
the signature of Junius, have been the object of so much
public curiosity. The late Mr. Suett, of Drury-lane
Theatre, confessed to me upon his death-bed, that he was
the author of those justly celebrated epistles. This I am
ready to verify upon oath before a Magistrate, whenever I
shall be so required. The period which my dear friend
was pleased to prescribe, till the expiration of which I was
not at liberty to reveal his secret, being at length elapsed,
no longer any motives of delicacy toward the dead exist
to prevent my satisfying the curiosity of the living. Here
then let the question rest for ever. After this candid
disclosure, the silly claims attempted to be set up for
Hamilton, Boyd, Shelbourne, &c. vanish in course. Hence-
forth let the laurel rest upon the true brow. Those who
are disposed to cavil, as such will always be found in the
clearest cases, may alledge that in the confessedly genuine
letters which yet remains of Mr. S. there is no resemblance
to the elaborate style and terse antithesis of Junius. Let
such consider the difference of a short note carelessly
scribbled upon any common occasion, perhaps a letter of
gaiety to a theatrical friend or boon companion, and the
meditated effusions of a writer sitting down to impress
posterity with a permanent picture of the passing politics of
his day. Those who were admitted to Mr. S.'s interior
confidence (I believe I may say I was in his heart, as his
image will be in mine till its latest beat), will recollect

246

several peculiarities in the avowed politics of that gentleman strongly corroborative of the claim here set up for him; his strong suspicions of something hollow about the character of the Marquis of G——y, the popular idol of the day; his moderate admiration (to express it in the most favourable light) of the Rockingham party; his personal aversion to a certain Great Personage; above all, they will remember the singular confusion which seemed to pervade his expressions (in general so clear) with regard to the question of General Warrants, a subject upon which, after all, it is doubtful whether our dear friend had made up any very clear or consistent opinion. I have the honour to be, Sir, your humble servant,

HENRY AUGUSTUS HUMPLEBY.

No. 1 *Ratcliff-Highway.*

["Examiner," July 4th, 1813. Hazlitt, in *The Conversation of Authors*, discloses that "Junius" was a topic (intolerantly handled) at Lamb's evening parties of this period.

"The late Mr. Suett" was one of Lamb's favourite old actors, but under the less venerable style of Dicky Suett; he was "the Robin Good-Fellow of the stage," whom no one but Lamb would have thought of "proposing" as the severe and massive author of *Junius* (just as only Lamb could have put it about that Lord Castlereagh was the author of *Waverley*). The solemn equivocations ("let the laurel rest upon the true brow," etc.), the dry affected *Gentleman's Magazine* style, tripping up at the awful alliteration of "impressing posterity with a permanent picture of the passing politics of his day," strengthen the main claim to Lamb's authorship; and finally the humorous management of the succession of parentheses is Lamb's mark, with the "&c." after the string of famous names.

Ratcliffe Highway was just then notorious for the frightful murders of 1811, and Mr. Humpleby's name seems to tell us that the letter is a *hum*.]

CHARLES LAMB
ON
THE NEW COMEDY, " DEBTOR AND CREDITOR "

HAVING put off seeing Mr. Kenney's Play to so late a date, it is with an ill grace, though with great truth, that we advise such of our readers, as have not had that pleasure, to see it as soon as they can. We have been much gratified by it. Not that during its representation we were so much struck with any of its passages standing out and claiming a present interest above the rest. We have been *partially* more tickled at several modern comedies (in themselves very inferior productions) which we could name. But the result upon our minds, when we got home, was, that we had seen (we are going to use a coarse phrase, but a more applicable does not occur) our money's-worth. In counting over again our sum of amusement, we could not help feeling that we had scarce given the piece credit enough while it was acting. We accused ourselves of the same sort of neglect which we accuse ourselves of uniformly to departed friends. We wanted, if possible, to see it over again the same night, to make up with it.

We the rather insist upon this our feeling, because we think that the want of prominence of parts in this Play has been the cause that it has scarce received its due meed of praise (though by no means a niggardly one) from our brother journalists. Equable and gentle interest—gentle but not without strength, kept up throughout the piece—has been mistaken for mediocrity ; or rather, the difference may have been felt, but found not quite so easy to express. Rough excrescencies and jutting points, are the pegs to hang critical notes upon ; as in Landscape criticism, it is the out-stretching promontory, the abrupt rock and mountain, that calls for distinct admiration :—while the quiet yet fruitful valley lies low, and tells no tales of its own beauties.

If for nothing else, yet for this alone, we should be heartily grateful to Mr. Kenney, for the boldness with which he has brought out Mrs. Jordan in one of her own parts. We say *her own*—for we think that almost all modern play-writers, that have availed themselves in late years of this actress's rare talents, have strangely mistaken her bent. They have put her upon a mixed farrago of fine ladyship and sentiment ; the two things which her nature has been ever most abhorrent from. We have seen the curious struggles which she has made to naturalize sentiment, i.e. mere lip-goodness, verbal virtue, to her mouth. She has no sounds to express a self-reflecting virtue by. She has not an artificial tone ; and when she brings out any set sentence of philanthropy, any one may see that she is giving the lye to her own honest nature. The commonest artificialist on the Stage has in this particular the advantage of her. When we say she never did or could play the *Fine Lady*, we mean it to her honour. Her mind is essentially above the thing. But if the term *Lady* implies any thing of graceful or delicate in the highest sense of those female attributes, in that best sense it is due to her. She is one, not of Congreve's, or Sheridan's, but of Shakespeare's *Ladies*. Those who remember her in *Viola* in the *Twelfth Night*, or have seen her in *Helena* in *All's Well that Ends Well*, or can call to mind her sisterly admonitions to *Laertes* in the early scenes of *Ophelia*, will know that we mean to deny nothing of true grace or propriety in behaviour, look, or utterance, when we refuse to Mrs. Jordan the praise of acting what is commonly called fine Ladies' parts.

Barbara Green is a child of nature—she is not, as has been falsely stated, a copy of *Miss Hoyden*—there is this only in common with the two characters, that each speaks (to use a homely phrase) what comes uppermost. But in *Barbara* it is the *pure Nature* from within bubbling up in

249

clear streams, healthy and delightful : *Hoyden* is a fountain of turbulent and muddy waters. Mrs. Jordan certainly shewed by her acting that she had a very different sense of the two characters. With all possible openness and frankness of manner, there was nothing clownish or ungainly, not one hoydenish trick, about *Barbara Green*. Only there was *the girl*, exact in her *teens*, as true to life as ever ; by what art she still contrives to cheat us we know not, but it was perfect deception throughout ; there was *the girl*, whom you might fancy not to have done growing.

Sampson Miller is the second character in consequence in the piece ; a most ticklish one, but contrived with the skill of an adept. A bruiser by profession, but always delivering lectures of morality to fashionable gentlemen. Placed as a kind of servant at a milliner's, where—as a neighbour whispered us in the pit—among the ribbons, flounces and furbelows, he cut pretty much such a figure as a bull in a china shop. Yet by the force of abstinence, of giving him just no more to say than is absolutely necessary ; by shewing him for a brief moment and then withdrawing him ; by *economising the humour*—that wise parsimony which few of our dramatic prodigals have courage to observe—he was brought through, not only with safety but with evident effect to the piece ; we believe almost entirely by this art of knowing the *proper quantity*. The actor who played *Samson Miller* so identifies himself with every part that he plays, that we were almost in danger of forgetting his professional claims upon our notice. Nothing can be more perfect than his *Samson Miller* ; it is of a piece throughout, *teres et rotundus*.

Mr. Liston's part is a pleasant amplification of the part of *Lubin Log*, in Mr. Kenney's farce of *Love, Law, and Physic* ; subtracting some of the more palpable vulgarities, and superadding the *poetical faculty*. We doubt if it is prudent in Poets to expose their craft on the stage. There are prose heads too many before the curtain, who are beforehand with their contempt. The word *author* has been bandied about in prologues till it has fallen in consideration lower than *gipsy* or *beggar*. Sham supplications have been reiterated, till they pass for real; and the stupid, gaping auditory literally fancy a man with a rope round his neck, patiently attending to receive from their dullness a pardon or a whipping. Be this as it may, this graft from the bay tree was no unpleasant accession to the parent log. It gave a burnish to the self-complacency of Mr. Liston; never was true internal satisfaction more gloriously expressed than in that gentleman's face. Some actors use great straining and effort to be expressive; they move their muscles by prodigious levers; he does it by a single thread, by a film, and by that film we (the poor silly spectators) are infallibly caught like flies.

We must just notice the satisfaction we had in seeing Mrs. Powell in the part of *Jesse's* mother. The sight of that Lady who was once, and is still, for aught we know, the finest woman on the stage, on the same night with Mrs. Jordan, brought forcibly to our minds the times when they played—the one *Olivia*, and the other *Viola*, in *Twelfth Night*, with Dodd, and Palmer, and *Bensley*, and *Suet*, at the old Drury Lane Theatre. *Where are the rest gone?*— We shall not easily forget the graceful deportment of Mrs. P. in that character; her elegant way of fooling away the time in questions with her fool, so like a high Lady unbending, carelessly beginning and carelessly giving over. We have seen *Olivias* since, who have vied wit with the *Clown*, and kept up a studied bandying of logic, seemingly upon the same equal ground as *Beatrice* holds argument with *Benedick*, as if the question were who should say the smartest things. But we are reminded of the time. We are not reviewing the *Twelfth Night*. While this has been under our hands, we have had put before us a poetical compliment to Mrs. Jordan on her performance in the very Comedy we have been noticing. We hope we do not encroach upon the *greater Editorial functions* in subjoining it, particularly being short.

THALIA TO MRS. JORDAN

On her performance of BARBARA GREEN, *in the New Play of*
DEBTOR *and* CREDITOR

Once more a girl—with girlish frankness blest—
A maiden frolicking in maiden's vest—
What charm is this that locks up Envy's tongue ?
What art preserves my Fav'rite ever young ?
In happy hour thou comest to maintain
The almost sinking glories of my reign.
My sister Muse,* flush'd with her late accession,
Had seized the Stage, and threaten'd long possession ;
Her rites restored with rapture she had seen,
And all she lost in SIDDONS, found in KEAN.
Let others boast the deep tragedian's line,
Thou from thy cradle hast been mark'd for mine.
Too humble, or too prudent to aspire
To the proud buskin, and the tragic fire,
Some natural tones, which reach'd the quiet heart,
Were all you practised of the *moving* art.
Nor with less caution in the comic act
You shunn'd th' aspiring, chose the safer tract,
Resign'd the tempting scenes of polish'd life
For half-bred *Hoyden*, and plain *Jobson's wife :*
Content, though travelling on lowest ground,
In company with NATURE to be found.

* Melpomene.

"Examiner," May 8th, 1814 ; having been announced
for "next week" on April 20th.

[Lamb contributed an epilogue to "Debtor and Creditor,"
printed with the play in 1814.

Among the several pieces of evidence which identify the
above appreciation as Lamb's, the principal is the allusion
to *Twelfth Night* as performed "at the old Drury Lane
Theatre." The reader may judge by a citation of Lamb's

THALIA TO MRS. JORDAN

" On Some of the Old Actors " (1823) how close the parallel
is with the passages on Mrs. Jordan and Mrs. Powell above :

" Those who have only seen Mrs. Jordan within the
last ten or fifteen years, can have no adequate notion of
her performance of such parts as Ophelia ; Helena, in All's
Well that Ends Well ; and Viola in this play "—i.e. Twelfth
Night " at the old Drury-lane Theatre two-and-thirty
years ago " . . . .

" Mrs. Powel (now Mrs. Renard), then in the pride of
her beauty, made an admirable Olivia. She was particularly excellent in her unbending scenes in conversation
with the Clown. I have seen some Olivias—and those
very sensible actresses too—who in these interlocutions
have seemed to set their wits at the jester, and to vie
conceits with him in downright emulation. But she used
him for her sport, like what he was, to trifle a leisure
sentence or two with, then to be dismissed, and she to be
the Great Lady still " . . . .

Bensley, Dodd, Palmer and Suett, of course, are portrayed
at full length, together with Mrs. Powell and Mrs. Jordan,
in the 1823 essay.

These similarities altogether certify that Lamb wrote
the paper now reprinted, and one striking identificatory
mannerism may be mentioned in addition—the sudden
emphatic question, during the retrospective mood in the
last paragraph, " *Where are the rest gone ?* " That is Elia's
voice, so memorable in " Blakesmoor in H——shire " :
" Then, that haunted room—in which old Mrs. Battle
died—whereinto I have crept, but always in the day-time,
with a passion of fear ; and a sneaking curiosity, terror-
tainted, to hold communication with the past. *How shall
they build it up again ?* "]

CHARLES LAMB

ON

SUB-PULPIT ORATORY

Being the first of a Series of Critiques which we propose
giving upon the principal Parish-Clerks of London, and
within the Bills of Mortality. After which will follow,
Sketches of the Lives and Characters of some of the
leading Organists, Churchwardens, and Pew-openers

Mr. Moses Mims, Parish-Clerk of St. Brides, Fleet-Street

The office of Parish-Clerk is one of extreme venerable-
ness and antiquity. Next in dignity to the Clergy, saith
Leland. Semi-ecclesiastic, according to Camden. Witty
Fuller likeneth him in his Church History to the bat, half
bird half beast, yet so as there is more in him of the former
than of the latter ; his clergy wings do outweigh the laic
or mouse part of him. He is the mouthpiece of the
congregation, saith Hooker. Mouth of mouths, according
to Bishop Bull ; the connecting link between the minister
and people. Cousin twice removed to the Vicar, saith
another ; note, that the Curate is betwixt. Bell-wether
to the flock, saith Bishop Andrews, speaking it in honour.
Spelman doubteth whether he be not entitled to a portion
of the lesser tythes, say a tenth.

From all which expressions, though some of them seem
run up into a height of metaphor and allegory greater
peradventure than the matter soberly considered will bear,
we may yet gather, in what kind of estimation antiquity
hath held the function, and deduce a kind of pattern or
ideal (as the modern phrase hath it) by which to try the

254

pretensions of the several candidates, who shall be brought in succession before the bar of our critical tribunal.

Mr. Moses Mims (Rev. Mr. we had almost written) hath long been an ornament to the Farringdons, both Without and Within. This Gentleman (for so he undoubtedly is, one day in seven) is arrived at that period of life when the troublesome passions are beginning to subside, and a man may carry a sedate and grave look without suspicion of hypocrisy. He is two and forty years of age, by his own reckoning; his wife says, four and forty. It does not much matter. His countenance is staid and composed, but by no means forbidding. Nay we have seen it, at the publication of a marriage banns, or when some rich man's child hath been christened, relax into a sober simper, not unaptly resembling the smiling looks of St. Brides herself, when at Easter, or some other holy festival, she is hung round with greens, and sparkling red berries between. His stature is above the common height of man, inasmuch that when he standeth up in his place, his tall figure hath been known quite to eclipse, and shut out from the view of the congregation, the person of the Rev. Mr. Manley Wood, who officiates in the reading desk two foot above him. Mr. Wood, we are sure, has too much good sense to be disconcerted by these unintentional and merely physical approaches to equality. The effect is nevertheless embarrassing, for we seem to have lost our Reader. He is, as it were, awfully snatched from us. Mr. Mims's voice is clear and sonorous; he commandeth a fine mellow tenor when he singeth, and he giveth out his first lines with a full magisterial dictation. But how shall we do justice to his Amen? Compared with his manner of pronouncing that final, conclusive, sealing word, as we may call it,* the prayer does not seem fully ratified, legal, we might say, till that final stamp is put upon it. Compared with his, all the Amens which we have ever heard in town and

* Is not some part of the sentence omitted at this point in the
"Examiner"?—Ed.

country, parochial, extra-parochial, cathedral, regular or dissentient, Church of England Amens, Presbyterian Amens, Popish Amens, Calvinistic, Lutheran, Armenian, Moravian, Wesleian, Huntingdonian, &c. Amens, have been, to use a familiar phrase, not worth a button. They were finical, drawling, sentimental, devoid of any true savour, unctionless. He doth indeed, as Mr. Thomas Brown in the last age nicely expresseth it, " curl " the word. It is as if you heard the old Sea God wind his " wreathed horn." No man alive is worthy to " say Amen, when he does cry God bless us." Mr. Mims must forgive us, but we cannot help noticing one fault among so many excellences ; it is his unwarrantable pronunciation of two Hebrew words, " To the Chirping and Serping," as nearly as we can catch from a hasty recitation ; for he seemeth to have some doubts, and to quicken his utterance, when he cometh to this passage, as men reading do when they are wavering. We are no great Hebraists, and we have heard it whispered that this gentleman has made it the amusement of his leisure hours, such as he can spare from his twofold occupation of Parish-Clerk and Green-Grocer, to study the Talmud. Possibly his pronunciation may, in that case, be remotely derived from Rabbinical tradition ; but he should remember that his auditors are not Hebrews, but plain Fleet-street and Black-friars Christians, who expect the words to be given in the common Anglicised fashion, in which they have been accustomed to hear them ; that is to say, trisyllabically. We cannot conclude without noticing a practice which seems to be peculiar to Mr. Mims, and which we cannot help thinking very praiseworthy ; which is, his accompanying every emphatic clause in the sermon with a graceful waving up and down of the hand, as if to point it out to the attention of the auditory. We have seen judicious Leaders of the Band regulate the time at Oratorios and Sacred Music, to the inferior musicians, in a similar method. This hath an excellent effect. Yet we doubt if it be a custom which we could

256

recommend universally. It may be right in this parish, wrong in the next. Generally it may be given as a rule, that where the Preacher's manner is cold and unanimated, as it is to a most surprising degree in both the Morning and Evening Preachers at St. Brides, the Clerk would do well to adopt this method of rousing a supplementary attention, in the absence of loud tones and awakening gestures. Where the Preacher is what they call evangelical, this sub-gesticulation is less called for.

DION JUNIOR.

(The subject of our next communication will be Mr. William Wicks, Assistant Clerk and Sexton at St. Andrews Undershaft. Little Knight, Christ-church, Newgate-street, who succeeded Hensman, will follow.)

["Examiner," August 22nd, 1819; in allusion to a series of criticisms of "Pulpit Oratory" by a writer signing himself "Dion."

Readers of this appetising, half-Hogarthian sketch will scarcely require that the indications of Lamb's authorship be insisted upon; the blend of actual antiquarian knowledge with smiling enjoyment of character and manners, indeed the nature of the parody here latent, would not be anyone's but his; he alone would quote in this spirit and on this occasion his Camden, Fuller, Andrews, Bishop Bull, etc., or gather from Sir Thomas Browne, Wordsworth on *The World is too much with us*, and *Macbeth* the phrases due to communicate Mr. Mims's great Amen. But the very name Mr. Moses Mims has an Elian affinity and consonance, and ranks for odd suitability with his Juke Judkins. The reference to "Little Knight" of Christ-Church, Newgate Street, "who succeeded Hensman," is a product of Christ's Hospital recollection. Mr. Lucas says that he could not discover whether Lamb "practised religious forms"; but the above paper, if it is his—and there can hardly be an

" if "—implies that he knew more about the services of the City churches than is usually imagined.

" A Correspondent who is disappointed at not seeing more articles on the *Parish Clerks,* is informed that the author did not intend to extend his joke further on that momentous subject."—" Examiner," September 5th, 1819.]

CHARLES LAMB

ON

THE REPAIR OF ST. PAUL'S

MR. E. V. LUCAS in his edition of Lamb's " Works "
(vii, 987) collected as " possibly Lamb's " eight lines
under the title " On a Visit to St. Paul's." These
lines Mr. Hutchinson reprinted in the Oxford edition, with
the note, " The attribution may be regarded as all but
certain : see ' The Tombs in the Abbey ' "—where Lamb
introduces an angry note on the charging of twopence for
admission to St. Paul's. The source of the epigram, noted
by both Lucas and Hutchinson, is the " Examiner " (from
the " Traveller ") of April 8th, 1821.

Now these eight lines, with a difference of one word,
are the concluding portion of a poem which had appeared,
without a signature, in the *Morning Chronicle* of March 9th,
1821. The full production is quite in Lamb's style, and
should replace the fragment in new editions of his poems :

THE REPAIR OF ST. PAUL'S.

David's wise son, renown'd in sacred song,
Ere yet 'twas known that kings could do no wrong,
Refus'd to leave his Maker in the lurch,
Nor built his Palace till he'd built a Church ;
But modern Priests have no such saintly call,
Build Fulham first, and then repair St. Paul.

Oh, could the air dispens'd from circling stove,
Warm as a Bishop's zeal or Christian love,
Dispens'd through stair-case, passages and hall
Of that Right Reverend house Episcopal,
With comfortable warmth, O ! Paul, pervade
The damp, dull mould'rings of thy chill arcade !

But ah ! I fear the comforts of the see
Will ne'er extend, unhappy Paul, to thee—
Though travelling eastward, they have reach'd as far
As the new mansion in St. James's-square.

What can be hop'd from Priests who, gainst the Poor,
For lack of two-pence, chain the church's door ?—
Who, true successors of the ancient leaven,
Erect a turnpike on the road to Heaven ?
" Knock, and it shall be open'd," saith our LORD ;
" Knock, and pay two-pence," say the Chapter Board :
The show-man of the booth the fee receives,
And GOD's house is again a " den of thieves."

An amusing letter on this same subject, and to be read in
connection with the poem now given and with the essay
" On the Tombs in the Abbey," was later printed in the
" Examiner " of March 7th, 1824.

INDEX TO PART I

BARNES, THOS.
his labours and powers 36
strong on Coleridge's " Remorse "
36
has the measure of Hazlitt 42
" Parliamentary Portraits " 36, 43

BLAKE, WILLIAM
his Exhibition discommended 9-11

BROUGHAM, HENRY
defends the Hunts 19
defends them again 25-26

BYRON, LORD
his " Address on the Opening of
Drury Lane Theatre " 29
illustrated by Stothard 54
his lyrics in the " Examiner " 55
" our Noble Friend with all his
faults " 61
monody on Sheridan 64
innocent morality of " Don Juan "
93
" Don Juan at Shooter's Hill " 117
notices of his death and nature 121

COLERIDGE, S. T.
disclaims lies in the *Courier* 19
his " Christabel " attacked 58
his " Lay-Sermon " shouted down
58

COLLIER, J. P.
" Criticisms on the Bar " 86

FIELD, BARRON
an early contributor 3
poem in Wordsworth's manner 29
poem in Lamb's manner 66
reviewed by Lamb 105

HAYDON, B. R.
the hope of the Hunts 10
his paintings good in parts 28
on the Elgin Marbles 65
his influence on Keats 69
" he killed his mother " 74
offers to adorn churches 86
" Christ's Entry into Jerusalem "
104
declines sadistic reputation 110
an admirer of Woman 110

HAZLITT, WILLIAM
abominates country character 41
his view of Iago 42
share in the Round Table 49-51, 65
his theatrical notices 53
onslaught on Lake Poets 58
fury against Wordsworth 59
on Coleridge and Southey 58, 69
his Shakespeare Characters
eulogized 74
his lectures commended 83
on country character again 91
differs from the Rev. W. B. Collyer
115
on Shelley's Christian spirit 116

HUNT, JOHN
trials for libel 12, 14, 19 24-26,
107, 108
in Coldbath Fields Prison 32
calls for Z 77
sued by Stockdale the mad pub-
lisher 88
a sound writer 107
confronts " the Royal gamecock "
107
his speech at trial, 1821 108
returns to Coldbath Fields 108

261

INDEX

HUNT, JOHN (*continued*)
his admiration of Shelley 114
awaits trial for publishing " The
Vision of Judgment " 117, 121
excludes Leigh Hunt from
" Examiner " 122

HUNT, LEIGH
on American foreign policy 6
on Sheridan's politics 6
on the O.P. riots 8
ridicules the Laureateship 13, 38
on Shakespeare 15, 64
condemns Moore's " M.P." 18
defends Negro Civilization 19
campaign against the Regent
21-24, 31, 45, 49
trial for libel 24-26
on the school of Gay 26
describes Mrs. Siddons as Lady
Macbeth 27
discovers Hampstead 27
on barracks in Dover Cliff, 27
praises Byron with reservations
29, 93
imprisoned in Surrey Gaol 31-36, 44
records the Englishman's Dialogue
45
feels discomfort in release from
prison 48
one of the " Round Table " 48-50
on Munden 52
dissatisfied with Kean 53
his unhappy Byroniana 54, 61
after Waterloo 55
states cause of Napoleon 56
not afraid of Wordsworth 57
welcomes Keats, Shelley and Reynolds 60
his poetic gifts 61
recants about Sheridan 64
on Shelley's law-suit 67
fosters the poetry of Keats 68, 81
his mock funeral of Southey 70
cinematographic style 71
against Chinese decorations at

HUNT, LEIGH (*continued*)
Drury Lane 72
on the true sublime 73
notices Shelley's " Proposal for
Putting Reform to the Vote" 74
on Shelley in Ireland 75
assailed by Z 75
cannot get at Z 76
gives up looking for Z 76, 77-80
loyalty to Keats, 1818 80-82
on " The Revolt of Islam " 83
condemns " George Barnwell " 84
his delight in Mozart 72, 85
looks at the world, 1819 88
on Lamb's genius 89, 109
on Gifford's anatomy 92
hails " Rosalind and Helen " 93
his great industry 93
fails to foresee Mr. Ford 94
discovers the Fire-Threatener 96
recuperates at Wimbledon 97
invents " Literary Pocket Book " 98
founds the *Indicator* 98
anti-Laureate again 99
on Procter's treatment of
" Isabella " 100
welcomes " Lamia," etc. 101
venerates " The Cenci " 103
compliments Miss Tree 106
removes to Italy 109
challenges the *Quarterly* on Shelley
112
his note on Shelley's death 114
his " Wishing-Cap " 117-121
his estrangement from John Hunt
122

HUNT, ROBERT
his career 5
falls foul of Blake 9
still dreams of Historic Paintings 87
on the Englefield Vases 102

KEATS, JOHN
his " To Solitude " published 60
in " Young Poets " 60

KEATS, JOHN (*continued*)
several sonnets published 68
his " Poems " reviewed 68
his " Endymion " reviewed and
discussed 80-82
his subject " Isabella " considered
100
Hunt and Lamb on his " Lamia "
volume 101
possible home of his Grecian Urn
102
his death and Hunt's illness 109
his " Lines in the Highlands "
printed 113

LAMB, CHARLES
" Poor Gentlemen " 14
incensed against Prince Regent 21,
22
feels guilty of part of the libel 37
epigram probably his 43
lines not his 66
theatrical notice 83
many contributions in 1819 89-91
receives a pair of green breeches 91
his " excellent Works " displayed 89
his championship of Keats 101, 102
epigram ascribed to him 105
his Russell Street evenings 118
at Novello's 120

LINWOOD, MISS
her Old Masters in needlework 12

MOORE, THOMAS
his opera found wanting 18
" Tom Brown " 63

REYNOLDS, J. H.
in " Young Poets " 60
his article on Keats 81
a comment on it 82
"One, Two, Three, Four, Five" 92

ROBERTSON, HENRY
writes on the opera 3

SHELLEY, P. B.
his princely offer 35
in " Young Poets " 60
" Hymn to Intellectual Beauty " 67
Westbrooke *v.* Shelley 67
" Proposal for Putting Reform to
the Vote " supported 74
reviews Godwin's "Mandeville" 75
tactics in Ireland 75
" Ozymandias " appears 82
" Revolt of Islam " explained 83
defended from scribbling ruffians 93
his " Cenci " saluted 103
on " Queen Mab " 110
again shielded from northern reviewers 112
"To a Skylark" reprinted entire
113
his death 114
his admirers and his destroyers
114-116
" Queen Mab " cut short 115
honoured by Hazlitt 116

SMITH, HORACE
his Ozymandias vein 66

SOUTHEY, ROBERT
" the laurel planted on his primitive
head " 39
" glorious, natural Bob ! " 44
damned by Hazlitt 58, 69
obsequies arranged for 70
phrenological development taken
by Hazlitt 71
avoids the lyre 99

WORDSWORTH, W.
his " Excursion " reviewed by
Hazlitt 41
flirts with the " Examiner " 57
his visions after Waterloo 57
dissatisfies Hazlitt 59
his " Peter Bell " disrespectfully
used 92